EFFECTIVE ADVOCACY

BEFORE

ADMINISTRATIVE TRIBUNALS

ANDREW J. ROMAN B.A., LL.B.

MEMBER OF THE ONTARIO BAR

D1384595

CARSWELL
Toronto ■ Calgary ■ Vancouver
1989

Canadian Cataloguing in Publication Data

Roman, Andrew J.
  Effective advocacy before administrative
tribunals

Includes index.
ISBN 0-459-33461-1 (bound)   ISBN 0-459-33471-9 (pbk.)

1. Administrative courts — Canada.   2. Representation
in administrative proceedings — Canada.   I. Title.

KE5029.R65 1989   342.71′0664   C89-094314-1
KF5417.R65 1989

© The Carswell Co. Ltd. 1989

Table of Contents

Foreword

With the growing complexity of government, administrative agencies are playing an ever increasing role. These agencies perform many functions: licensing, investigating, conciliating, adjudicating, policy formation, reporting and advising to Cabinet. The decisions and actions of such bodies on these and other matters affect a variety of individual and public interests. Therefore, it is no wonder that more and more interests groups are seeking to be heard by administrative agencies.

In this book, Mr. Andrew Roman concentrates upon administrative tribunals that require a public hearing. A hearing before an administrative tribunal resembles a trial, but requires special skills and techniques. It is these that Mr. Roman addresses in this book. He does so with the insight and understanding that can only be had by one who has been there.

Given the nature of a public hearing, one's imput into the tribunal's decision-making process will be only as effective as the advocacy employed to put forward a client's case. Advocacy before an administrative tribunal shares many attributes with advocacy before a court. In both fora, the guiding principle is the art of persuasion. What distinguishes a good advocate in any forum is the ability to get to the heart of an issue in a manner that vastly simplifies the work of the tribunal. These are attributes which the book seeks to promote.

The author explains in detail how to aproach the various steps involved in the making of submissions, including the establishing of a litigation strategy, retaining of lawyers and expert witnesses, and the protecting of the right to participate fully. The supplements to this book cover such matters as the law of administrative procedure, the law of evidence and the question of costs.

Yet, perhaps the most interesting segments of this book are those devoted to improving one's skill in making motions, conducting a cross-examination and presenting a final argument. Having been on both sides of the bench, I can say that Mr. Roman's suggestions are very much to the point.

In general, this book will be welcomed by the profession and interest groups alike. Both will appreciate this attempt to deal in a practical way with the principles of advocacy peculiar to Canadian administrative tribunals. The author brings to this task a special combination of talents, both as lecturer of many years in advocacy skills at universities across the country and as an experienced advocate in administrative matters before courts and various tribunals.

Mr. Roman has succeeded in creating in one volume a concise and comprehensive review of all aspects of a public hearing. Lawyers and interest groups will find this book a useful guide on all aspects of advocacy before administrative tribunals.

The Honourable Justice John Sopinka
Supreme Court of Canada
July, 1989

Acknowledgements

Although I am the principal author of this book, it is largely the result of a collective effort spanning a number of years. I am, of course, solely responsible for the end result, as well as the delay.

I would acknowledge first the Consumers' Association of Canada, whose General Counsel I was from 1973 to 1976, for encouraging me to think systematically about advocacy and for publishing my first book on the subject, *How to Prepare Cases for Administrative Tribunals*. A major contribution was also made by the Donner Canadian Foundation, which provided substantial funding to The Public Interest Advocacy Centre (whose General Counsel I was for 12 years, until last month) to develop and conduct a major advocacy training programme across Canada. Without that grant, this book would not have been possible. Under that grant, the Centre was able to retain Nancy Peterson as its advocacy training coordinator. Not only did she serve admirably in that position, but also pestered me relentlessly and entirely with justification for some years thereafter to get me to complete this book.

Dan Maas, of the British Columbia Bar, was kind enough to work with me for a summer for remuneration which was as embarrassing to us as it was unjust to him, while he did much of the background research and even prepared preliminary drafts of several of these chapters. A similar debt of gratitude is owed to Mark Hemmingway of the Ontario Bar who, among his other duties at the Centre, edited most of this manuscript and wrote preliminary drafts of a few chapters.

Considerable financial assistance was provided by the Federal Department of Consumer and Corporate Affairs, without which I could not have taken the time from my other duties to devote to the numerous drafts through which this book has emerged. Thanks are also due to The Public Interest Advocacy Centre and to its sister organization, The Public Interest Research Centre, for allowing me to take the time from the other duties for which these organizations have retained me to complete a work of this sort.

Acknowledgements would be incomplete without recognizing Carol Denman of Atchison & Denman, court reporters in Toronto, for putting up with my handwriting and with endless changes. I must thank my secretary, Danielle Pepin, who provided assistance on this book for so long that I am chagrined to say that she was divorced, fell in love again, remarried, and had a child who is now three years old, all while I dithered with this manuscript. Last but by no means least, I would thank Lois Shelton, now articling in B.C., for considerable editorial and computer assistance.

In closing, I must apologize to my long-suffering wife and children who were awakened on more mornings than they care to remember by my size 12 shoes clumping down the stairs at dawn to do a bit more "final editing".

Andrew J. Roman
Toronto
July, 1989

Preface

Although there are more than 100 boards, commissions and tribunals (the three terms are interchangeable) established by the federal government, and perhaps 50-60 or more in the average province, how to participate in hearings before such tribunals is not taught in any regular university course, in any law school or in any bar admission course. There is a small group of regulatory lawyers but the vast majority of the legal profession and the general public can be expected to feel rather lost when participating for the first time at a tribunal hearing. This book attempts to fill a real, urgent need to help overcome such feelings.

The book is directed at two categories of readers: the non-lawyer who wishes to learn more about tribunal advocacy, with a view to participating; and the lawyer or law student with limited or no experience in this forum. To cover this broad a range of readers some compromises had to be made. Some parts may be a bit elementary for lawyers, others a bit technical for non-lawyers. Hopefully, if the style of writing is sufficiently readable and the topics are covered in sufficient depth, most readers will be content.

In general, the easier chapters are near the beginning. Lawyers may want only to skim these. The more difficult subjects are covered in the second half of the book. Non-lawyers may find these more sophisticated than necessary for the particular tribunal before which they wish to appear. Nevertheless, most readers should find most of the book of some interest and, hopefully, a useful source of reference.

I have struggled mightily but with limited success to avoid the use of sexist language and to ensure the equal treatment of both sexes. My next-to-final draft made frequent use of "he or she" and in alternate chapters referred to expert witnesses or lawyers as "she" and "he". This was found by the editors to be more irritating than progressive, so I re-edited the whole work to use the male pronoun only, and would ask the reader to credit me with non-sexist values, if limited writing skills. We all know that today almost as many participants in the tribunal process are female as male, so when I use "he", please take it as a short-form for "he or she".

The first six chapters are intended to provide a basic orientation for those who know very little about the regulatory process. These chapters may also be of interest to readers who understand the principles of regulation, but may have no intimate acquaintance with the procedures and practices employed by tribunals. Supplements and Forms have been provided so that verbal descriptions of procedural devices or documents in the text will be made more realistic by actual illustrations. The basics of the law applicable to tribunals is also briefly summarized.

A major feature is the description of royal commissions, judicial inquiries and advisory boards. For the inexperienced participant, very often the first and only exposure to the tribunal process is to such a special tribunal considering a particular project or issue of local concern. Since these tribunals differ significantly in their operations from the on-going tribunals, and often operate on very tight deadlines, a complete road map is essential at the outset; otherwise the participant can get lost at virtually every stage.

A chapter-by-chapter description of the contents follows.

Chapter 1: INTRODUCTION

An understanding of what is and what is not effective advocacy is essential to everything which is to follow. Similarly, it is necessary to explain what kind of legal creature an administrative tribunal is, and how it stands with one foot in the government and one in the courts.

Chapter 2: THE STAGES OF A PUBLIC HEARING — ONGOING TRIBUNAL

This chapter explains, in detail, every step of every stage of the public hearing, and even describes what goes on after it.

Chapter 3: THE SPECIAL SITUATION OF ROYAL COMMISSIONS, JUDICIAL INQUIRIES AND ADVISORY BOARDS

Such tribunals are normally set up with special legislation and procedures. This chapter encourages the would-be participant to become actively involved before this legislation is passed, to ensure that the mandate is broad enough and the procedures appropriate to permit effective presentation of the viewpoints of all interested parties. The "state of the art" was greatly advanced by the Berger Royal Commission, and has continued to develop rapidly, yet so little has been written about it that those responsible for the creation of new commissions might also benefit from this chapter. A complete description of each stage of these inquiries will be provided.

Chapter 4: WHAT ARE THE ISSUES IN A HEARING?

Various examples are used as illustrations.

Chapter 5: LAWYERS, CONSULTANTS AND EXPERT WITNESSES

Retaining lawyers, consultants and expert witnesses is an extremely difficult process, and the choice one makes can significantly affect the outcome of the hearing. This chapter is intended to provide a guide to working with such experts.

Chapter 6: AN INTRODUCTION TO ADMINISTRATIVE ADVOCACY

This chapter is intended to give would-be advocates an awareness of the benefits and pitfalls. Those who have the necessary commitment will be encouraged to develop the required skills.

The balance of the book is directed to those who have already read the first six chapters, or who are sufficiently familiar with the regulatory process to be able to participate without such introduction. It is hoped to be useful to a wide audience, comprising public interest groups and students of law, accounting, business or economics, as well as regulatory agencies, government officials and members of the practising bar.

This book is intended to serve as a guide to doing one's own advocacy before both ongoing and special tribunals. It will describe and illustrate the various stages and techniques of effective regulatory advocacy, as well as provide some of the conceptual background necessary to be an effective advocate. Most of this information is not found elsewhere. Strong emphasis is placed throughout on ethical advocacy and the avoidance of games and shoddy tactics.

Chapter 7: USING THE RULES EFFECTIVELY

Unlike courts of law, regulatory tribunals have relatively few procedural rules, and those they do have are often ignored or applied very loosely. Some were drafted many years ago for a situation which is no longer relevant and have never been revised.

In the case of inquiries, special rules are often prepared by persons with very little knowledge or experience with the regulatory process. The purpose of this chapter will be to develop a sensitive awareness for the requirement of fairness to all parties, so that archaic or non-existent rules of procedure may be used imaginatively or supplemented by new rules proposed by the parties, to achieve the ends of a full and fair hearing.

Chapter 8: ESTABLISHING AND PROTECTING THE RIGHT TO PARTICIPATE FULLY

There is a great deal of needless concern as to whether or not public interest groups without a proprietary or pecuniary interest in the outcome of a hearing will be granted standing to participate. This is a serious problem in the United States, where most of our regulatory literature originates; not so in Canada.

While standing is easy to obtain, some tribunals make a practice of treating non-commercial interveners as having less importance than businesses and giving them fewer procedural rights. Hence, protecting the right to full participation before the tribunal and preserving rights of appeal to the courts are important considerations.

Chapter 9: WINNING THE BATTLE FOR INFORMATION

Given the usually one-sided nature of the regulatory process, it is frequently a battle for information. This chapter will help win the battle.

Chapter 10: EXTENDING RESOURCES

Organizations with very limited or non-existent advocacy budgets can extend their resources by means of a judicious use of volunteers. On the other hand, failure to recognize the limitations of the volunteer role or an inadequate integration of roles of volunteers and professionals can lead to serious problems, and may in fact be counterproductive.

Some tribunals may award costs of participation. These can be very important in extending resources.

Chapter 11: CASE STRATEGIES

Far too few people, including lawyers, recognize the necessity of developing an overall strategy for the case. It is easy to become mesmerized by the volumes of complex technical evidence, which may result in unnecessarily hiring experts to deal with it or giving up in horror. Alternatively, parties, particularly the inexperienced, may be confused as to their appropriate role in the process and may fail to develop a workable strategy. None of the specific techniques to be used make any impact except in the context of an effective overall strategy.

A case strategy sounds extremely simple, but is perhaps the most difficult part of the entire process. The chapter illustrates the pitfalls of incorrect strategic planning and suggests techniques for correcting it.

Chapter 12: OPENING STATEMENTS AND FINAL ARGUMENT

In many hearings the volume of evidence is so overwhelming that at the end of it everyone is bored and confused. It is the purpose of final argument to persuade the tribunal to view the evidence and the issues in the way suggested by the advocate. Techniques for doing this are illustrated.

Of particular importance is the technique of writing the final argument before the case begins and using a summary of it as the opening statement. This will ensure that the advocate has thought his way through to the end of the case and knows what he wants the tribunal to order, and why. Both content and form are discussed in the chapter.

Chapter 13: MOTIONS AND OBJECTIONS

Even more than in the courtroom, timely and persuasive motions and objections influence the outcome of the case. Once a sense of the purpose of the hearing and of fairness is developed, non-lawyers can make motions and objections every bit as effectively as lawyers. This chapter should make a major contribution to the confidence of the non-lawyer, as the mystique of motions is one which frequently deters or inhibits effective participation.

Chapter 14: CROSS-EXAMINATION — PREPARATION OF STRATEGY

Many neophyte cross-examiners launch into cross-examination without any strategy but to attack. The result is usually an objection from the opposing counsel or even the chair, which flusters and often defeats the questioner. Alternatively, some useless information may be obtained and much useful information will not. Hence, this chapter will develop the skill of preparing a cross-examination strategy, integrated with a strategy for the case as described in Chapter 11.

Chapter 15: CROSS-EXAMINATION — PREPARATION OF QUESTIONS

Once the strategy for cross-examination has been determined, it is important to be able to draft questions which efficiently and accurately abstract the information sought or effectively attack credibility. Problems, such as keeping track of the answers to questions as asked and relating these to transcripts and to final argument, are also considered.

Chapter 16: CROSS-EXAMINATION — GAMES WITNESSES PLAY AND COUNTER-STRATEGIES

Most experienced expert witnesses test and frustrate the cross-examiner by refusing to answer questions directly, if at all. The games witnesses play can be analyzed into categories, with counter-strategies to extract the necessary information while turning the tables on the witness.

Chapter 17: CROSS-EXAMINATION — LAWYERS' TECHNIQUES

Regulatory lawyers have designed techniques for making witnesses presenting perfectly sound evidence appear to be ignorant and inept. These can usually be neutralized by effective counter-strategies described in the chapter.

Chapter 18: HOW TO PREPARE AND SUBMIT EVIDENCE AS A WITNESS

The preparation and submission of evidence is an art. Being able to write learned journal articles is not necessarily helpful background. Similarly, the oral presentation of evidence requires specialized skills. This chapter provides an introduction to both.

Chapter 19: THE MANAGEMENT OF A MAJOR REGULATORY CASE

A major regulatory case, whether one is participating as an applicant or an intervener, requires extensive management, otherwise the deadlines and sheer volume of paper can easily get out of control. This chapter describes the tools and techniques and characteristic lead times in each stage of a major regulatory case.

Chapter 20: APPEALS — TO THE COURTS AND TO THE
        POLITICAL PROCESS

The overwhelming majority of appeals from regulatory agencies are unsuccessful. In many cases this is so because the appellants have failed to anticipate the need for an appeal, during or even before the public hearing. Also it is not commonly known that the legal and political avenues of appeal are in some cases mutually exclusive.

The techniques and kinds of arguments which tend to be successful in the courts are very different from those used in the political process. Techniques for developing each are covered.

SUPPLEMENTS

The   ‸ry chapters may appear a bit technical, a   ‸ description of the law
of adm   able for the
sake o   ire, but may
not be   e complexity
of th   apters should
prov   ommon sense
will   onfidence and
enc

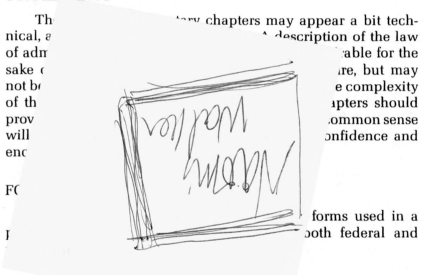

FC

                                          forms used in a
                                          both federal and

1

Introduction

1. WHAT IS ADVOCACY?

Most issues on which government agencies are allowed to
render decisions affect the private or public interests of individuals or organizations. But most government agencies are not
designed to hold public hearings before making decisions.
Certain agencies which usually are intended to do so are known
as "administrative tribunals" or, simply, "tribunals". These tribunals take many forms, govern many types of public and private
issues and vary radically in their procedures. They may be long-
standing permanent bodies dealing with a broad range of
questions or they may be one-time *ad hoc* agencies created to
consider only one significant question (e.g., the environmental
aspects of a new pipeline or the deaths of babies at a hospital).

Effective advocacy is persuasive. Since what may persuade
one person may have the opposite effect on another, no one
technique and no single advocate can be universally persuasive.
However, in general, good advocates share certain qualities. They
appear to be controlled, calm and confident (regardless of how
they may feel inside). They sound positive and optimistic rather
than negative and despairing. Their approach is thoughtful,
logical and analytical, examining carefully the various options
open to the tribunal. They are highly self-disciplined and
prepared to work hard to understand the evidence, even if it is
technical, so they can relate it to the relevant public policy
arguments.

Effective advocacy requires commitment to long hours of

hard work and learning. It cannot be achieved merely by indulging in the wish to vent one's spleen. Nor is it likely to work without some basic knowledge of how the hearing process operates, a bit of legal background reading and an understanding of "the tools of the trade".

This book hopes to provide the would-be advocate with as much of the necessary information as can practically be conveyed without actually experiencing a hearing. It is principally designed for use by individuals and groups considering involvement for the first time in a tribunal's process, and for lawyers just beginning tribunal advocacy. The first six chapters are intended to give a general introduction to administrative tribunals and their procedures. This will assist in determining *whether* one should become involved in the process and, if so, indicate what financial, professional and other resources one should need. The remaining chapters provide a comprehensive introduction to the techniques with which administrative advocates should become familiar. First-time participants in administrative tribunal proceedings should find that these materials enable them to participate more constructively and effectively.

Most decisions made by government agencies are not made by administrative tribunals. Individuals who wish to have their interests considered by agencies other than tribunals will find relatively little assistance in these materials. However, as it is often difficult to determine whether the statutory agency is in fact a tribunal, some care must be taken in making this initial determination.

2. WHAT ARE ADMINISTRATIVE TRIBUNALS?

There is no foolproof test to determine whether a government agency is or is not an administrative tribunal. Courts of law have applied various tests, not always consistent with each other and often confusing. One cannot completely rely on the agency's own description or even the opinion of its lawyer. A particular agency may be an administrative tribunal for the performance of some of its duties, but not for others.

Probably the best initial determination can be made by the name and the operation of the agency. Most agencies known as a "board", "tribunal" or "commission" are administrative tribunals. If individuals are entitled to appear at the hearings of such agencies, the initial determination is safer. For example, agencies which resolve specific questions after holding hearings and are administrative tribunals include: landlord/tenant and labour relations agencies; workers' compensation, immigration and unemployment insurance appeal boards; environmental assessment boards; public utilities boards; municipal zoning and planning boards; and some licensing agencies. It should also be noted that some bodies which are not part of the government, such as those which govern the professions in each province (e.g., colleges of physicians and surgeons, the law societies, architectural institutes, etc.) may be given powers of regulation by provincial statutes and, in exercising those powers, are administrative tribunals.

Perhaps the most difficult determinations are required when considering agencies which regulate industries or licensing. If the function of such an agency is mostly one of management or the mechanical application of legally required procedures, it is probably not an administrative tribunal. Nevertheless, it is frequently best to proceed as if an agency is an administrative tribunal until the question arises.

If there is some doubt about whether you are approaching an administrative tribunal, you can start by asking employees or other representatives of the agency. If you are told the agency does not conduct itself as an administrative tribunal, you may then consider further research or obtaining a legal opinion from a lawyer who specializes in administrative law.

In determining what requirements a tribunal must fulfil and whether there are procedural protections for individuals wishing to be heard by a government agency, the Supreme Court of Canada[1] listed four factors to be considered:

1. the language and context of the relevant statutory provisions;
2. whether the rights and obligations of individuals are affected;
3. whether competing parties have adversarial stances; and
4. whether general decision-making rules are to be applied in resolving specific questions.

---

[1] M.N.R. v. Coopers & Lybrand Ltd., [1979] 1 S.C.R. 495, 24 N.R. 163, 78 D.T.C. 6258, [1978] C.T.C. 829, 92 D.L.R. (3d) 1.

Although these functions were listed as helpful in determining whether a specific agency function is "judicial" or "quasi-judicial", they also indicate the extent to which the agency must afford parties procedural fairness. This is explained more fully in Supplement 1.

There are almost no generalizations which hold true of all administrative tribunals; they vary greatly in size, purpose, function and powers. Nevertheless, in dealing with any particular tribunal, it is helpful to have some general knowledge of the background and purposes of administrative tribunals in Canada.

The court system in Canada is based on some 800 years of precedents and traditions, while administrative tribunals are a relatively new creation. The first regulatory tribunal in Canada was the Board of Railway Transport Commissioners, created in 1903. Increasingly throughout the twentieth century, the various levels of government in Canada are creating agencies to do work and make decisions which would otherwise be made by ordinary public servants in the executive branch of government. Wide powers have been delegated to administrative tribunals, for several reasons, including:

1. *Independence and impartiality*: some decisions should be, to some extent, separated from the politics of government;
2. *Expertise and specialization*: the creation of an agency to make certain types of decisions or recommendations exclusively permits the selection of individuals with special skills and knowledge, who can continue to accumulate valuable expertise while working with the tribunal;
3. *Reducing government burdens*: as society grows more complex, demands on government continue to grow, prompting the shifting of some responsibilities to peripheral agencies; and
4. *Public access*: better decisions are made when decision-makers are aware of the relevant concerns and interests of those affected, including the public at large.

Lawyers, public interest advocates and others appearing before administrative tribunals should always bear in mind that, in one sense, tribunals need interventions to justify their existence. Occasions may arise when the advocate has to remind the tribunal of this. As long as the advocate does not unreasonably delay or complicate the proceedings, causing unnecessary expenditure of public funds, tribunals should be supportive of and encouraging to individuals interested in participating.

There are several other generalizations about administrative tribunals to be noted. In Canada tribunals are frequently under-staffed, under severe funding pressures and time constraints, and subject to relentless public and government scrutiny. They are heavily lobbied by corporations or individuals whom they regulate and are concerned that if too many members of the public become involved in their processes, this will complicate their jobs even further. All these factors may influence the performance and decisions of tribunals.

3. RELATIONSHIP BETWEEN THE TRIBUNAL AND GOVERNMENT

It has been said that a tribunal has one foot in the legislature and one in the court of appeal. This is quite different from a court of law.

Through legislation governments can create tribunals, alter their responsibilities or even dissolve them. Legislation, however, requires the approval of Parliament or a provincial legislature, and the legislative process tends to be slow and controversial. Hence, governments are often unwilling to allow legislation to be the sole means of influencing the policies and activities of tribunals. The Cabinet, or the minister, is sometimes given the power to interfere with tribunals on an ongoing basis. This is a major difference from the situation in the United States, where such tribunals have greater political independence.

In Canada, in some situations the Cabinet or the responsible minister has the power to make regulations which can affect the duties or responsibilities of the tribunal. With a few tribunals such as the National Energy Board (NEB), some of their functions do not permit them to make a decision but merely to report to the Cabinet which, if it approves the report, thereby makes it a decision. (This gives rise to the interesting questions whether the Cabinet can refuse to approve an NEB report *without* making it public and whether it can send it back to the NEB with an indication as to what changes it would require to grant approval.)

Other federal tribunals, such as the Canadian Radio-Television and Telecommunications Commission (CRTC), can have their decisions set aside by the Cabinet at any time, on a complaint by any person, or even on the Cabinet's own initiative. Similar provisions are found in several provinces.

Finally, for a limited number of tribunals, the Cabinet is empowered to issue so-called "policy directives" to the agency with the intention that they be binding. Examples of this include the CRTC at the federal level and the British Columbia Public Utilities Commission provincially. These directives, however, can give rise to a number of complex bureaucratic and legal problems, the description of which is beyond the scope of this paper.[2]

It is important for the advocate to remember that the tribunal may not be the last or even the most important step in the whole process. Indeed, it may be little more than the slow way to the minister or Cabinet. This underlines the importance of preliminary research to determine who has the final decision-making authority, and whether directives or successful appeals to cabinet are common. For a citizens' group with limited resources, the decision as to whether to focus on the tribunal or the Cabinet may be crucial.

4. RELATIONSHIP BETWEEN THE TRIBUNAL AND THE COURTS

Tribunals are subject to appeal not only to government ministers or to the Cabinet, but also to the courts. However, the grounds of appeal are different. A minister or Cabinet will not overturn the decision of the tribunal on the basis of a question of law; Cabinet overrides are normally confined to major errors of policy. On the other hand, the courts will limit judicial review to questions of law or jurisdiction, and will not become involved in the merits of the actual issue before the board. It is not the function of the courts to second-guess the board as to whether its decision was right, but merely whether it was legally proper.

If the court concludes that the tribunal exceeded its jurisdiction or made a decision by means of a process which was

---

2 These problems are described more fully in my article "Government Control of Tribunals: Appeals, Directives and Non-statutory Mechanisms" (1985), Queen's L.J.

unfair, the decision will be quashed. If the tribunal adopts an unfair procedure during the course of a hearing, relief may be obtained from the courts in the form of a quick order known as "prohibition", to prohibit the board from proceeding further in this manner or, alternatively, an ancient order called "*mandamus*", to compel the tribunal to treat the parties fairly and lawfully. The legal rules governing judicial review and the rights of parties to hearings are described in Supplement 1. This is for background purposes only, as the right to present such a court application on behalf of a group is limited to lawyers. However, even among lawyers, only a small number specialize in administrative law, the branch of law under which judicial review applications are taken. Accordingly, someone requiring a judicial review application, or even procedural advice without going to court, should seek out a lawyer thoroughly experienced in administrative law.

2

The Stages of a Public Hearing — Ongoing Tribunal

1. ONGOING VERSUS ONE-TIME TRIBUNALS

There is an important distinction between two kinds of tribunals: ongoing tribunals which have regulated an industry or area of activity, perhaps for decades; and one-time special tribunals which usually take the form of royal commissions, judicial inquiries or special one-hearing advisory boards.

Ongoing tribunals will tend to have a permanent staff, many of whom have worked for that tribunal for several years. The tribunal members, usually appointed for five to ten-year terms, are frequently re-appointed and also tend to have lengthy tenure. Many of the companies or Crown corporations appearing before them have been doing so since the tribunal was created. For example, the Canadian Transport Commission (CTC) (now called the National Transportation Agency (NTA)), Canada's first tribunal, has been regulating the Canadian National Railway and Canadian Pacific Railway since 1903; it has also regulated Air Canada and every other airline in Canada since their creation; until 1975 (when jurisdiction was transferred to the Canadian Radio-Television and Telecommunications Commission (CRTC)), the CTC also regulated Bell Canada and British Columbia Telephones.

Not surprisingly, regulatory agencies with a long tradition and slow turnover of staff and members tend to become fixed in their ways. The hearings before such agencies tend to appear a bit "clubby", in that the same lawyers and the same witnesses appear there on behalf of the same parties, case after case and year after year. The first appearance of a new consumer or environmental group can appear to be almost like someone entering a private club without an invitation. The outsider is regarded at first with some suspicion, or even hostility. If this group is going to force new viewpoints and interests to be taken into account in what has been a fairly stable series of ongoing relationships, there will be concern on the part of all of the traditional parties, as well as the tribunal, that the new presence will be disruptive. For these reasons, all but the most extraordinary grievance or problem presented by the new intervener is likely to be received less than sympathetically. Only responsible, persistent and effective intervention will gain acceptance for the new group.

No amount of moral self-righteousness will compensate for a good track record before the tribunal. Even if the new group is impeccably virtuous, the tribunal members are more likely to accept it after they have seen it a few times. So, one should not expect to achieve too much the first time before this kind of tribunal. One's views will only be given the weight they deserve if seriousness and determination are shown through repeated intervention.

By way of contrast, the one-time commission is expected to last for at most a year or two, and will have staff and commissioners whose work is normally in other areas. The staff will be hired from consulting companies, or seconded from government departments. The commissioners are usually judges, lawyers, senior public servants or others with special expertise or experience in the field. The members of these tribunals are often the "movers and shakers" who are expected to be able to accomplish an intensive and innovative study of a field in a short time. This situation is in distinct contrast to that of members of on-going tribunals whose members are sometimes selected on political grounds and may have little or no expertise (at least initially) in the subject matter they are expected to regulate. One-time tribunals, however, pose their own special problems.

First, it is expected that one-time tribunals will discover the solution to some immensely difficult problem in what often proves to be an unrealistically short time period. Because of timing and budget pressures they tend to spend very little time planning and organizing the hearing before they start, and give little thought to the procedures they should use. Quite commonly, they will hire a counsel with an extensive background in the courts but little or no experience with public inquiries, and will accept unwaveringly this lawyer's advice as to the appropriate procedure to use. The lawyer will probably simply copy procedures used by the courts or by other tribunals studying quite unrelated questions. For example, an inquiry conducted by Commissioner McQuaid of Prince Edward Island into issues such as the cost and price of electricity provided on the island by Maritime Electric was modelled after the MacDonald inquiry into alleged wrongdoing by the Royal Canadian Mounted Police. Serious procedural problems were created because the informal procedure desirable for a meaningful discussion of electricity prices is not necessarily the same as the formal procedure required in a crime inquiry, the major concerns of which include the protection of the reputations of the innocent and the preservation of national security.

Leaving aside such notable exceptions as the Royal Commission of Inquiry into the Mackenzie Valley Pipe Line (Berger Inquiry), the West Coast Oil Ports Inquiry (Thompson Inquiry) and the Beaufort Sea Environmental Assessment conducted by the Federal Environmental Assessment Review Organization (FEARO), each of which took special and elaborate steps to encourage full-scale involvement and participation by all potentially interested groups such as native and environmental groups, most one-time inquiries tend to be bogged down with the archaic procedures of the police or crime investigation model for which such inquiries were first established early in this century. This seems especially so if chaired by a judge. Even when such inquiries are willing to listen to the public, the intention seems to be more to encourage public opportunities for "blowing off steam" than to foster meaningful and effective public participation. The former can be accomplished through a few informal evening sessions in different communities — a travelling road show in which anyone and everyone would be listened to for 15 minutes; the latter requires a great deal more thought, organization and effort, not to mention money.

From this description of the two kinds of tribunals, it should be clear that effective advocacy may be quite different before each.

With the on-going tribunal, in the early 1970s the principal concerns were simple questions of access: to full participant status, to information, to the right to confront an adversary and ask questions. While some of these battles are not yet over, in the tribunals most commonly frequented by public interest groups in the late 1980s — public utilities boards at the provincial level and the NTA/CRTC/NEB (National Energy Board) at the federal level — the war has largely been won and the "club" has been opened to admit groups who represent the victims of new construction projects or the payers of higher rates. Having opened the doors, and even having won a few significant victories, the consumer or environmental advocate's concern for the 1990s will be how to enlarge upon and consolidate these victories so as to ensure that, as the novelty wears off, there is no reversion to the earlier closed door situation.

With one-time inquiries, however, the problems are as individual as the tribunals themselves. Since they appear not to follow any tradition, but to "re-invent the wheel" each time a new commission is created, all the old battles of access must be fought anew. There is a "grapevine" among regulatory tribunals; in the public utilities field there is CAMPUT (Canadian Association of Members of Public Utilities Tribunals) and, more generally, CCAT (Conference of Canadian Administrative Tribunals) to provide some direction to administrative tribunals. But there is no comparable on-going body to study and disseminate information about royal commissions. Thus environmental groups, for example, have experienced the frustration of having to fight repeatedly for the right to participate effectively before each new public inquiry. Although such battles severely drain the human, financial and legal resources of community groups, there is still no assurance that new public inquiries being created will not adopt procedures more appropriate to a criminal investigation in England in the post-World War I period than to an inquiry into electrical rates or broadcasting or Arctic oil drilling today. The only solution is the amendment and updating of the federal and provincial public inquiries legislation to take into account the present realities. However, a necessary precondition to such reform is political recognition of the need.

2. GENERAL INTRODUCTION TO PUBLIC HEARINGS

(a) What is a Public Hearing?

Although the term "public hearing" conveys an image of one or more persons hearing a case in public, the term has no precise legal definition. Indeed, there have even been public hearings where it has been considered necessary to hear some portions of the evidence *in camera*, which means in the *absence* of the public. Also, as will be discussed below, some public hearings are conducted partially or entirely in writing. Barring special circumstances, however, a public hearing is to be heard orally and held in public.

(b) Standing

Normally, any member of the public with an interest in the matter should be permitted to participate. The standing issue is discussed fully in Chapter 8, but it is important, for introductory purposes, to be aware of it. Although questions have been raised from time to time as to the "standing of ordinary members of the public" to participate, today this concern would not appear to be based on solid legal grounds. In the first place, the law of standing, even in courts of law, has been greatly liberalized by the Supreme Court of Canada in the last several years. Today, anyone with a genuine interest in a question can commence a legal action to question the legality of government behaviour, even without being "directly affected", if it appears improbable that anyone else will do so.[1] Thus, even in courts of law, which tend to be far more formal than tribunals, the question of standing is becoming increasingly unimportant as a barrier to access.

It is arguable that standing has no relevance whatsoever to the administrative process because the work of tribunals is so different from that of courts of law. The legal concept of standing does not exist at large but is a meaningful concept only with

---

1 *Re Elizabeth Fry Society of Sask. Inc. v. Sask. Legal Aid Comm.*, [1988] 2 W.W.R. 168, 72 Sask. R. 1, 32 C.P.C. (2d) 62 (Sask. C.A.); *Min. of Justice of Canada v. Borowski*, [1982] 1 W.W.R. 97, 24 C.P.C. 62, 24 C.R. (3d) 352, 12 Sask. R. 420, 64 C.C.C. (2d) 97, 39 W.R. 331, 130 D.L.R. (3d) 588 (S.C.C.); *Finlay v. Canada (Min. of Finance)*, [1986] 2 S.C.R. 607, [1987] 1 W.W.R. 603, 23 Admin. L.R. 197, 17 C.P.C. (2d) 289, 71 N.R. 338, 33 D.L.R. (4th) 321, 8 C.H.R.R. D/3789.

reference to the particular kind of legal action contemplated. The question must be: "Does *this* plaintiff have the right to take *this* action against *this* defendant?"[2] Tribunals do not grant judicial remedies and do not have "plaintiffs" and "defendants" in the conventional legal sense. Thus, the real question before a tribunal is quite different: who may participate in the public hearing? The right to participation is in the discretion of the tribunal, but it is expected that this right will not be arbitrarily denied to any person who has any interest in the matter.

What is meant by an "interest" is a complicated legal question, but to summarize the more modern view, virtually any legally recognized interest will do. The strictest test (derived from the law of public nuisance) is that an interest must be a "proprietary or pecuniary interest, or an interest greater than that of the general public". Even that can be met if the individual is a user of the service involved and pays its rates. The purpose of a rate increase application is to take money out of customers' pockets and put it into the pockets of the utility. Thus, the pecuniary interest of a public utility in its rate case is exactly equal to the sum of the pecuniary interests of all its customers.

More difficult theoretical questions arise with large public projects, the economic and environmental impact of which will be felt by more than the owners of adjacent land. Consumer, native or environmental groups claiming to represent the public interest are not likely to be able to meet the strict public nuisance test. Nevertheless, as the validity of importing the public nuisance standing test from its legal context into standing before administrative tribunals is questionable,[3] in the last decade it has become customary at least to permit, if not actively to encourage, public participation in such public hearings. Accordingly, if someone raises a standing challenge at a public hearing, a strong argument can be made that public participation is now the norm at public hearings, and that departure from this norm should only be made in extraordinary cases, where special circumstances so justify.

---

2 *A.G. Nova Scotia v. Bedford Service Comm.*, (1977), 72 D.L.R. (3d) 639 at 645, 18 N.S.R. (2d) 132, 1 M.P.L.R. 204 (C.A.), per Chief Justice MacKeigan. This case was later reversed by the Supreme Court of Canada, but on other grounds: [1977] 2 S.C.R. 269, 19 N.S.R. (2d) 310, 14 N.R. 413, 80 D.L.R. (3d) 767.

3 *Thorson v. A.G. Canada (No.2)*, [1975] 1 S.C.R. 138, 43 D.L.R. (3d) 1 at 3, 1 N.R. 225.

(c) Preserving Efficiency

If public participation is the norm, one might well wonder why public hearings do not get out of control (in one Bell Canada rate hearing in 1978, for example, there were some 3,500 'interveners'). The simple answer is that most interveners are not parties in any meaningful sense. In the Bell example anyone who wrote a letter of complaint about higher rates was classified as an intervener. Although every such intervener would theoretically have the right to cross-examine every witness and even to appeal the decision, this never happens. The reason, of course, is that participation in public hearings is a very expensive and time-consuming process. In fact, in that 1978 hearing there were no more than five or six *active* interveners, and the rest were simply persons who had written a letter complaining about higher rates or some aspect of service quality. Had the standing of each intervener been challenged and a hearing held to determine the participation of each, and possibly appeals taken from some of these, it might have taken several years before the substance of the hearing would have been reached. By treating standing as a non-issue, the hearing took only the normal length of time.

Experience in this and in other hearings has shown that the length of the hearing does not vary with the number of interveners. A hearing that is hotly contested by two or three active parties may take months or even years to conclude, whereas another with thousands of members of the public formally designated as interveners may be concluded with only a few days of public hearings. If there are numerous active interveners at a public hearing, such as in some of the pipeline cases before the National Energy Board, again, little can be done to restrict the number of participants. Rather, order is kept and undue delay avoided through a number of basic chairing techniques.

First, there is usually a rule against repetitive cross-examination. Thus, if a counsel for party A uses a particular line of questions, counsel for party B will not be permitted to repeat them; the chair of the hearing panel will say that the Board is satisfied that it has enough information on the record on that subject. Since the number of genuinely different and relevant issues is normally quite limited, after an extensive cross-examination by one or two of the major parties there tends to be very little, if anything left for the others to question. Hence there is no point in creating a battle to exclude interveners. The rule against repetition is much more effective.

Second, final argument at the conclusion of the case may be required to be presented in writing rather than orally, or may be given a time limit, such as 30 minutes. This also saves time when there are numerous parties. In summary, then, there are various ways to strike an appropriate balance between efficiency of process and public participation. Increasingly today, this is being done by encouraging intervention while maintaining efficiency through appropriate hearing procedures.

(d) Hearings in Writing

All hearings used to be held entirely orally. That is no longer the case. Increasingly, portions of hearings are being conducted in writing. Rare is the tribunal which today will require, or even permit witnesses to read lengthy briefs or statements "into the record". Instead, these are simply filed and copies provided to all the other participants. Likewise, if oral testimony on some technical issue (e.g., financial reports or scientific equations) would be excessively time consuming, the witness may be asked to provide a full written report instead, perhaps in the form of a response to a written interrogatory (discussed in detail in Chapter 9), with this serving as the basis for what should be a much more efficient cross-examination process. Also, at the end of lengthy hearings, rather than allowing two-day final addresses, the custom is increasingly to allow perhaps an hour, with a full, written argument to present the rest of it.

As startling as it may sound, one is not necessarily entitled to an oral hearing at all. Some tribunals may conduct the entire hearing, or virtually all of it, in writing. Which tribunals may do so, and under what circumstances, is a complex legal question which cannot be discussed here, but the issue is raised for two reasons. First, so that those unfamiliar with the process will recognize that sometimes part or all of the public hearing will be carried out in writing; second, so that someone requesting a public hearing who is brushed off with the argument that hearings are too slow and costly can reply that because much of it can be in writing, that need not be the case.

Hearings in writing are efficient, but are not a cure-all and create their own problems. Because oral questions from the tribunal are greatly reduced or eliminated, the preparation of the written submissions is an exhausting process. There will be a tendency to try to anticipate every possible question the tribunal might have and to answer them all. It would be disastrous if the whole case were lost merely because the advocate mistakenly took for granted the acceptance of some point of argument. Thus, what might otherwise have been a short oral argument tends to become a major written treatise, which can be very costly for the participants.

Despite the often greater length of written presentations, the quality of scrutiny of the evidence will not be the same unless full cross-examination is preserved. Any experienced expert witness will ask, when requested to prepare a memorandum, whether it will be subject to cross-examination. If the answer is "yes", the whole approach will be different. Broad generalizations will be eliminated or carefully qualified, calculations will be triple-checked, and insupportable conclusions or inferences deleted. In other words, quality control will be rigorous and the tribunal will receive the best possible evidence that the best available witnesses can supply. To do any less is to risk humiliation on cross-examination.

If there is to be no cross-examination that risk is gone. It is then no longer as important to present the best possible evidence or even to retain the best witnesses. As quality control declines, so does quality. There is an increase in exaggeration, posturing and statements outside of the witness' expertise. The tribunal which congratulates itself on avoiding the formalism of cross-examination by doing it all in writing will have hearings which, though speedy, may lack the focus and depth essential to making the right decision.

From the parties' viewpoint, the small oral portion of a hearing which is primarily written may also be unsatisfactory because it soon becomes evident that the tribunal members have not read all the written submissions, despite the usual assurances to the contrary. This is suspected if the tribunal fails to ask any of the obvious questions and is confirmed if, as is so often the case, the questions asked reveal ignorance of the contents.

It is well known that a tribunal will ask its staff to prepare briefings for the members, summarizing what the staff member regards as the important part of someone's submissions. If there is a lot of evidence this work may be undertaken by different staff members, whose summaries may be inconsistent. Since experienced participants do not trust the ultimate decision-makers to read all of their submissions, they will try to find other ways to ensure full attention to their views. One will be to stretch out the oral presentation to repeat, in different words, virtually everything submitted in writing. This is not always easy to prevent or resist, and can negate much of the time saved by insistence on submissions in writing. Even worse, it may encourage parties to seek meetings with staff and members to try to persuade them in private. (The disadvantages of this kind of meeting are discussed later in this chapter).

In the final analysis, there is no effective substitute for an oral hearing, or at least one in which the written portion does not preclude a full opportunity for a focused oral clash of views, to confront one's adversary on points of difference in evidence or argument. That does not mean that everything must be done orally. Certainly, affirmative statements of witnesses are better presented in writing a week or more before the witness is to testify. But if oral questioning is precluded or seriously restricted, the indispensible minimum oral element has been undermined and at least one side will tend to feel that a fair opportunity to attack the arguments of the other has been denied.

(e) The Idea of "Filing a Brief"

The assumption is commonly made by those new to public hearings that one participates by "filing a brief" and then appearing to read the brief aloud, or to "speak to it" by paraphrasing its contents. Where this idea originated is a mystery, but to equate intervention with filing a brief is a misconception. Although a tribunal will allow someone to file a brief if that is requested, this form of submission is exceptional. Normally, when a hearing is announced, a quick deadline is given for the filing of intervention statements, usually just called "interventions". Contrary to what is feared when the shortness of the deadline is announced, these are not expected to contain the total of an intervener's evidence but merely a short summary of what the intervener's position will be at the hearing. It is not necessary to provide any more at this preliminary stage. Indeed, it would be unwise even to attempt to present evidence before the evidence of the applicant has been formally presented and tested by cross-examination and questioning from board members.

Unfortunately, the confusion between an initial intervention statement and the entire intervention often leads to panic and cries for an adjournment or extension of the deadline. The typical question is: "How can we possibly get our group together and prepare a brief in 30 days?" Of course, an intervention statement is normally only a two or three-page statement of one's position. If an intervener cannot even state in two or three pages who it is and why it seeks to intervene, it is seriously questionable whether the group is sufficiently mature and organized to be able to accomplish anything useful at the hearing itself.

Nor is a "brief" normally filed at any stage. Rather, hearings are usually divided into two phases, evidence and argument; so important is this distinction that it will be discussed in depth in Chapter 11 on "Case Strategies". A brief can present problems for the tribunal because it usually contains a mixture of statements of evidence and argument. For reasons which will become clear as the reader proceeds through this book, it is recommended that briefs not be used at all, or if they must be, then only as a last resort.

(f) The Hearing as the "Tip of the Iceberg"

The oral hearing itself is often only the tip of the iceberg. Hence, this chapter covers both the pre-hearing and post-hearing stages.

3. THE PRE-HEARING STAGE

(a) Pre-application Meetings with Cabinet and Tribunal

As will be clear from the previous chapter describing the relationships between the tribunal and the government, most tribunals do not operate in a political vacuum. The knowledgeable applicant, particularly one seeking permission to construct a major project, will have meetings with senior officials and Cabinet ministers well in advance of any application to a tribunal. Where a so-called "mega-project" is involved, the several industries which would supply raw materials, machinery, tools and consulting services to the project also carry on extensive lobbying campaigns to persuade all levels of government of the importance of the project. Where this happens, the intervener can anticipate severe direct and indirect political pressure on the tribunal to license or approve the project as quickly as possible. Although virtually nobody else can hope to compete with this level of political pressure and lobbying, nevertheless, it is important to begin one's efforts at this pre-hearing stage by expressing concerns to the appropriate ministers. For example, if the representatives of a pipeline company were attempting to recruit the support of the Minister of Energy, Mines and Resources, the prospective intervener might seek the support of the Minister of the Environment for environmental concerns or, if the project might result in higher prices, the Minister of Consumer and Corporate Affairs.

Just as there are meetings with government officials, there are usually meetings with the tribunal. While some meetings between the applicant's and tribunal's staffs to discuss the procedure for the application are inevitable, serious ethical and legal problems are raised if such meetings discuss its substance. Nevertheless, there is a deplorable tendency for some tribunals to permit members of the regulated industry to lobby its members before a hearing in the guise of seeking guidance as to the appropriate content of their applications. Sometimes this is done a bit more subtly, through the staff; in other cases, the tribunal members meet directly (although usually secretly) with the applicant. Although the courts have repeatedly denounced this practice as giving rise to a reasonable apprehension of bias on the part of those not invited to these meetings, the practice continues, either through sheer ignorance of the law or the expectation that, if both parties to the meeting keep quiet about it, no one will be caught.

From the applicant's point of view such meetings are very useful, of course, because they are an opportunity to conduct a "dress rehearsal" of the public hearing. It may well be told which aspects of its application are incomplete or which are unsatisfactory and must be changed. Once the tribunal has participated actively in helping in the preparation of the application, and the applicant has met all of its requirements, the tribunal is much more likely to approve the application. For the tribunal to do otherwise would, in the circumstances, seem virtually immoral. The more the applicant can persuade the tribunal to provide detailed pre-hearing criticism of its application, the greater the likelihood that the tribunal will feel obligated to grant its approval.

Such pre-hearing meetings are also useful for the tribunal. Through meeting with the applicant it can avoid accusations of being aloof, theoretical or "living in an ivory tower". Board members have a need to appear informed and co-operative, which is enhanced by meetings with the industry. (The solution, of course, is not to avoid ever meeting with the industry, but to have such meetings in public, or at least to make them open to all interested parties who may wish to attend, so that they do not appear to be exclusive or behind closed doors.)

Tribunals dislike having to reject an otherwise worthy application merely because of some minor defect or flaw, which can be corrected. Hence they may feel that if they warn the applicant of this flaw in advance, the problem can be corrected before the hearing. If the deficiency is more fundamental, such prehearing meetings can avoid the public embarrassment and considerable expense of having to turn down the application and require a fresh application to be submitted many months and perhaps millions of dollars later.

In short, assuming that such meetings are not discovered, a secret pre-hearing bargaining session and rehearsal reduces the risks of an unpleasant hearing for both the applicant and the tribunal. Since most of the active parties at regulatory hearings tend to be members of the regulated industry who are competitors of the applicant, or major customers of the industry who are for that reason regularly before the tribunal, they are unlikely to be "whistle blowers" even if they do find out, as they may wish to obtain the same benefit next time. At the very least, they will be reluctant to create a scandal for the tribunal for fear of being perceived as trouble-makers, thereby losing the tribunal's goodwill.

Merely because some people are willing to participate in

such questionable activities does not mean that groups which purport to represent some aspect of the public interest should do the same. It is not suggested that one should never speak to any member of a tribunal outside of the formal context of a public hearing, but it must be remembered that members have the responsibility to make decisions with detachment and objectivity similar to that of a judge in a court of law. While it may be acceptable to speak to a member of the tribunal on some question of procedure, one must absolutely never discuss the substance or content of an application before, during or even after a public hearing until the decision has been made and released to the public.

One may, on occasion, meet a member of a tribunal at an airport, government reception, or even private lunch, where he or she initiates a discussion which moves dangerously close to the taboo subject — the content of a public hearing before the tribunal. One should immediately change the subject, firmly and obviously. In the face of a persistent desire to discuss the hearing, one can only say, as tactfully as possible, that one would not wish to risk the appearance of having compromised the tribunal member's objectivity.

(b) Applications

After extensive preparation, the first formal step is taken through the filing of an application. Some tribunals have elaborate rules as to what constitutes an application; others have none. Unlike courts of law in which trials are started by means of standardized pleadings, both the style and content of applications vary greatly between tribunals, and sometimes even within the same tribunal. Thus a British Columbia Telephone Company application for a rate increase before the CRTC may be quite different from an application filed by Bell Canada for the same thing before the same tribunal, and also quite different from the application by British Columbia Hydro for a rate increase before the British Columbia Public Utilities Commission.

This diversity is not necessarily due to a lack of consistency. The broad range of policy and public interest considerations taken into account by many tribunals means that no standard form application can address every concern. Also, since no particular application can contain an infinite amount of information, to some critics it will always appear incomplete.

In some tribunals, no distinction is made between an application and the evidence submitted in support of it. Before such tribunals, the application contains all the evidence. In others, an application, like an intervention, may be a relatively short document summarizing the arguments and evidence to be submitted by the applicant at the public hearing; the evidence itself would not be made public until some time before the public hearing or, sometimes, only at the hearing itself.

(c) Deficiency Letters

A deficiency letter is a letter from the tribunal to the applicant setting out the deficiencies in the application. This does not mean that a tribunal will inform an applicant at this pre-hearing stage what aspects of its proposal it may like or dislike; rather, information which the applicant has omitted will be requested.

Usually, the application will not be treated as ready to set a date for public hearing until all significant deficiencies have been satisfactorily remedied. Some tribunals schedule and call a public hearing for a fixed date and require the applicant to provide deficiency responses prior to that date. The latter procedure is less fair because it encourages applicants to prepare hasty, superficial responses and precludes the tribunal from putting a second round of pressure on the applicant to provide satisfactory responses if the initial attempt to resolve the deficiency is inadequate. It is also prejudicial to an intervener, which needs some time with a completed application to be able to prepare a full response.

From the intervener's standpoint, deficiency letters are useful for another reason. They help to flag the concerns of the tribunal, or at least of its staff, in time to do something about it. Deficiency letters and responses are part of the application or evidence and, as such, are normally put on the public file in the secretary's office, or in some other public file available to interveners. Since this part of the applicant's evidence is prepared last, and usually under the greatest time pressures, it will probably contain the most errors. It may also show areas of the case which the applicant thought were weak and may have wished to avoid discussing. Deficiency responses thus provide a potentially fertile ground for cross-examination.

(d) Notice of Application/Public Hearing

Once the tribunal is satisfied that any deficiency letters have received adequate response, a public notice is usually issued to inform the public that the application has been filed and that there will be a public hearing.

Such notices differ widely in their quality. Some merely provide the date, time and place of the hearing, and a brief description of the subject. Others contain a brief summary of the application (i.e., what the applicant is asking for) and indicate where and how one may intervene. Public notices such as those of the National Energy Board sometimes even go so far as to describe the particular procedures intended to be used for the public hearing, if these differ from or supplement those set out in the Board's Rules of Procedure.

(e) Interventions

The word "intervention" has two meanings: one, the participation in the case by a party other than an applicant; and second, the document filed by the intervener to respond to the application. To avoid confusion, we will refer to the latter as an intervention statement.

An intervener in its intervention statement may support, oppose or seek to modify an application. Depending upon the rules of the tribunal, this may be done in one of two ways. If the rules of the tribunal are fairly informal, they may require the applicant to submit all its evidence in advance, as part of its application; such a tribunal may expect the intervention statement to contain all the evidence to be submitted by the intervener. If the hearing is a longer one, or the tribunal is simply more formal, the intervener, like the applicant, would probably be expected to file an initial statement summarizing its general position, but certainly not containing all the evidence.

Under the latter procedure, which is generally preferable, the intervener would wait until all the evidence of the applicant, including all the cross-examination on it, had been concluded. Then, if it was felt necessary to present evidence, the intervener could do so; otherwise, the presentation of the case would be completed in final argument.

Until the interveners have seen and tested the evidence of the applicant it is often difficult for them to know what evidence of their own, if any, they should introduce. For this reason, a tribunal which requires that all the evidence of all parties be submitted before the evidence of the applicant or proponent has been heard is more likely to prolong its hearings with needless or premature evidence. Such a tribunal is perhaps a bit insensitive to the needs of interveners, or has simply failed to recognize that most of the relevant evidence (as distinguished from argument) in most cases is likely to be in the possession of the applicant.

As some tribunals have rules prescribing the content of an intervention statement, anyone planning intervention should obtain a copy of the tribunal's rules of procedure, and should certainly follow to the letter any rules dealing with intervention statements. If there are no such rules, and even if there is no rule or other formal recognition of the right to intervene, it should not be assumed that no intervention is possible. On the contrary, the would-be intervener should prepare and submit an intervention statement; there is a good chance that if it is properly prepared, it will be accepted and permission to intervene granted. Such an intervention statement should set out at the top the name of the tribunal and the name of the public hearing, or its subject-matter, as drawn from the public notice. It should then set out clearly and concisely, in consecutively numbered paragraphs, the name of the intervener; the nature of its interest in the subject-matter; whether it supports, opposes or wishes to modify the application; the reasons for its position; and the decision or order sought. A sample intervention statement is included in the Appendix containing Forms at the end of this book.

(f) Pre-hearing Conference

Many tribunals will, prior to the public hearing, hold a conference of parties to discuss and resolve procedural matters. Tribunals which do not do this perhaps should, as they may well spend a great deal of expensive time on opening day discussing procedural matters which would better have been resolved earlier.

Most pre-hearing conferences will include discussions by parties as to what facts they are prepared to concede without strict proof, what witnesses the parties intend to call and how long they expect their evidence to take, arrangements for transcripts, days of the week or hours of the day during which the hearings will be held, adjournments for holidays or to permit preparation of the next phase of the evidence, and so on.

Additionally, the pre-hearing conference may provide the opportunity to hear motions about the responses to interrogatories.[4] If the time between the pre-hearing conference and the hearing is sufficient, it can be useful at this stage to resolve disputes about interrogatory responses so that those ordered to be provided will be received well prior to the public hearing. It is also useful for the applicant to know which interrogatories it will not have to respond to, so that those persons who would otherwise be preparing the replies can be employed in other ways.

4. THE HEARING STAGE

(a) Location

Most provincial tribunals sit in the provincial capital. Federal tribunals sit in Ottawa, but in special cases regional hearings may be held. Some tribunals have a policy of hearing applications affecting a particular region or city "on location". Thus it should be noted that if there is sufficient interest, it is possible to request that the tribunal "come to you", rather than vice versa.

(b) Setting

Tribunals will conduct their sessions in a variety of formal and informal environments. The author has seen them use everything from vacant courtrooms to hotel ballrooms, church basements, legion halls and even a log cabin. Despite the informality of the setting, most tribunals will maintain some element of formality in requiring witnesses to testify under oath

---

4 Interrogatories are written questions to which written answers must be provided, usually before the hearing. For a discussion of these, see Chapter 9.

and, usually, to be subject to cross-examination. The tribunal members will normally sit at one end of the room behind a table on a raised platform. Before them, in several possible variations of an L-shaped table arrangement, will be counsel and witnesses for the various parties and, usually off to one side, the court reporter who uses shorthand or an electronic dictating machine or short-hand machine to record every word that is said (later to be turned into a typed transcript). Depending on the size of the hearing and the number of participants, there may be several rows of tables for parties not at the moment presenting and, also, toward the back of the room, several rows of chairs for the audience. If it is a federal tribunal there is usually a soundproof booth located at the back of the room or in one of the corners for the translators. They provide simultaneous translation in both official languages, which can be heard either by earphones available at any one of the tables or audience chairs, or by means of special portable pocket-sized receivers which can be borrowed without charge at the door.

(c) Opening Motions

In a well-organized tribunal, at the opening of the public hearing, the chair normally asks: "Are there any preliminary matters?" This is a call for motions. Issues which have not been satisfactorily resolved at the pre-hearing conference can now be raised again, as well as any new procedural questions which have arisen since then. Additionally, "preliminary matters" include routine housekeeping such as the filing of exhibits of evidence on behalf of witnesses to be called, the submission of interrogatory responses where these have been delayed or have just recently been requested, and so on.

An invitation to discuss preliminary matters is often made at the opening of every day's hearing by the tribunal, and sometimes, at the early stages of the public hearing, even at the opening of the afternoon session. This makes it possible for the parties to raise procedural questions at regularly scheduled intervals so as to avoid interrupting the presentation of the evidence. Even if the chair forgets to allow the presentation of preliminary matters, any party can raise a hand or otherwise interject at the opening of the proceedings to request that such an opportunity be provided. Alternatively, if the tribunal has no such procedure, a request (through board counsel or the secretary) should be made in advance so that the chair can anticipate the request.

(d) Opening Statements

Some tribunals encourage opening statements by each of the parties, so as to afford an opportunity to explain what their case may then be, in light of their having examined the evidence of the applicant and the replies to the interrogatories. Other tribunals discourage or even refuse to allow opening statements.

Opening statements can be very useful (assuming that time limits are not abused), unless a large number of parties are active at the hearing, simply to focus the tribunal's attention again on the issues. Tribunals which do not permit opening statements tend to have more frequent arguments during cross-examination as to the relevance of this or that question. The person presenting the opening statement (which should be no more than five or ten minutes in length) should set out what the party intends to prove, as well as which areas will be covered in cross-examination and which by the party's own evidence, or in final argument.

(e) Sequence of Evidence

The applicant normally presents evidence first, followed by the interveners. If an intervener raises new points of evidence not covered in the original evidence of the applicant, the latter will usually be permitted to provide rebuttal or reply evidence. This is to be confined solely to the new evidence raised by the interveners, and is not to be abused as an opportunity to present new evidence not raised by the interveners, or to rehash and shore up evidence presented earlier.

A few tribunals still use the old-fashioned method of presenting evidence, an oral question and answer format between the lawyer and the witness or, alternatively, the witness alone reading aloud a long prepared statement. Since reading aloud is very slow, this wastes a great deal of time. The majority of tribunals now have what is referred to as "canned" evidence: a written memorandum containing the evidence is made available to the other parties, usually at least a week in advance. Complex, voluminous evidence that may require a considerable amount of time to analyze is sometimes circulated even months ahead.

The presentation of a witness' evidence has three stages: examination-in-chief, cross-examination and re-examination. Examination-in-chief is the affirmative presentation of evidence. Where this is done orally, the witness steps into the witness box (if there is one) or sits at the table reserved for witnesses, is duly sworn, and presents the entirety of the evidence orally. If the more modern method is used, the witness simply swears that the evidence that has been distributed in advance was prepared by him personally or under his supervision, and is true and accurate to the best of his knowledge and belief. In some cases, cross-examination begins immediately, with the written evidence serving as the substitute for examination-in-chief. In other cases, the witness may be permitted a brief oral summary or highlighting of the evidence before cross-examination.

After cross-examination has been completed, counsel for the party calling the witness is permitted re-examination. The purpose of re-examination is merely to clarify points which were raised during cross-examination on which the record may have been confused or ambiguous; it is not to introduce new evidence or to repeat evidence already presented.

After the first of the applicant's witnesses concludes his examination-in-chief, he is then cross-examined in turn by each of the parties present who wish to cross-examine. Thus one witness may be cross-examined by a large number of parties. Re-examination, if done at all, is usually very short. Then the second witness for the applicant would go through the same procedure, and each successive witness, until the applicant's case has concluded. Then the same procedure would be used with each of the witnesses of each of the interveners in turn.

The sequence of witnesses and cross-examiners is usually set in advance at the pre-hearing conference. It may be in alphabetical order, or by seniority of counsel or by type of client (e.g., governments may be first or last). Nevertheless, for particular reasons, certain parties may wish to cross-examine particular witnesses out of their usual order, for example, due to the need to catch a flight to another city, or whatever. Changes in the sequence of cross-examination can usually be arranged amicably between the parties, and communicated to the board counsel. Where board counsel does not play this role (or the board has no counsel), the chair determines the sequence. In the rare cases in which an agreement is impossible to achieve, board counsel or the chair may be asked to arbitrate.

(f) Motions During Hearing

As mentioned earlier, motions during the hearing can be made at the beginning of the proceedings each day, or after the lunch break. As well, in special circumstances it may be impossible or undesirable to wait until the next normal time for motions. It may be, for example, that a witness is refusing to answer a particular question, or has been evasive or non-responsive. In the circumstances, the only remedy the cross-examiner has is to request the chair to order the witness to answer the question properly. Such an order usually must be requested by motion. Hence, where necessary, motions can be made throughout the hearing.

(g) Sequence of Argument

The distinction between evidence and argument is crucial to an understanding of the public hearing process. Although a more detailed discussion of the significance of this distinction is found in Chapters 6, 11 and 18, it is important, at this stage, to be aware that evidence is basically the presentation of facts (or the opinions of experts, which are a species of fact) and is usually subject to cross-examination. Argument is simply the presentation of counsel (or someone performing that role for the party) and is not subject to cross-examination.

Argument as a type of submission can occur at any stage, as, for example, the argument of a motion. When presented at the end of a case, it is often referred to as final argument but, sometimes, this is shortened to just "argument". The purpose of final argument is to persuade the tribunal, at the end of the day, that the order sought by that party should be granted. Final argument is usually presented orally, but in some cases, if the evidence has been exceptionally long and complicated, it may be presented as a written brief or as a lengthy written argument with a short oral summary.

Since the applicant has the burden of proof, and has presented its evidence first, its final argument comes first. Counsel for the applicant is followed by counsel (or other presenters, where parties do not have counsel) for other parties, usually in the same sequence as they cross-examined the applicant's witnesses, until all of the parties have presented arguments. Then, counsel for the applicant is given the opportunity to make a final reply, confined to refutation of the arguments raised by the intervenors. New issues cannot be raised in final reply; otherwise other counsel would object and seek an opportunity for a further reply.

(h) Cost Awards

A limited number of tribunals have the power to award costs. These are mostly public utilities boards determining rates and the CRTC in its telecommunications hearings. Submissions in relation to costs would normally be made as part of the final argument, if not sooner. (A detailed discussion of how to obtain costs before those tribunals which can award them is discussed in Chapter 10.) The decision as to whether or not costs should be awarded is normally made as part of the main decision in the case. The actual amount of costs awarded is not normally decided at the same time, but is delegated to commission counsel or some other person whose function it is to assess the reasonableness of the expenses and counsel fees incurred by the interveners.

(i) Meetings with Cabinet and Tribunal

Most people are now aware that it is unethical and improper to lobby tribunals with respect to a particular regulatory hearing before or during the public hearing, but it is sometimes assumed that one may do so after the hearing but before the decision is released. There is no basis whatsoever for this view. If the attempt is to influence the outcome of the decision by any communication outside the public hearing, it is improper at any stage, up to the time the decision is released. It makes no difference in morality or in law whether the illegitimate influence is sought to be exercised before, during or after the public hearing. For further explanation, see the discussion on bias in Supplement 1.

5. THE DECISION

The decision of a regulatory tribunal normally has all the force of law, and is as binding on the parties as if it were made by a judge. Behaving in a manner which violates that decision renders the person liable to a contempt charge, which can, upon conviction, be as serious as contempt of court.

The decision or order should not be confused with the reasons for decision. Some tribunals issue decisions with no reason given — a licence or other order sought is simply granted or denied, or granted with certain conditions attached, but with no expressed reasons. Other tribunals write lengthy and complex reasons for decisions, similar to those of a court of law, dealing with issues of policy, evidence and, where relevant, law. These reasons for decision may be accompanied or followed by a formal order. Usually, if there is an order separate from reasons, the former is what is binding, the latter merely explanatory. Therefore, while one can appeal a decision or order, one cannot appeal what are merely reasons.[5] For a discussion of appeals, see Chapter 20.

Tribunals are not bound to treat their own decisions as precedents and, therefore, can follow or decline to follow their own previous decisions.

---

5 For a discussion of appeals, see Chapter 20.

3

The Special Situation of Royal Commissions, Judicial Inquiries and Advisory Boards

1. SPECIAL LEGISLATION

A royal commission, judicial inquiry or other special one-time inquiry requires either a special Act or Order-in-Council (a formal order of the Cabinet) to create it. Most provinces have a *Public Inquiries Act*, which covers public inquiries within the province in general. However, a particular public inquiry may be established either by a special Act designed for that inquiry alone, or by means of an Order-in-Council appointing some person(s) to conduct an inquiry under the *Public Inquiries Act*. In whatever form the inquiry is created, it is important for any would-be participant to read the legislation or Order-in-Council carefully to understand fully the scope of the inquiry's mandate.

Unlike courts of law, regulatory tribunals and particularly royal commissions and judicial inquiries have no inherent powers. They only have such powers as are expressly stated in the legislation which creates them, or other powers necessarily implied to carry out their purposes. Usually the terms of reference of such inquiries are very broad, but there are occasions when they may be too narrow, or may be interpreted too narrowly by the commissioner. For example, a commission given the power to weigh the costs and benefits of some proposal may interpret this mandate as including only economic costs and benefits, and may be unwilling to look at environmental or social costs and benefits. Once the terms of reference have been made public, changes are unlikely, as they will appear as admission of error on the part of the minister and department responsible for the drafting. To avoid such problems it is very important to learn about the government's intention to create an inquiry as early as possible, and to make submissions with respect to the mandate of that inquiry immediately.

2. SPECIAL PROCEDURES

Some inquiries use procedures as formal as a court hearing a criminal case, especially if headed by a judge with that kind of experience. Others, particularly if headed (for example) by a retired professor from the local university who has had no prior experience conducting an inquiry, may be quite informal, and even disorganized.

The procedure is usually not set by the enabling legislation or Order-in-Council but by the commissioner, at the beginning of the inquiry. Therefore, procedures which facilitate the participation of one's client should be advocated vigorously when the rules are being prepared. This necessitates an unusually active stance on the part of public interest groups. It will probably be unsatisfactory to wait to complain until procedures have been drawn up. Once that happens everyone's ego will get in the way and the draft rules will be treated as though they had been carved on tablets of stone. Hence it is desirable to do some reading[1] and talking to persons knowledgeable in the field to determine what kinds of procedures are most desirable.

Perhaps the best Canadian inquiry model, encompassing both informal and formal hearings, was provided by the Berger Commission. It has been further developed and modified to suit particular circumstances by a succession of other more recent commissions. In the full-scale Berger-type hearing, the public hearings are of two kinds. There are informal community hearings in which the commissioner travels to a number of communities, holding hearings extending into evening hours to encourage participation by private individuals after work. No cross-exam-

---

1 Especially R.J. Anthony & A.R. Lucas, *A Handbook on the Conduct of Public Inquiries in Canada* (Toronto: Butterworths, 1985).

ination is permitted during these hearings, to be careful to avoid intimidating ordinary members of the community who are not experienced witnesses. In this way, people without formal academic training or expertise in a particular subject are nevertheless permitted to provide real and practical information based on their own life's experiences. In many situations, the long-term experience of such witnesses is given more weight by the decision-maker than the findings of some highly trained expert given a small budget and short time in which to become an instant expert on an area in which he has never lived.

In addition to the informal community hearings, such inquiries hold fairly formal hearings in several cities, with full scale cross-examination and extensive testimony by expert witnesses from every imaginable scientific discipline. Participants are given the choice of attending the community hearing, the formal hearings or both. In this way, each kind of participant may be given an opportunity to attend the hearing using the kind of procedure with which each is most comfortable. Moreover, neither the opportunity to encourage community participation nor the need for complex technical analysis is allowed to become predominant to the effective exclusion of the other.

Generally, inquiries following Berger have adopted his innovation of using a community hearing as part of the overall hearing. The danger, however, is that such community hearings become token events which, it is felt, cannot be avoided in today's climate of public participation, but are not taken very seriously. During the Berger hearings, Inuit and Indian hunters were able to tell the inquiry, from their own personal experience, what had happened to the game in recent years, and what was likely to happen given a major construction project. On the other hand, consider community hearings held by a commissioner examining the costing and pricing of electricity in the province, or of telephone rates and service quality. While each individual customer might have an anecdote or complaint about some feature of the service, it is most unlikely that these observations will be of great value unless they can be systematically organized and presented to indicate where the bulk of the problems lie. Even then, it is an open question how much this will help the commission to determine whether this is a reasonable viewpoint in light of the costs involved in running such a service and the efficiency of management in doing so.

In summary, community hearings can become a sort of modern ritual which cannot be avoided; to fail to have a community hearing might appear elitist and insensitive to community views. On the other hand, if public participation is limited only to such an informal community hearing, without a formal hearing with interrogatories and cross-examination, it is likely to have very little influence on the decision.

In the early 1970s it was thought that public hearings involving interrogatories, cross-examination and final argument were too sophisticated for ordinary citizens, and that, therefore, their participation should be discouraged, if not formally precluded. Nevertheless, a number of events occurred which changed this. One of these was a fairly innovative attitude exhibited by the National Energy Board (NEB), and particularly by its then chairman, Marshall Crowe. In such hearings as he chaired he would permit anyone to cross-examine, whether they knew how to do so or not. He generally found that for the first little while, inexperienced cross-examiners would flounder around. However, with a little assistance from Board counsel or from the Chairman in wording questions, their skills soon improved. More importantly, they quickly learned the difference between evidence and argument, and learned how to question witnesses without arguing with them. Since many of the points such individuals wished to bring forward were really matters of policy or opinion rather than simple technical content, their cross-examination tended, with experience, to become relatively short. The NEB members simply had to be patient while the neophyte advocates progressed rapidly up the "learning curve".

Also, in 1975, the Canadian Radio-Television and Telecommunications Commission (CRTC) (in some respects the tribunal on which many others have modelled their procedures) conducted a major hearing on the procedures and practices it would use in telecommunications cases. The CRTC had expected a wide range of views from participants as to the kinds of procedures they would like, and had anticipated that consumer groups would advocate less adversarial, informal procedures. It was startled to find how much unanimity there was about the ideal procedure. Consumer groups battled side-by-side with telephone companies for the right to cross-examine each other's witnesses and to preserve other fairly formal procedures which permitted some real clash between the parties. The need to confront one's adversary and to be able to obtain answers to one's questions was generally considered to be so important a vehicle for arriving at the truth that the modest difficulties in learning to handle such procedures seem well worth the effort.

The CRTC adopted the procedures recommended and it would appear that, in spite of the inevitable arguments as to how they should be implemented in particular cases, all parties have been satisfied with them. Nevertheless, royal commissions still continue to be created under a *Public Inquiries Act* model as if the experience of the last decade had not taken place. And each such inquiry "re-invents the wheel" in asking would-be participants what procedures to adopt. Today, serious interveners reject proposals for "informality" if this is a euphemism for a denial of interrogatories and cross-examination.

The typical consumer or environmental group will have among its active members persons with post-graduate degrees in economics, engineering, mathematics or biological sciences. Their knowledge will often equal or exceed that of the major industrial or governmental participants. It is often much easier to teach a member of such a group how to ask questions in lawyer-like ways than to teach a lawyer groundwater engineering, metallurgy or rate structure economics. One only has to watch lawyers fumble with technical details at hearings, even with questions whispered to them by technical advisers at their sides, to recognize how very few of them have even a working understanding of the technical aspects of these cases.

Since 1980, funded initially by a seed grant provided by the Donner Canadian Foundation, the Public Interest Advocacy Centre has conducted advocacy skills training seminars for many of the major consumer, native and environmental groups in Canada. The Centre's experience in these training sessions has been truly amazing. While not every participant has had the capacity or dedication to become a skilled advocate, a sizeable proportion have, and in a remarkably short time. All it takes is an enthusiastic would-be advocate who is prepared to exercise sufficient self-discipline to put in a day or two of advance reading and to spend two or three days in an intensive training session.

With this training, anyone with average intelligence and a good knowledge of the subject-matter will probably learn enough about procedure and practice to be able to function before most inquiries. The combination of background reading, formal lectures, video tapes and role-playing exercises serve to telescope a great deal of learning into a very short time.

From the foregoing it should be clear that there is no need to confine public participation to token community hearings. Public interest groups, whether they are broadly representative of the community at large or only of the interests of a limited number of members, can provide a useful service to the inquiry.

First, they can expand the resources and staffing of the inquiry by making available to them persons with expertise who would not normally be present. These include both the members of the group themselves and such national and international experts as they may bring to support their cases. This contribution can be particularly useful if funding is provided by the appropriate level of government, or in one way or another by the tribunal itself (how this might be done is considered under the general subject of costs, in Chapter 10 and in Supplement 3).

Second, public interest groups can make the adversary system work better. It seems peculiar to design a decision-making procedure employing an adversary process and then to have virtually no adversaries; or to have the adversary role played by commission counsel, with all of the constraints that are implicit in a relationship in which the commissioner and staff must remain neutral. While the commissioner is always free to reject the evidence of public interest groups, if it is not available it obviously cannot be chosen. Thus a commissioner is much more likely to fall prey to being in fact, or at least appearing to become, "captured" by the very institution being examined.

Finally, public interest groups can help an inquiry by focusing and collecting community information, including complaints. Without detracting in any way from the authenticity of the complaint of the individual citizen, such viewpoints have far greater utility when they are aggregated, analyzed, and based upon a sophisticated knowledge of the costs and problems of providing the service involved.

3. TIMELY SUBMISSIONS

With an on-going tribunal, if one fails to obtain a satisfactory hearing in a particular matter, often there will be a future opportunity: the next hearing. With a royal commission, of course, if the hearing is not conducted well the first time, there will be no further chance. Also, because of the tight time constraints normally imposed on royal commissions there is little opportunity to correct procedural mistakes as the inquiry progresses. This makes imperative timely submissions when the legislative mandate and procedures of the commission are being drafted.

Timeliness is crucial to resolve any procedural problem. For example, even if the company or agency which is the subject-matter of the inquiry has filed a great deal of evidence before the public hearing phase, or throughout, there is a likelihood that this will fail to deal adequately, or at all, with some of the issues of concern. Also, much of the information filed will usually be simply what the company has on hand, and may be of limited relevance, or incomplete. It may be necessary to compel the company to conduct new studies especially for the purposes of the inquiry, and to have these studies made available in time to permit examination to determine whether they are adequate or whether they have to be done again, or at least supplemented by further data.

In these situations, information is power, and companies or government agencies being investigated will be reluctant to given up any power. Thus there will be a tendency for their first batch of information filed to be full of innocuous documents and self-congratulatory clichés, with rather limited substance. Such "studies" as they will prepare in response to requests for detail will show remarkably little improvement over their original evidence unless it is made clear by the commission that sanctions will be applied for failure to provide more meaningful evidence.

For all of these reasons, intervention in a special inquiry or royal commission requires a participant to have a well-developed sense of strategy and to know what procedure it wants. It must be quick off the mark in lobbying for the right terms of reference and procedures, and must very rapidly assess the likelihood of useful evidence being made available to it without some special motion. It may be helpful to prepare a flow chart setting out the important dates of the inquiry at which certain information is scheduled to become available, and to work with that to ensure that the information needed is provided before it is too late to be useful in the inquiry.

4. FUNDING AND COSTS

There is no issue of greater importance to the effectiveness of advocacy groups than the scarcity of financial resources.

"Funding" refers to grants made to participants (usually to those who could not otherwise afford to participate) from the government creating the inquiry, either directly or through the budget of the inquiry itself. "Costs" refers to an award made by the tribunal (sometimes partly before, but usually at the end of an inquiry) of the costs of participation, to be paid by the company or agency which is the subject of the inquiry. From the standpoint of the group receiving it, so long as there are no strings attached and it is reasonably timely, it makes no difference in what form the money comes. However, there are all sorts of ideological and philosophical arguments for and against both funding and costs.

Funding provided by the government has the advantage that the donor has a predictable amount to pay in advance, can select a recipient on the basis of demonstrated responsibility, and can allocate funding as it wishes among various groups competing for it. It avoids some of the problems of having the person conducting the inquiry also administering the funding, and precludes the occasional, outraged cry of the subject of the inquiry that "we not only have to come here to have these busybodies snooping into our affairs, we also have to pay these self-appointed guardians of the public interest for the privilege".

The disadvantage of having the government administer the funding is that it renders it liable to the accusation that those selected for funding are political favourites, or tame and harmless groups, while those more controversial applicants likely to provide the most effective opposition are frozen out. It is also possible, where the source of the funding is government, that groups will expect larger amounts than might otherwise be the case and, if they spend it before the case is over, may well return and expect more. Once the government has committed itself to funding a particular participant in a case, it becomes very difficult to cut it off three-quarters of the way through simply because the inquiry took longer than was originally expected. They all do.

One advantage in having the commissioner handle the funding directly is that it de-politicizes the question. As well, the person conducting the inquiry is presumably in the best position to know, because of direct expertise in the subject-matter, which interveners have the best grasp of the subject-matter, appear the best organized or are otherwise most likely to make a useful contribution. On the other hand, the accusation is just as likely to be made that those who were funded were those who appeared initially to favour the commissioner's personal views and, thus, that the commissioner was encouraging the evidence he wished to hear while precluding that which he did not. To put it bluntly, the accusation can be made that costs can be used as a way of manipulating the hearing to achieve a predetermined result. What may be worse, the commissioner who bestows funding on some groups but excludes others may be seen to acquire a certain responsibility for the quality of the evidence they submit. If they appear to have been "paid" to prepare and submit this evidence, it may be much more difficult for the commissioner to reject it as having no value. The parties opposed in interest to the groups being funded are likely to be concerned about this.

Another problem with funding (regardless of source) is selection, from among several competitors, of the right group to fund. Obviously, if half a dozen groups each approach the inquiry seeking a massive amount of funding to advocate essentially the same position, to give it to each of these would be a waste of money. One technique which has worked is to bring the groups together to form an umbrella group or coalition which would specify in advance the common core of their concerns and their differences, if any. Once a responsible executive committee or coordinator has been selected for the umbrella group funding can be provided to it as such, or to the most apparently responsible member of the groups, subject to the condition that it be used for all of the members of the umbrella group and not merely for the immediate recipient.

Mr. Justice Bayda (now Chief Justice of the Saskatchewan Court of Appeal), when conducting his inquiry into uranium mining in Saskatchewan, introduced a most successful innovation. Funding was provided to environmental groups through the budget of his inquiry, but he avoided the pitfalls of administering the funding himself by delegating the task to a three-person committee chaired by a professor of engineering, which made the decisions as to who should obtain how much funding. Presumably, had applicants for funding been dissatisfied with these decisions, they may have appealed to the commission. However, from all accounts the system worked well.

The awarding of costs has the important advantage that it can be tied in some way to effectiveness of contribution (and expenses actually incurred). If a group does not make a useful contribution to the hearing, presumably it would not be awarded all of its costs and, perhaps, in an extreme case, might receive none of them. This should be a sufficiently strong incentive to use the money well and to conduct oneself responsibly. However, the situation is more complex than that.

If costs are all awarded at the end of the hearing, a group which initially does not have sufficient resources to participate would be excluded even if it could anticipate that it would recover some (undetermined) portion of its costs at the end of the hearing. Paradoxically, it might even be argued that a group which can afford to participate actively throughout an entire commission hearing without an award of costs is so wealthy that it probably doesn't need such an award at all. Thus, such commissions as have awarded funding or costs usually have provided a significant portion of the funds in advance, and the rest in a series of payments throughout the case. While it may be desirable to hold back some portion of the money to ensure good performance right to the end, clearly, most of the money will have to be paid out when the evidence is being prepared, which is before the results are seen.

As noted earlier, costs are subject to the philosophical objection that, having done nothing wrong, the payer should not be required to pay for the costs of those who would oppose it. This argument has been countered by the recognition that it is not necessary to have done something wrong to be ordered to pay costs. Rather, such an order can be justified on the basis that the legislature has deemed this inquiry necessary in the public interest, and not because the person whose conduct is being considered is immoral. It is the very existence of the activities themselves, and their nature, which necessitated the inquiry. Accordingly, it seems reasonable that those who carry on that activity cover the reasonable costs of participation in the inquiry. Since the group seeking the costs would not be put to this expense were it not for the existence and activities of the entity being studied, an order to pay such costs can simply be seen as a "cost of doing business". As the costs award is made by someone whose orders have the force of law, the cost will be deductible for income tax purposes and, therefore, perhaps half of it will really be paid by the taxpayer.

Just as with funding, there is a danger that costs can be used, or can appear to be used, to manipulate the results. Knowing that the chair has the power to award or deny costs, a group being denied procedural fairness may hesitate during the hearing to bring the inquiry into a higher court to complain. Conversely, it may be, or may appear to be, that the chair will award costs to those public interest groups which seem most critical and negative. Why pay someone who argues that the proponent is substantially right? Its own lawyers can do that.

If, on the other hand, the appointment of the commissioner was a retirement present for past services or an opportunity to become known to advance a political career, the chair may want his relationship with the entity being studied to be largely supportive, and may hesitate to allow a group of citizens to confront it. Or the chair may simply be intimidated by the economic and political clout of the corporation or department before him, and may decide that the path to safety lies in denying the confrontation sought by the consumer group. In these circumstances the consumer group has a problem: if it is docile, as the commissioner wants, it may be awarded its costs at the loss of its effectiveness and self-respect; if it continues to fight aggressively for what it believes is right, especially if it takes its fight to a higher court or to the media, it risks retaliation from the chair in the form of a denial of costs. Funding from the government, at least, is not subject to the requirement that popularity with the chair be maintained. The same is even true of pure funding provided in advance by the commission itself.

Another problem with costs which consumer groups have to face is what happens if the evidence of one of its witnesses is not accepted. No evidence, however well prepared, is ever perfect. There may be nothing substantially wrong with the evidence, but the opinions of equally learned experts may frequently differ, and the commissioner must choose between them, often on rather intuitive or subjective grounds. The evidence of one expert witness may be rejected in preference to that of another without the former being necessarily "wrong", simply because the latter had a bit more experience or was for some reason slightly more persuasive. In these circumstances, there may be a danger that when costs awards are being decided at the end of the case, the public interest group will be given short shrift.

The payer of the costs may argue that it should not have to pay for evidence which the commission "rejected". While this argument undoubtedly appears sound from its stand-point, it makes the person calling the witness virtually a guarantor that the witness's evidence will be accepted. It also places the reputation of the witness at risk.

Consider, hypothetically, what would happen if the commission rejected the evidence or the case of the company and accepted instead the evidence of the public interest group. Would it then be acceptable to argue that all of the company's witnesses and lawyers should not get paid, and have the commission so order? Of course not. Surely the best any party to an inquiry can be expected to do is to present evidence of reasonable competence and quality having regard to its resources and the available time and expertise. The function of interveners is to participate, and to do so reasonably and responsibly, but not necessarily to "win" in the conventional sense of that term as it is used in ordinary law suits.

By and large, and subject to remarkably few disappointments, those tribunals which have made a practice of awarding costs, as well as those royal commissions which have awarded them, have been content with the results. Over the past 15 years, as public interest groups have become more sophisticated, the quality of intervention has improved. Many public interest groups have acquired considerable staff and volunteer expertise — so much so that their staffs are frequently recruited by corporations, government departments and law firms. The typical Canadian consumer or environmental group of the late 1980s is likely to be run by a board of directors made up of stock brokers, corporate lawyers, university professors and scientists as well as the now largely mythical "little old lady in tennis shoes". Its staff is likely to be every bit as expert as its board. Through formal and informal "networking" linkages, they have affiliations with and access to other groups across the country, or even around the world. Their resources to mount a major intervention before a royal commission may be severely constrained, but given access to reasonable resources through funding and costs awards, they can frequently make an extraordinary contribution to a commission of inquiry which must tap a lot of the available expertise in a short time.

5. INEXPERIENCED COMMISSIONERS

Since it is very rare for anyone to be asked to conduct more than one royal commission, by definition, almost all commissioners are inexperienced in the subject area. Some, however, have had experience in directing inquiries in related fields as judges or chairing an on-going tribunal. Others, while possessing some technical knowledge of the subject-matter they are to inquire into, have never chaired a public hearing in their lives, and perhaps have never even been to one.

Problems of appointments usually fit between two extremes. One is the commissioner who is a good judge in a courtroom but will never really be able to come to grips with the technical subject-matter in sufficient depth to be able to write a persuasive report; the other is a great technician or scientist who cannot keep order at a public hearing, and is equally unlikely to produce a useful report. Each of these areas of inexperience gives rise to its own peculiar problems.

The judge will probably remedy any lack of technical expertise by hiring an expert adviser or consultant. He is also most likely to accept the consultant's advice, in which case, if the consultant's views are favourable to one side, it will prevail, and if not, that side probably does not have a chance. In this kind of inquiry, while the judge always has a veto over the adviser if something is obviously wrong, the chances are that in most of the grey areas, the adviser will dominate the thinking of the inquiry while the judge handles the procedure at the public hearing.

The other kind of inexperienced commissioner will typically go one of two ways. He or she will either hire counsel (too often one who has had no experience with royal commissions either, but who will try to impose a rigid crime inquiry model) or will try to avoid anything to do with lawyers. The author has seen a number of commissions in which the chair virtually abdicated responsibility for making procedural decisions to the commission counsel. For all practical purposes, then, the public interest groups' rights of participation have been defined and administered by someone who is likely to have little professional experience with, or sympathy for, public interest groups.

The few commissions which have tried to dispense with lawyers entirely ("Let's avoid all that formalism and legalism") have soon found themselves adrift or in serious trouble. Some of the parties — particularly corporations or government agencies — insist on being represented by counsel to protect themselves. The scientist-chair without counsel has to defer to their arguments or risk a morass of court actions causing him to miss the reporting deadline. After the chair has been through the chastening experience of learning that procedural fairness (or even a powerful corporation's view of it) cannot be dispensed with, there is a tendency to be more cautious.

What is worse, procedural insensitivity and inability to chair a hearing often go hand-in-hand. When the hearing is permitted to wander out of control, and discussions ad nauseam about a broad range of irrelevant subjects are allowed, the corporate participants will soon complain that this is expensive and irritating; the public interest groups may find such protracted participation impossible to sustain, and may be absent for important parts of the hearing where their absence may be exploited by other parties. Tough, experienced, knowledgeable chairing — so long as it is fair — is clearly in the best interests of all parties. Unfortunately, not all appointments are of this calibre.

What can one do when confronted with one of the inexperienced types we have been considering? Once again, advance preparation appears to be the only answer. Familiarity with the workings and procedural rulings of other major royal commissions, particularly those active in studies in related areas, will put the advocate in a better position to offer guidance and useful advice to the chair. Also, reading a basic text in administrative law (for example, that of Professor Mullan[2]) and the lone text on public inquiries,[3] should amply equip the advocate to understand both the basic requirements of a fair procedure and the application of those requirements to the objects of the particular inquiry.

6. INQUIRY/GOVERNMENT RELATIONS

Success before an inquiry requires some knowledge of the relationships between the government which created the inquiry and the probable outcome. Perhaps it is belabouring the obvious, but it must be recognized that royal commissions and inquiries are created for a variety of political purposes, not always to find the solution to the problem. Also, in some cases, "the problem" which the government may wish the inquiry to solve is not the same as the public's perception of it. For example, in some cases the government may well recognize that public opinion is so strongly divided about what to do on a matter that there is no political appeal in coming down on either side of an issue. To illustrate, non-medical drug use appeared to be a problem of growing seriousness in the late 1960s and early 1970s. The government of Canada created a royal commission on the non-medical use of drugs. The government of the day must have known that there were really only two policy alternatives: to prosecute vigorously those who used illegal drugs, or to legalize the use of those drugs. After the royal commission spent three years studying the problem the government neither accepted nor rejected its recommendations; it set up an internal group to study them. Since then, the commission's report has sunk into the bureaucracy without a trace. Nevertheless, from the government's viewpoint, the commission can be considered an unqualified success because it diverted public attention and criticism from the government's unwillingness or inability to make a decision, enabling it successfully to study the problem to death within the bureaucracy it controls. There was a similar experience with a special federal task force on pornography.

---

2 D.J. Mullan, *Administrative Law*, 2nd ed. (Toronto: Carswell, 1979).

3 Anthony & Lucas, above, note 1.

In other instances, such commissions may serve a useful purpose even before they are finished doing the job they were given. In 1978, then-Premier Bennett of British Columbia instituted a royal commission to determine whether uranium exploration and mining should be permitted in the Province. There was an obvious competition in values and interests between those who thought that uranium mining was immoral or hazardous to the health of miners and to adjacent properties and drinking water, and those who considered it an important potential economic resource to be exploited. This commission was just starting to reach full speed, with a number of expert studies commissioned but not yet completed, when the Premier made the public announcement that he had concluded on the basis of such evidence as was already available that there ought to be a ten-year moratorium on uranium mining in the Province, and he closed down the inquiry. It had already served its purpose.

Some commissions seem to be designed to fail. In the spring of 1982, following an election in Prince Edward Island in which an emotional response to nuclear power had been a major issue, the government of then-Premier Lee created a royal commission under the Honourable Melvin McQuaid to look into a number of aspects of the provision of electrical power by Maritime Electric. This inquiry was given virtually no staff, the commissioner was a retired judge with no particular expertise in electricity, and he was given the task of investigating five major phases of electrical generation and pricing that could have kept an experienced public utility board and its staff going for several years. Nevertheless, the required reporting time was approximately five months after the inquiry began.

From the standpoint of a public interest group, serious questions must be asked as to whether participation in special inquiries can serve any useful purpose. If the real purpose of the inquiry for the government (which, after all, will receive the recommendations of the commission and decide what to do with them) is simply to distract the public, or to provide a political excuse for some action it has already decided to take or to avoid taking, why should a public interest group, with its very limited resources, devote the usually massive effort required to participate? If the inquiry is really unlikely to change anything anyway, it may be that the most effective stance the public interest group can take is to refuse to lend its reputation, dignity and effort to the process.

But let us not be too hasty. It is not always easy to tell beforehand whether the public inquiry will turn out to be a significant event or merely another dismal charade. In most cases, the commissioner appointed is sincere and well-meaning, and perhaps unaware of how the government intends to use the report. The government can make no advance commitment to the commissioner to adopt the advice to be given. There is also always the fear that if one does not participate one's interest will not be taken into account, and a recommendation or decision may be made in which one's views are ignored.

In other cases, participation may be justified on the ground that whether or not the commission reaches a conclusion which is favourable, and whether or not the government acts on its conclusion, the process itself is what counts. The preparation and presentation of sophisticated evidence supporting one's viewpoint, presumably with attendant publicity, sometimes is considered to be worth the effort alone.

While the decision as to whether or not to participate in each royal commission must be made on its own merits, some general considerations can be suggested. First, consider why the government created the royal commission — not necessarily the stated reason, but perhaps the answer to the question: "In what way does the government hope to benefit politically from this royal commission?" Second, one can ask why the particular commissioner was appointed. What (if any) are his or her postcommission ambitions? Are they likely to be advanced or retarded by encouraging or discouraging the presentation and acceptance of one's viewpoint? Finally, one can look at the reasonableness of the time frame and resources available to the commission in light of the range and scope of the subject matter it has been assigned to investigate.

On balance, the author's experience with or knowledge of several royal commissions has been negative. In most cases, any part of the report the government does not like is unlikely to be accepted. This is especially true if a new government is elected after the commission is created but before it reports. Those with the resources to do so will persuade the government not to accept recommendations inimical to their interests. Hence, even total victory at a royal commission hearing can be fairly easily circumvented at the political level, at which public interest groups, despite their fantasies to the contrary, normally have very little clout. Moreover, it is usually fairly easy to give limited weight to the findings of royal commissions because they are often given so little time and money with which to investigate a complex question, resulting in a report which may be superficial in some important aspects. Sometimes the government has been careful to select a commissioner whose views are already known to it, or who can be subtly influenced to present a report favourable, or at least acceptable to the government. This is especially likely to be so if the commissioner wishes to avoid the report merely gathering dust on the minister's shelf.

Given the wide variety of on-going tribunals and the other forms of input into the political process, a public interest group's decision to participate in a royal commission should only be made if the group considers that alternative and more effective ways to have its views recognized are unavailable.

7. AFTER THE REPORT

In many cases, unsophisticated participants will tend to see the report as the final event, after which they can go back to life as usual. Realistically, however, it is only the beginning. If one has struggled hard for months, or perhaps years, to influence the recommendations of a report to government, surely it is of some importance whether or not government acts on those recommendations. If the recommendations are more favourable to one viewpoint than another, most probably the unhappy party will attempt to discredit the report in any way it can. Conversely, of course, the party to which the report is generally favourable will naturally want to support its recommendations and to urge the government to implement them as quickly as possible. Thus it is important to protect one's victory, if that's what it was, or to try to ensure that defeat before the royal commission never turns into concrete government action.

4

What Are the Issues in a Hearing?

In every hearing potentially an infinite number of subjects can be discussed in what tends to be a very limited time. It is most important to have a clear sense of direction and purpose when approaching a hearing, and this can only be done if you know what the issues are. In a court of law it is easy to know what are issues and non-issues. They are determined by the law itself. Not so before a tribunal.

In general terms, an "issue" may be defined as something which stands between the parties, that is, about which they disagree. As parties may have a wide range of disagreements, not all issues are relevant to the hearing. Hence, when we use the word "issue", we will confine its meaning to those issues which are relevant.

What does "relevant" mean — and relevant to what, or to whom? That depends on a number of considerations, not all of them easy to define. The problem with the word "relevant" is that it begs the question "relevant to what"? In other words, "relevance" requires context. Also, "relevance" is like "importance" — it tends to be somewhat subjective. To make matters worse, it also permits questions of degree: some things are plainly irrelevant and others unquestionably relevant, with controversy about everything between.

Relevance may appear to vary with the way in which the potential issue is described. For example, in a hearing to determine whether proposed electricity rates by Manitoba Hydro are reasonable and just, an environmental group seeking to raise as an issue the telecommunications policy of the government of Canada may appear to be merely frivolous. On the other hand, if a federally chartered telecommunications carrier intervenes to complain that Manitoba Hydro's rates to it for electricity for a proposed new use are unfair, it may become relevant in that context to argue that such a proposed use is contrary to the telecommunications policy of the government of Canada. Thus, almost any argument or evidence may be relevant or irrelevant, depending upon the context of the interests sought to be advanced and the statutory mandate of the tribunal. Once a relevant argument is made, if it is opposed, then there is an issue.

Knowing what the issues are is more than merely theoretically important. Virtually any question one may ask of a witness in cross-examination can be challenged by counsel for that witness with the objection that the question is not relevant to any of the issues in the hearing. To defeat this objection, one must be able to show that there is something that has been put in issue to which that question relates. Similarly, an applicant can refuse to respond to an interrogatory on grounds of alleged irrelevance. To persuade the tribunal to compel a reply requires a successful argument that the information sought is relevant to some question in issue.

It should already be obvious that no exhaustive definition of "the issues" is possible, but certain questions do tend to arise more often than others. Accordingly, and for the sake of illustration only, a number of the issues which frequently arise in various different kinds of cases are set out below. While some of these are similar, or at least overlapping, sometimes putting an issue one way rather than another way can be important, as it includes a broader or a narrower question.

1. ENVIRONMENTAL ASSESSMENT CASES

Most environmental assessments require a proponent of a project to file an environmental impact statement (EIS) at some fairly early stage. There is usually a government review of this EIS, which is also made public, followed by an opportunity for public comment on both the EIS and the review. A partial list of the questions that might become issues in these cases includes:

1. Is the definition of "environment" consistent with the Act or regulations? This is important because some statutes include the human as well as the physical environment. Hence an issue may arise as to whether socio-economic considerations have been omitted.
2. Is the assessment complete? In many cases only a few of the impacts have been considered, and several of the obvious ones ignored.
3. Have realistic alternatives been considered? There is a tendency for an EIS to consider only environmentally worse project alternatives, while ignoring better alternatives or the option of doing nothing, that is, of preserving the status quo.
4. Have all the benefits and costs been considered and quantified? In many cases, the EIS considers and quantifies economic benefits, while merely listing environmental negatives. Usually, with a bit of effort, some quantification can be applied to these negatives as well, which may well result in the total social costs outweighing the total social benefits.
5. Are the environmental mitigation measures proposed realistic and, also, likely to be implemented? In many cases it is quite apparent that the proposed mitigation measures are so expensive that they will never be implemented. Alternatively, sometimes all we have is a recommendation of a consultant that they be implemented, with no undertaking by the proponent that, should the requested permit be granted, these mitigation measures will actually be implemented.
6. Has adequate field work been done? There is a tendency to base an EIS on literature surveys or comparisons with other areas, the comparability of which may be unknown. In other cases, two or three months of field work (usually in the summer when the weather is favourable) may be done to permit the claim of on-site experience, whereas appropriate biological study methods may require at least one full year's data.
7. How have the trade-offs between economic and environmental issues been made? It is quite common to conclude that an alleged X dollars of economic benefits versus certain (usually unquantified) negative environmental impacts demonstrate that the project is worthwhile and should be permitted. But what is the right amount of economic advantage to offset what amount of environmental degradation? This is not a technical

question capable of being resolved merely by technical expertise: it is simply a value judgment in which technical experts are no more expert than any other member of the general public. Accordingly, a properly constructed EIS and assessment should do no more than indicate the relative impacts, positive and negative, and leave it to the decision-maker to decide whether the benefits outweigh the costs.

2. MAJOR PROJECTS

It should not be forgotten that the advocacy of major projects is itself an industry in Canada. Exploiting the myth of the untapped riches of our last frontier, a small army of lawyers, accountants, expert witnesses and business managers make a handsome living inflating and flying trial balloons. Whether the project ever sees the light of day may be a matter of relative indifference — their money is made in presenting it. Unfortunately, governments, like mythical emperors, are all too susceptible to being sold a magic suit of clothing and to insisting on wearing it long after its lack of coverage has become evident to everyone. Perhaps the intervener playing the role of the child who has to point out the emperor's nakedness may be aided if the following issues are kept in mind:

1. Does this project appear to make financial sense today? Many projects take years in planning, and are initiated at a time when economic forecasts are moving in a certain direction. For example, the time frame for planning a major hydro-electric project is at least ten years. Ten years ago most forecasts of annual per capita increase in electrical consumption showed continuing rapid growth rates. At that time, proposals for major nuclear plants in Ontario and New Brunswick, and hydro electric plants in Quebec, Manitoba and British Columbia were being advanced. Since then we have again learned the lesson that trees do not grow to the sky, as annual consumption increases dropped from five or six percent to one or two percent. Projecting what will happen in the next decade may be difficult, but the economics of a situation with compounding annual increases of one to two percent is considerably different from that at five to six percent.

2. Have the cost relationships changed? A major argument in favour of, for example, nuclear power is the low cost of fuel versus that of fossil fuel methods of generation. However, the major cost of nuclear plants is the cost of capital to construct them. Thus, at a time when oil is X dollars per barrel and interest rates are Y percent, the nuclear plant may seem the clear winner. However, at a time when the price of oil may have dropped to 60 percent of X, while the cost of capital has risen to 200 percent of Y, the winner may have changed. In a world where commodity prices and capital costs may fluctuate rapidly, assumptions about relative costs should always be questioned.

3. Have all costs been taken into consideration? Projects are frequently justified on the basis of the construction cost to the applicant, without consideration of who will bear the cost of the social problems created. For example, new schools, roads, hospitals and sewers may have to be built. Who will pay for these? There may be a rise in the incidence of crime, family breakups or unauthorized hunting and fishing in wilderness areas. Native land claims and lifestyles may be jeopardized. Also, spent nuclear fuels may have to be stored for thousands of years in radiation-proof facilities. These things are not costless. Have their costs been properly estimated and included?

4. Who benefits and who pays? It is quite often argued that the benefits of a proposal exceed the costs. Even if this were true, those who benefit often bear virtually none of the cost, while those who bear all of the cost obtain virtually none of the benefits. This raises important issues of equity and income redistribution. What should be done to ensure that those who benefit also compensate those who do not? Is proper compensation even possible (e.g., in native land claims situations)?

5. Will the project still be necessary at the time it is scheduled to be completed? Since many major projects may require as many as five or ten years to complete, it may be that either the supply-and-demand situation or the life expectancy of the technological advantage of the project may be exceeded. Was the project simply started too late? In the circumstances, it may be preferable to cut our losses while we can rather than to build something which may cost billions and never return

a reasonable profit. Evidence that bankers and other prudent financiers are unwilling to finance the project without government subsidy or credit guarantee is usually a dead giveaway.

6. How realistic are the forecasts? The only thing one can know for certain about a forecast is that it will be wrong. What remains to be determined is by how much and in what direction.

Essentially, all decisions about major projects are decisions about the future. Yet there are no "facts" in the future. Thus what the proponent must show is that its view of the future is likely to be accurate, and that the status quo should be changed to reflect this view.

All crystal-ball-gazing is a hazardous exercise, even when it is backed by the most modern forecasting techniques. However, the forecasting techniques used are not always the best available. For example, one of two assumptions must be made: that change in the future will continue at the same rate as in the past, or that it will change at a different rate but by an amount that is predictable. Both of these assumptions are open to question and difficult to prove. Even the most complex computer modelling, involving potentially dozens of variables, is only as good as its ability to track results. Of course it can usually track past results with some degree of accuracy because that was how it was constructed. Whether it can track future results is a completely different matter.

To the extent that the future need for a major project, at the time it will be completed, is justified by forecasts based on a certain vision of the future, the accuracy of the vision is always potentially in issue.

In many cases, several of the key numbers upon which the forecasts have been based are simply assumed. There is no way to prove or disprove them. In other forecasts, certain important numerical relationships are assumed. Where this is so, the sensitivity of the final result to relatively minor changes in the assumptions or other input data can be an important issue.

3. ROYAL COMMISSIONS AND SPECIAL INQUIRIES

It is usually said that the issues before a royal commission depend upon its mandate, but that is not always very informative. Usually its mandate will be so broad as to cover potentially a very wide range of issues, which must be narrowed down to a more manageable level. Hence, fairly early on, one of the major issues is: what is this inquiry all about? Or, to put it more conventionally: how should the commission's mandate be interpreted?

Depending upon the task of the inquiry, perhaps some of the issues considered above in the context of environmental assessment cases or major projects will also be issues. In addition, the special problem-solving task of most royal commissions gives rise to certain special issues.

1. How does the proposal or subject matter under consideration relate to known or anticipated government policies? Since the government must ultimately approve any recommendation of the commission if it is to be implemented, the commissioner is not likely to want to come to a conclusion which is contrary to government policy unless there is overwhelming evidence that the policy is wrong and should be changed.
2. How does the proposed recommendation of the commission (or task force) coincide with the decisions or policies adopted by regulatory tribunals? It is difficult to find an area of activity today which is not subject to regulation by some tribunal. It may be that one of the reasons why the commission was created was to find a new policy when existing regulation has "painted itself into a corner". On the other hand, it may be that the existing regulators' policy is considered sound, but is for some reason opposed by some of the participants before the commission, so that indirectly the *ad hoc* commission is being asked to recommend the way to gain acceptance for a regulatory policy. Thus, arguments presented to a royal commission should be seen in the broader context of the decisions of existing regulatory regimes.

4. LICENSING HEARINGS

Although public participation in simple licensing hearings

tends to be somewhat uncommon, some major projects such as pipelines are regulated by means of a licence called a "certificate of public convenience and necessity". Similarly, broadcasters and cable television operators are licensed by the Canadian Radio-Television and Telecommunications Commission (CRTC). In most cases, if the company has been in operation for a while, the practical question is not whether the licence should be revoked; this almost never happens. Also, it can virtually be taken for granted that a licence will be issued to any major project that seeks it, and that a licence will not be revoked in the absence of gross negligence or near-criminal conduct. For example, out of the thousands of broadcasting licenses that have been granted, in the entire history of the CRTC since 1967, only three licenses have been revoked.

The major issues in a licensing hearing centre around the terms or conditions of the licence, and how licences can be enforced if they are breached.

Unfortunately, licensing is a most inadequate form of regulation for most activities beyond the simple one of carrying on a trade or profession. If a licence is granted following a process of formal education and apprenticeship, with perhaps further licensing for specialization at a higher level of expertise, the decision to license an individual — whether taxi driver, plumber or brain surgeon — may not have enormous public consequences, assuming the average level of competence in the trade or profession to be reasonably high. Likewise, as there will be numerous licences, the revocation of a single licence is rather insignificant. However, when a pipeline company or cable television company is licensed it is expected that hundreds of millions, if not billions of dollars will ultimately be invested. Large segments of the population become dependent upon the new licensee. The revocation of the licence becomes virtually unthinkable, so the licensing decision is substantially irreversible.

That being the case, there is little or no clout left to the regulatory agency should the licensee fail to perform as promised. Can the National Energy Board (NEB) tell someone who has built a several thousand mile long pipeline to "pick up your pipe and go home"? Can the CRTC tell a major cable operator to rip all the wiring down and to cease providing service to perhaps hundreds of thousands of subscribers until a new public hearing can be held and a new licensee appointed? Clearly, such treatment is so draconian as to be impossible. Since the tribunal does not usually have the power to fine or otherwise discipline the licensee, there is really not a great deal it can do if the original promises made to obtain the licence are not met. In the absence of rate of return regulation (under which both the quality of service and the profit permitted to the regulated company can be controlled) regulation of complex enterprises merely through licensing is largely an illusion.

Against this background, the issues which might be considered in licensing cases follow.

1. Is what the applicant promises financially feasible? It is easy to promise virtually anything in order to get the licence (as our Pay-T.V. experience shows), even while knowing that these promises may not be financially feasible. After the licence is obtained and the glorious promises are admitted by the successful applicant to have been unrealistic, normally the licence is not revoked; instead, the agency modifies the licensee's commitments to what it can achieve while earning a good profit.

2. How will the regulatory agency know whether or not the promises are met? In some cases, the promise to spend a certain proportion of revenues or a certain amount of dollars is dependent upon questionable cost allocations or an exercise in creative accounting. Unless the regulatory agency can regularly audit the books of the company and verify its allocation techniques, there may be no way to know whether or not the financial commitments are being met. In the circumstances, it may be necessary to recommend a segregated fund of dollars as an insurance scheme or up-front cash payments to ensure that there is no way in which financial commitments can be evaded.

3. Who is really paying for the financial commitments of the applicant? It has become fashionable in broadcasting hearings to promise, for example, increased expenditure for research and development, multilingual community programming, and a whole host of other goodies. However, it is always easy to be generous with other people's money. A proposal which

looks generous if it is coming from profits of the applicant may on closer scrutiny prove to be nothing more than bribing customers with their own money.

4. Is the proposed benefit really a benefit at all? For example, it is common in broadcasting take-over cases to offer to provide a whole range of new service-quality improvements through improved hardware. In some cases these may have been promised earlier, and should have been installed by the outgoing licensee. If that is the case, the issue might be whether this should be deleted from the list of benefits as simply an unfilled obligation of the outgoing licensee which passes to the incoming one.

5. Is the proposed purchase price reasonable? In many cases the transfer of a licence (or, technically, the assets or shares of a licensee) results in a windfall profit to the seller through a huge purchase price paid by the buyer. Where this happens, will the new owner raise rates or reduce service quality in order to make a reasonable profit?

6. What if the licensee goes bankrupt or cannot afford to fulfil the conditions of the licence? In a licensing decision of the Yukon Territory Water Board in the spring of 1982, this question arose in the context of the abandonment plan for a major mining operation by the Cyprus Anvil Mining Company at Faro, Yukon. The firm of chartered accountants retained by the Board as consultants recommended a combination of insurance and a sinking fund (in which a certain portion of the ultimate abandonment costs would be set aside every year, growing with both annual contributions and compounding interest). In such cases the objective is to provide sufficient financial security to satisfy those with a duty to protect the public interest that the necessary money will be available when it is needed, without creating an immediate financial burden for the company which would make the project uneconomic.

The tougher the economic climate, the greater the risk that quick profits may result in the original owners of the licensee taking their money out and doing well, with subsequent shareholders and perhaps the general public left "holding the bag" when the benefits begin to decline and the costs increase. Where the characteristics of a licensed activity are such that the benefits or profits to the licensee tend to decline over the lifetime of the project while the costs and risks to the public increase, the question of premature abandonment is often an important issue.

5. RATE CASES

Rate cases normally involve a very broad range of economic and non-economic issues. To deal with these in a coherent fashion, they have been subdivided into categories. First, the economic issues are generally divisible into two broad questions: whether the applicant needs increased revenues and, if so, which customers should pay for them.

The applicant's argument in favour of increased revenues generally begins with the assertion that rapidly rising costs as a result of cost inflation, increased demand for service or the need to upgrade technology have outstripped the company's ability to pay for them at current rates. If the requested rate increase is not granted, financial ratios and the ability to borrow, modernize and provide service to customers will be impaired, and everyone will suffer.

When it comes to opposing the requested increase in revenues, consumer groups tend to work together. Up to this point in the hearing they have a common interest. However, when it comes to distributing the burden of the increase (if one is to be granted), the coalition of interveners usually falls apart and each competes with the other to avoid the bulk of the burden. Residential customers argue that business customers are not paying their fair share and *vice versa*; rural customers submit that the inferior quality of the service they receive justifies their paying still lower rates, while the applicant itself will strive to keep rates low for those services facing competition.

In principle, and apart from areas of competition, an applicant should be indifferent as to which customers its money comes from, as long as there is enough of it. Nevertheless, most public utilities will tend to take strong, sometimes doctrinaire stands as to how the rate burden should be distributed, perhaps simply because they have always done it that way.

There are two basic ways in which the burden can be allocated: on the basis of costs, or using some non-cost principle.

The latter, in practice, is similar to what economists euphemistically refer to as the "inverse elasticity principle", which might more colloquially be expressed as "sticking it to those who can least avoid it".

In most rate structures there will be a combination of these two principles rather than an application of either principle exclusively. Each principle can be very difficult to apply in practice, and to combine them is even more difficult. Discussions in the rate area tend to sound like those of the ancient metaphysicians discussing how many angels can dance on the head of a pin.

If rates are based on "costs", this term itself has so many meanings as to be virtually meaningless without a precise definition. By costs, do we mean economic costs or accounting costs? This is an important issue because accounting costs are actual historical costs on the company's books, while economic costs are not. This does not mean that accounting costs are in some way more "accurate" or use less arbitrary assumptions than economic costs. Indeed, they can vary quite substantially depending on a large number of management judgments and also upon which of several different generally accepted accounting principles are used. Economic costs are described as forward-looking rather than historic, and dynamic rather than frozen at a point in time. Nevertheless, they tend to produce results in a broader range. For example, in a hearing considering whether Ontario Hydro should adopt marginal cost pricing, it was learned that there are more than 20 "correct" ways of calculating marginal costs.

Most of us are used to thinking about "cost" as having a precise meaning: something costs what we pay for it. In the more complex costing systems of public utilities, costs are "imputed" for items which require no cash outlay, such as depreciation for technological obsolescence, the "calculation" of which can be quite arbitrary. Therefore, we can obtain little information from the simple statement that rates are based on costs. This just begs the question: what do we mean by "costs"? The answer is very much a matter of judgment.

"Value-of-service" pricing sometimes used by utilities tends to be equally arbitrary. The value of a glass of water to someone dying of thirst in the desert may be infinitely high; its value to someone standing beside a tap may be virtually zero. Although Canadian telephone companies traditionally have argued, on value-of-service principles, that telephone rates should be higher for those living in large cities because they can reach more telephone numbers with their basic service, it is generally conceded that there is no evidence whatsoever to indicate that customers in larger cities actually call a broader range of numbers than customers living in smaller cities. Indeed, the whole edifice of value of service pricing rests on such unverified assumptions.

It may be interesting to note that in some American states, value of service principles are not used to set basic rates, and the monthly rate for basic telephone service is higher in smaller communities than larger ones because it costs the company more to provide service in smaller communities, where wires must be strung over greater distances and, generally, the population density is lower. In other United States jurisdictions and in Canada, the price of telephone service to the customer increases with city size based on the value of service principle just mentioned. Thus, two completely contradictory results have been given legal recognition and validity virtually side by side. And this is but one of many illustrations of the arbitrariness inherent in all rate setting.

The usual statutory requirement that public utility rates must be "reasonable and just" requires consideration of both economic and non-economic principles. This conceptual mish-mash, which is implicit in most rate decisions, requires participants and regulators to be schizophrenic. Somehow, we try to combine two mutually contradictory principles in the very same rate case.

The first principle — the prevention of cross-subsidization — is that no one should pay for another's telephone service. This can only be achieved if rates are based strictly on costs (assuming, of course, that we can agree on what is meant by "costs"). The second principle — the duty to provide service even to customers whom it is unprofitable to serve (e.g., those in remote areas) — is based on the policy that even these consumers are entitled to service in return for the utility's privilege of a monopoly in more lucrative areas. This second principle clearly requires rates to be higher or lower than costs to provide cross-subsidy of unprofitable areas by revenues from profitable ones.

When it serves its purposes, an applicant for a rate increase will argue that the rates it proposes for a particular customer class must be increased to bring them closer in line with "costs". Customer groups opposing such increases will reply that in accordance with some other definition or way of measuring costs, they are already paying their fair share and that the applicant has overstated its costs of providing service to them. When this argument is unlikely to succeed by any measurement of costs, or when costs are impossible to estimate, they usually fall back on the other principle, that public utilities must not be permitted to indulge in "cream-skimming" by serving profitable customers only.

The duty to provide service is justifiable from the standpoint of fairness to the utility so long as the average return earned by the company on its profitable and unprofitable services is reasonable.

The provision of service at below cost (where cost can be meaningfully determined) must be carefully controlled, to prevent unfair price discrimination. In particular, any cross-subsidization in rates must be considered "socially acceptable". The categories of socially acceptable cross-subsidies have never been defined, but the term is usually taken to include assistance to remote and rural areas which could not otherwise have service, low income subscribers for whom telephone service might otherwise be a hardship, and the special requirements of the handicapped or of Inuit and Indians living in isolated communities and in part on the land, for whom efficient and affordable telephone service might mean the difference between life and death.

While the pricing of service based on cost and socially acceptable cross-subsidization are conceptually incompatible, their simultaneous use appears to have created few problems in practice. Perhaps this is in part because costing is still so unsophisticated and inherently subjective that we have very little hard knowledge of what anything costs, and rate structure change, in practice, has tended to be a series of small incremental departures from past rates. But socially acceptable cross-subsidization is only the first of a newly emerging series of non-economic rate issues. In the electrical utility field, one such issue has been so-called "life-line" rates, which allow low income consumers to pay a low basic monthly rate in return for a limited electricity consumption. Such rates are usually justified on the non-economic but important social principle that if a service is important enough for the legislature to deem its provider a public utility, it is an essential service; and access to essential services should be virtually a matter of right. A parallel to this principle is found in telephone rates, through keeping low the cost of installations so as to render less onerous the entry rates for access to the system. A whole other major category of non-economic issues centres around the quantity and quality of service provided.

If the customer's duty is to pay the bills, the utility's duty is to provide the service. But what level of service are we entitled to for any particular amount of payment? With telephone service, are we entitled to a directory, to yellow pages? To have a service installed within any particular time period if we move? To have our telephone service repaired if it is out of order within any particular time period? To any particular level of accuracy in billing? To what class of customers and in which amount should the telephone company be permitted to charge security deposits? Issues such as whether the advance payments policy of Bell Canada and British Columbia Telephones are, as administered in practice, unfairly discriminatory against the poor have been issues in telephone rate cases along with literally dozens of other service quality complaints.

There appears to be an emerging recognition that the telephone company tariff (which is, formally, what the regulatory agency regulates) is a kind of contract between the telephone company and the customer. On the one hand, the telephone company is entitled to receive its revenues; on the other, the customer should be entitled to a certain level of service. Just as a merchant selling a ten-pound bag of flour for five dollars can change its effective price by selling an eight-pound bag for five dollars, the telephone company which keeps its prices the same but reduces the quantity or quality of service can bring about a rate increase. Therefore, unless the service quantity or quality is regulated as closely as the rates, the utility could evade regulatory scrutiny. Indeed, the day may not be far off when service quantity and quality standards are written right into the tariff, with rebates to customers not only if there is a total service breakdown, but also if service quality falls below a tariff standard for a significant period of time.

With gas and electrical utilities, the range of service quality problems is not as acute, but service quality can still be relevant, e.g., held orders for installation, repairs after outages, correction of billing errors and credit collection practices. More subtly, both gas and electrical service is engineered to provide a very high level of reliability — higher than is necessary for most residential customers. For example, for each tenth of a percentage point of reliability beyond a certain point, the cost goes up enormously. Certain industrial customers may need a very high level of reliability for their processes, but the same level of reliability — and expense — is imposed upon all customers, whether they need it or not. The issue might then be: why don't those who want the higher level of service pay for it? Due to the difficulty of computing or estimating a dollar value for this, regulators almost universally ignore service quality cross-subsidies. Thus, there will usually be a service quality cross-subsidy from the bulk of ordinary users to those who have especially high service quality requirements. As the latter are normally large business or government customers, this cross-subsidy is the opposite of what is normally considered socially acceptable.

From the foregoing discussion it should be evident that rate cases involve a whole host of economic and non-economic issues, virtually as complex as our society itself. No simple listing of these issues is possible, as it would probably occupy many pages and still not be complete. One reason for this complexity is that the regulation of a multi-service enterprise such as a telephone company, with as broad a market of customers as society itself, involves an extremely difficult mix of economic, accounting, engineering and other technical judgments, as well as a whole host of rather subjective policy or value judgments. Obviously, not every rate case can involve a discussion of all of these issues, or even of a small fraction of them; otherwise it would never end. Hence many important issues may lie dormant and for years may be ignored; indeed, with the turnover of members on some boards, an entire generation of members may be quite unaware of them. Nor can a consumer group, even one with virtually unlimited resources, attack every issue at once. A careful selection of issues is essential. A partial list of issues follows.

1. Rate of return, although theoretically important, is in practice often a non-issue, especially during a period of rising or stable interest rates. This is because the rate of return is a maximum ceiling on the "profit" the utility can earn. If it earns more than this, it will be taken away by the regulatory agency and given back to subscribers. No regulatory utility in its right mind would ever allow itself, except perhaps accidentally, to earn more than its allowed rate of return.

   There is also considerable rhetorical advantage to earning less than the maximum permitted rate of return, because at rate cases the utility can argue that the company has consistently earned less than what the tribunal had considered a fair rate of return; stockbrokers and their securities analysts (for whom the sale of public utilities stocks is an important portion of their business) will usually join the chorus supporting the company's argument that profits are so low that no one will invest. Newspapers (and financial writers in particular) tend to report in exquisite detail the complaints of senior company officers and financial analysts about the low rate of return. All of this sympathetic cheering section is part of a public utility's usual public relations campaign to put pressure on the regulatory agency to give it more money.

   Of course, if the company finds between rate cases that it is starting to earn too much revenue in the sense that it is beginning to approach its maximum rate of return, the quick fix is to spend or invest some more money. In general, then, a regulated utility will always spend as much as its regulator allows, and then some, so as to arrive at a rate of return which is below its allowed rate of return. This is one of the unfortunate but apparently inevitable perverse incentives built into rate-of-return regulation.

   In cross-examination, the utility's financial witnesses will acknowledge that their rate-of-return calculations are based on an acceptance of the company's forecasts of revenues and expenditures and, to the extent that such forecasts might be wrong, their own forecasts of necessary rate of return would also be wrong. Since rate of return is really the "bottom line", one can fruitfully examine each of the lines above the bottom line and have as much effect as if one were to attack the bottom line directly.

2. Part of the rationale for a rate increase is that the public utility has a legal duty to provide service in both good and bad economic times, and that it cannot obtain all of the capital it needs to provide the necessary expansion and modernization of its plant simply from internal sources. Accordingly, it must raise capital on the capital markets to meet its service responsibilities.

This can often be a fruitful area of investigation for the consumer group, in that capital requirements are usually based on demand forecasts, with separate forecasts being provided for each kind of service. While local service tends to vary primarily with population growth and therefore to be fairly predictable, most other services are not. An examination of the telephone company's demand forecasts for long-distance and other services (particularly competitive services) may yield interesting results. The historical forecasting accuracy of the company should also be considered.

With electrical utilities, exaggerated demand forecasts have become notorious. There has always been a considerable lag before the declining annual increase in consumption has been recognized by the utility and put into its forecast. Since a utility which is expanding more rapidly generally offers more promotions and raises, and otherwise tends to be more interesting to work for, it is understandable that management, who is not, after all, personally paying for the expansion, will tend to exaggerate the demand for growth in the hope that it can become a self-fulfilling prophecy. The political masters of most electrical utilities (usually provincial crown corporations) also favour "mega-projects" like dam or nuclear reactor construction in the mistaken belief that such capital intensive projects "create jobs".

To the extent that the projected annual rate of growth can be demonstrated to be exaggerated, capital budgets can be reduced. While there may be some lag between the time the corporate decision is made to reduce the budget and the time it can be implemented (some equipment may be ordered years ahead), these leads and lags should be computed and justified by the utility so that there can be effective control over its capital budget.

3. A more difficult issue in the capital budget is whether it really

costs what the company says its cost to build what it wants to build. Who really knows what it will costs to build a pipeline or a nuclear plant? In the case of telephone companies, which may have literally hundreds of simultaneous small and large construction projects, who knows how much each of them should cost to build efficiently? It is very difficult to determine whether the $300,000 slated for the addition of lines at switching station X should really be $200,000, or whether the demand for expansion is caused by basic or competitive services. A major flaw of the regulatory system, for which there is as yet no solution, is that the regulator does not have the resources even to spot-check the accuracy of construction budgeting. We are all pretty much at the mercy of the company to provide reasonable figures.

When a great deal of the construction is done by the telephone company's wholly-owned but unregulated subsidiary, or unregulated sister company, there is a natural tendency to be suspicious that the construction costs have been exaggerated in order to put more money into the unregulated entity. To verify such a suspicion is virtually impossible at the present time, given available regulatory resources and techniques. The CRTC holds an annual Construction Programme Review to look into these questions in greater detail than could be done during the pressured situation of a telephone-rate application itself. While these reviews appeared promising at first, they have now become largely information-only sessions dealing with the process by which telephone companies engineer their construction programmes. Other things being equal, a good process will tend to lead to a good result, but other things are not always equal. In the absence of vigorous and effective external cost reduction pressure of the sort created by competition, there is no irresistible incentive to cut costs. Nevertheless, until we are prepared to provide regulatory agencies with the resources to scrutinize and at least to some extent to second-guess the construction expertise of the utility, a construction cost estimate will largely have to be approved as a cost if the utility says it is.

4. Another important issue is whether the company is employing the lowest possible cost of capital. Although this involves complex questions of corporate finance dealing with bond

ratings, debt/equity ratios, dividend payout ratios and the like, such expertise is available in Canada at a reasonable price, and the company can be challenged in this area. In spite of such evidence, challenges to a utility's efficiency in raising capital have not generally been successful. This is largely because the regulators have very little direct experience with raising capital themselves and, hence, very limited self-confidence in a potentially dangerous area. Thus, when the president or vicepresident of finance of the utility testifies at the public hearing that he was personally warned by the "gnomes of Zurich" or the underwriters on Wall Street that a company of comparable size earning its present rate of return would need to pay no less than Y percent for its money, regulatory commissions have tended to treat such anecdotal evidence as irrefutable.

Despite every possible economic blandishment, the author has not been successful in persuading any member of the investment community to provide testimony in this area on behalf of a consumer group, to contradict that of a public utility. Nor are there any known instances of such testimony anywhere in Canada. Hence the only witnesses who can be called to contradict the evidence of senior company officers and the stock brokers are university professors of finance, whose lack of "hands on" stock market experience may preclude their views from being given the same weight.

5. Revenues and expenses are perhaps the most fruitful issues for examination. Not surprisingly, revenue forecasts tend to be understated (on the argument that it is better to be conservative) while expense forecasts are overstated (this is also supposed to be conservative).

Usually there will be a bunching of forecast expenditures in the year in which the rate increase is sought so as to make it appear as an unduly expensive year, even though many of these expenditures are discretionary (for example, a sudden increase in the inventory of replacement telephone poles when there is no reason to believe that any more of them will fall down this year than last year). Similarly, allegedly reduced revenues as a result of alleged competition have often been exaggerations, as have the forecast reduction in long-distance revenues due to a generally unhealthy state of the economy.

An economist with mathematical modelling experience in the public utilities field, and preferably direct experience with the type of utility being scrutinized, can be most helpful. Even if such expertise is unavailable, someone willing to spend a few hours playing with a calculator and looking at the company's numbers, both historical and projected, will soon have little difficulty in finding a number of important questions to ask.

6. Rate structure and rate design issues are often the most likely to be fruitful. To argue that one group should pay more and another less relies more on questions of fairness and the kinds of social policies we wish to encourage than it does on costly technical expertise. Over the last decade, employing such arguments, the Public Interest Advocacy Centre has had considerable success in helping keep basic telephone rates down and improving service to low income consumers, the hard of hearing, the Inuit and Indians.

7. Management efficiency is another important and very difficult issue. In regulatory theory, the function of a regulatory commission is to be a surrogate for the forces of the market, which reward efficient companies and punish inefficient ones. In the absence of competition, the rate regulator is supposed to provide the same effect. It can do this by granting the company a higher or lower rate of return, or higher or lower rates, to force it to become more efficient. Specifically, expenses that are not considered prudent and necessary (e.g., the corporate jet once used by Union Gas) can be disallowed as expenses which will be recognized for regulatory purposes.

The effect of such a disallowance is to transfer the cost of such expenses from the customers of the utility to the shareholders. This will usually result in the expense being discontinued very quickly.

In regulatory theory, the utility has the duty to prove that its management is efficient, and that it is conducting its business at the lowest possible cost. In practice, hard proof of this is never required of a company, and the mere assertion that it is doing so is usually treated as sufficient. In effect, then, the onus of proving inefficiency falls on the interveners. This onus is extremely difficult to discharge, for at least two reasons. First, efficiency is never absolute: to demonstrate that the company is inefficient in relation to some external standard, an appropriate benchmark must be selected. Companies in competitive industries may be used as a standard of comparison, but where their technologies and products differ significantly from those of the utility, the danger of a misleading comparison is very high. Even comparing telephone companies only, differences in terrain and product mix can easily mask differences in efficiency and, in any event, as they are all regulated monopolies, it may be that we are largely comparing relative levels of inefficiency supported by regulation.

Added to these basic conceptual problems, we have the fact that the units of measurement of efficiency are by no means clear. While some fairly complex economic studies have been done showing historical trends in the "marginal productivity" of capital and of labour employed in the enterprise, such studies rest upon a fairly large number of controversial assumptions. Moreover, inter-company comparisons are difficult because the data is in many cases unavailable. Even if it were available, it would probably be measuring productivity changes in different input and output mixes. In other words, short of finding glaring examples of obvious inefficiency, a systematic examination of the efficiency of any public utility is likely to be beyond the resources of the wealthiest intervener and, therefore, not likely to be a very fruitful area of challenge in a rate case.

8. The "fudge factor" is not an openly acknowledged issue but, nevertheless, one which underlies every rate case. Since the applicant expects to have some portion of its rate increase rejected, perhaps simply because of the cosmetic need of the regulator to show that it is doing something, utilities will tend to ask for more money than they really need. This "fudging" can be expected in every aspect of the company's application: asking just a bit more on its permitted rate of reurn than is justifiable, over-estimating expenses, under-estimating revenues, and so on. The strategy appears to be that what one does not ask for one cannot receive and, if one should be so lucky as to receive all of what one asks, it is not very difficult to spend the unexpected gain.

For its part, the regulatory agency is also aware of the

game that is being played, but determining the magnitude of the fudge factor is difficult for all concerned. Yet in one application after another, the author has seen the applicant receive three-quarters, or even one-half of what it has been asking for and continue to survive, despite earlier cries of imminent catastrophe if the rate increase was not granted immediately in its entirety. In the end, the regulatory decision as to how much of a rate increase should be granted involves an unfathomable mixture of specific techniques (e.g., economics and accounting) and just plain judgment about credibility.

In a period when costs are rising, a smaller than required rate increase simply increases the frequency with which the applicant will re-apply; on the other hand, granting an excessive rate increase in the hope that another rate case can be avoided in the near future has usually not worked, with the "bonus" intended to buy more time simply disappearing into the general expenses. The fudge factor, then, can be dealt with both through the presentation of one's own expert evidence and also through common sense arguments in final argument. The failure to consider the fudge factor at all, however, leads to the risk that the utility will leave the hearing laughing all the way to the bank.

5

Lawyers, Consultants and Expert Witnesses

1. INTRODUCTION

Retaining lawyers, consultants and expert witnesses is an important matter; one's choice can significantly affect the outcome of the hearing. Hiring the wrong expert can actually do more harm than good. Not only may the evidence presented be less persuasive than the same point well made in final argument, but, if it had been expected that his services would be compensated through costs awarded by the tribunal, the failure to receive such costs can be most painful.

2. IS AN EXPERT WITNESS NECESSARY?

The first question is whether one needs an expert at all. This depends on the nature and scope of the proposed intervention. If there is a simple, non-technical point to be made, it can probably be made well enough through an intervention statement and in final argument. The danger, however, is in wrongly assuming a complicated point to be simple. For example, what will it cost the regulated enterprise to do what you propose? It is rather difficult to appear to be a responsible intervener when one advocates a solution the cost of which is unknown. Under some circumstances, then, where cost is likely to be an important issue, some expertise may be required.

Sometimes, precisely what one proposes may not be technically feasible, even though it sounds like a good idea in principle. However, it may be possible to do something quite similar which is technically feasible. Retaining the appropriate technical expertise can be very helpful in such cases.

Many public interest groups have available to them a considerable level of expertise on their own staff. Naturally, such resources should be used whenever possible. But not everyone with technical knowledge is a good witness. As experience in the witness box can make a critical difference, it may be desirable to hire an outside expert to testify to obtain the benefit of this experience, as well as the aura of impartiality which tends to surround independent witnesses.

Regulatory tribunals tend to place a great deal of emphasis on credentials. While two people may have equal knowledge about a subject, if one has a PhD in the subject and several years of consulting and testifying experience, greater weight will be given to his or her views. Since the object of all advocacy is to persuade the decision-maker, if the resources are available or can be obtained, participants in public hearings should take a pragmatic view of the retainer of experts. Some citizens' groups have a strong "anti-expert" bias, and struggle against what they believe to be the tyranny of expertise. While there is much to be said for this viewpoint in many aspects of life, it does not necessarily win hearings. Thus, the decision is whether the goal of an intervention is to strike another blow against the tyranny of the expert, or whether it is to achieve a successful result at the public hearing.

3. IS A LAWYER NECESSARY?

When deciding whether or not to retain a lawyer, many of the same considerations apply. If someone is appearing for the first time before an on-going tribunal, or if this is a one-time commission in which procedural issues are likely to be of importance at least initially, having an experienced regulatory lawyer can be most important. In many cases, at unpredictable times, complex issues of procedure or evidence arise in which someone without experience in administrative law may be at a severe disadvantage. Even if the lawyer is not in attendance in the hearing room throughout, availability at the right time can be critical.

Apart from emergency situations or portions of public hearings in which important procedural issues dominate, the full-time attendance of a lawyer is not indispensible to a successful intervention *provided* that the members of the group have themselves developed some advocacy skills and a working knowledge of procedure and the evidence in the case. Even reading this book and watching a public hearing for a few days can be of help. Attending an advocacy training session is better still.

Although a lawyer may not be essential, it does not follow that he will not be useful. To do an effective job in a public hearing involving issues and evidence of any complexity, no "one man band" is likely to be very effective. A division of labour and skills is often important.

In a complex hearing, someone must be responsible for coordinating the entire intervention. This may include the preparation of the intervention statement, interrogatories, affirmative evidence and cross-examination of the evidence of other parties; it may also require dealing with and co-ordinating the efforts of a person carrying out the central role at the public hearing (whether or not that person is a lawyer), with consultants and experts who may work in other cities; assembling, organizing and indexing the potentially hundreds of exhibits of evidence and dozens of volumes of daily transcript (perhaps 250 pages in each volume) as they come in, and so on.

The person(s) who is (are) to testify will have a major job: looking at evidence in previous hearings, reading and analyzing all of the evidence in this hearing, drafting and re-drafting a written memorandum to withstand cross-examination. The person fulfilling the principal advocacy role will have to be preparing final argument as the evidence proceeds; looking at the cross-examination of all witnesses by all parties to cull out relevant portions; preparing cross-examination (in consultation with one's expert witness); working with the expert witness in preparing affirmative testimony, and so on. In any major environmental, licensing or public utility hearing, there are simply not enough hours of the day for one person to do all of the witness and counsel work effectively, even if a person with such a broad range of knowledge and skills could be found. Since someone must play the advocate's role in any event, if resources are available or can be obtained, one might as well hire a skilled regulatory lawyer to do the job.

4. CHOOSING A LAWYER OR EXPERT WITNESS

Just as with expert witnesses, finding the right lawyer for the job can be time-consuming and difficult. Citizens' groups have frequently been disappointed in their selection of lawyers, for a variety of reasons. First, and most obviously, is their cost. People are shocked to discover that an experienced regulatory lawyer will probably charge at least $1,000 a day for each day in court, and at least $100 an hour for preparation; senior counsel may charge more than twice these amounts. While junior lawyers will have a lower hourly rate, often the more experienced lawyer will actually accomplish more work in less time, and thereby result in a lower total bill. The lowest hourly rate is not the only relevant consideration.

The writer has no desire to be an apologist for the legal profession, but in many cases lawyers' hourly rates only appear to be high if one does not consider their overhead component. In most other businesses in which persons are paid comparable salaries, as well as in government, if one took all the overhead and worked out a per hour basis, hourly rates would often be comparable or higher. For example, if one took salaries of university professors and added to it a fair share of the cost of the administration of the university, a fair market rent for the square footage cost of offices and classrooms, the cost of secretarial and other salaries, and divided all this by the number of hours spent teaching, the professorial cost per hour would be a good deal higher than a lawyer's. On the other hand, if the law firm were to bill its clients by charging separately for the lawyer's time, the secretary's time, the bookkeeper's time, office space, and each and every individual charge which comprises the hourly rate, the total bill would be the same but may not give rise to the same intuitive reaction that no one should be paid $100 per hour.

It is one thing to recognize that lawyers' rates are not necessarily too high. It is quite another to believe that legal services will always provide good value for the money. This depends primarily on the output and effectiveness of the lawyer, which is closely related to directly relevant expertise and advocacy skills. The fact that a lawyer may have spent 25 years arguing cases before the court of appeal does not necessarily mean that he or she will be skilled in presentation before a regulatory tribunal. The kind of highly technical knowledge required by some regulatory tribunals is fairly rare in the legal profession.

Even considerable regulatory experience before one tribunal does not necessarily translate to success before another where the issues and personalities may be different. In some situations a lawyer's success before one tribunal may be simply because of numerous appearances before it, and because everyone there knows, likes and trusts him. As a new person appearing before another tribunal, the first impression created may be crucial and it may not necessarily be as good as in the more familiar habitat. Also, although many skilled advocates are versatile enough to argue virtually anything, some, who have for years been working primarily for corporate clients, find it difficult to make the switch and to argue convincingly on behalf of, for example, an anti-poverty or an environmental group.

Some would advise that one should go to an enthusiastic young lawyer operating out of a hole-in-the-wall storefront office in preference to an older one who works in an oak-panelled office in an office tower. The reason given for this is that the young lawyer will probably be more anxious to acquire a reputation, more dedicated and hard-working, and a good deal cheaper. If everything else were equal, this might well be true. However, the lawyer in the high-rise office may have had many years of experience in difficult and tricky cases with heavy-weight lawyers on the other side. The young lawyer, while bright, may have done little more than simple automobile accidents and provincial court matters, with no experience opposing senior counsel. Sometimes even the prestige of a major law firm in and of itself adds credibility to a client group which otherwise appears powerless and is unknown to the board.

On the other hand, the fact may be that the senior lawyer has had all of the benefit of a patrician family up-bringing and private schooling, association with a prestigious law firm and membership in the right clubs, but has relied on bright juniors for many years and done little original work; or may have a condescending attitude towards non-corporate clients and little real sympathy for their cause.

Although one may tend to assume that a large law firm has depth of expertise in every area, this is rarely true. The number of lawyers in any province who have much experience handling public utility rate cases or pipeline applications can probably be counted on the fingers of both hands. In the end, the young lawyer's bill would probably be two-thirds to three-quarters of that of the more experienced counsel, and hence the saving in dollars may not be all that large. Therefore, it is necessary to look behind the stereotypes to find out with whom one is really dealing.

Hard questions should be asked as to directly relevant previous experience and, equally important, to the results thereof. There is nothing wrong with asking to see the transcript of a hearing in which the lawyer presented a final argument. Is the lawyer's presentation style compatible with that of the client group? In personal terms, would *you* feel comfortable inviting him to dinner or to a party at *your* house? Intuitively, and at a non-verbal level, how well and quickly do *you* and the lawyer understand one another? If there are some "bad vibrations", of whatever sort, why it this? If the whole relationship does not feel comfortable after an hour of discussion, it may well never.

Finally, no group should feel obligated to retain the first lawyer or expert it interviews. Comparative shopping is always important. Most lawyers are happy to have new clients. It is recommended that one shop carefully and insist on value for money.

In most major cities, lawyers are as highly specialized as are doctors. Just as no one would hire a foot specialist to do brain surgery, it is pointless to retain a company law lawyer or matrimonial lawyer to do an environmental case. Unfortunately, unlike doctors, lawyers do not normally advertise their special-ties, and in many cases provincial law societies have not even defined approved areas of specialty. For example, there are no certified specialists in "environmental law" or in "rate regulation". Thus, to determine how much a lawyer knows about these fields, a community group will have to ask how many such cases have been handled in the past, find out what the cases are, and determine whether they bear any significant resemblance to the case in which the group expects to be involved.

Designations for accountants and economists are just as confusing. A chartered accountant who has spent a great deal of time auditing companies is bound to have some peripheral knowledge of concepts of rate of return. Nevertheless, he may not be qualified to be an expert in cost of capital unless he has had either specialized training in the field at a post-graduate level or direct experience. Designations for economists are every bit as vague. Even one who has taught industrial organization (which includes regulation of the economy) is not necessarily qualified to analyze in detail the actual revenues and expenditures of a gas company. It would take him several weeks simply to catch on to the technical terms used in any industry, and usually it is too expensive to pay for his education.

In both Canada and the United States there is a very limited number of specialists in accounting and economics who are qualified in regulatory matters. Among these, the number who are really good at what they do (as distinguished from those who have simply participated in several cases) is as small as it is in any profession. Most of these are in great demand at all times, and must be recruited well in advance or they are likely to be unavailable.

In summary, finding and recruiting competent counsel and expert witnesses is one of the most important tasks of any group intending to conduct effective advocacy. The resources of the applicant and of most corporate interveners in these cases tend to be formidable. Public interest groups can never hope to compete on a witness-for-witness or lawyer-for-lawyer basis. Yet much of the corporate effort is undertaken from an abundance of caution, and often proves to be needless repetition or even "over-kill".

It is recognized, of course, that in a substantial percentage of cases, public interest groups will have no resources available to them — no experts, no lawyers. Some of the chapters which follow are intended to make it feasible for the more articulate members of such groups to do their own advocacy. In all circumstances, of course, one simply must try to do the best one can with what one has. However, where supplementary expertise in the form of appropriately qualified and sympathetic expert witnesses or lawyers is available, the potential benefit of such additional resources should not be discarded lightly.

5. GETTING THE MOST OUT OF LAWYERS AND OTHER EXPERTS

Getting the most out of lawyers and other experts can require considerable ingenuity. Set out below are a few suggestions for improving the chances of a satisfactory working relationship.

(a) Lawyers

Where possible, shop around and compare the services which can be offered by different law firms: check the reputation and the ability to deal with clients by talking to former clients, or others who know him.

Lawyers have a number of bad habits which are particularly annoying to public interest groups. The worst of these is not returning telephone calls — probably the most notorious failing of lawyers. It may be too much to expect telephone calls to be returned immediately or even the same day but, unless the lawyer is out of town at a trial (in which case calls can be returned in the evening) there is no excuse for an urgent telephone call not being returned within 24 hours, or a less urgent one within 48 hours. Yet it is not uncommon for some lawyers to allow client telephone call slips to pile up, and simply not to return them, communicating with their client only if and when caught without a chance to escape.

Other lawyers simply form their own impression of what is in the client's best interests, and do not ask the client's instructions as to what they would like argued. Such lack of communication may result in a client who attends the hearing feeling embarrassed as the lawyer makes some argument that the client is not at all happy with, or having to put the lawyer through the embarrassment of rushing up to say that the argument is wrong. However successful they may be with judges, lawyers who have these and similar communications problems with their clients are unlikely to exhibit the kind of sensitivity necessary to advocate effectively the rather subtle public policy arguments which must be used before regulatory agencies.

In what kinds of cases can lawyers provide service without a fee? Normally, a public hearing at which one would expect to be present over a 20- or 30-day period is not one in which it is feasible to request someone to provide volunteer legal assistance for the full hearing. It is simply unrealistic and unfair to expect any lawyer to give up that much income as a social contribution. At the other end of the spectrum, a one or two day case to be presented before a provincial supreme court or the Supreme Court of Canada is something for which it may be relatively easy to recruit lawyers, as the total effort, including preparation, is not likely to exceed two or three days.

If the group has any resources with which to pay a lawyer, it should. It is dishonest and immoral to pretend that a group has no resources in order to obtain what is in substance a charitable donation at the expense of others. Also, there is always the tendency to provide better service to the paying customers than to the non-paying ones; to leave until later in the day cases which come out of one's leisure time with one's family or friends. On the other hand, if it turns out that the client is receiving poor service simply because the lawyer is not being paid, it may be desirable to try to find another lawyer who is willing to provide better service.

Whose assistance should one seek? There is no easy answer. Individual personalities are more important than generalizations. The author has had considerable success recruiting highly respected senior counsel who could easily take their pick of cases. Such lawyers are usually no longer supporting young families and, as senior partners in their law firms, don't need to worry as much about partnership pressure to maximize their billings. The downside of such counsel is that they are frequently so busy that they are booked months ahead and have little flexibility in their schedules.

Nor is it always helpful to go to someone who is well-known to the general public. Some lawyers (particularly those practising criminal law or doing a bit of civil liberties work) have a flamboyant style which is virtually irresistible to the newspapers. But success with juries and skill at promoting oneself through the media are not necessarily attractive qualities in the eyes of more conservative regulatory board members whose backgrounds, typically, are in academia or government. There are all kinds of lawyers who are extremely competent, but who have never had a major profile in the newspapers, or have never become public figures through successful or unsuccessful attempts at electoral politics. Such lawyers may be the best for administrative tribunal advocacy even though their names are likely to be obtained only from other lawyers.

What if a client cannot afford to pay a lawyer's full fees? At a bare minimum, one will be expected to cover disbursements. These are out-of-pocket expenses which the lawyer must pay, such as transcripts, transportation expenses, photocopying and so on. On the other hand, if full fees are unaffordable, it is better at least to offer to pay something. This enables a lawyer to say to his partners (many of whom practise corporate law and are much less frequently requested to do charitable work) that the request is not a total donation because at least some fee will be paid. Since most law firms are familiar with legal aid, and have accepted it in principle, it will appear less strange or unusual to be requested to do work on a basis that is similar to that of legal aid.

At the opposite end of the senior practitioner is the enthusiastic young graduate just out of bar exams. Such a lawyer may be willing to work for community groups, especially if he is not yet very busy, since the public exposure which can come from a high profile regulatory case or appeal from a decision of a regulatory tribunal can be very good for his practice.

Midway between senior practitioner and the neophyte is the lawyer of five to 15 years' experience. It is this group which does the bulk of the cases, and is usually the busiest. As they have not yet "arrived" at the senior partner stage, they may be less likely to give away their time. They may have several young children and a large mortgage, with pressure from their juniors for salary increases and from their senior partners who want to take life a bit easier. Lawyers in this middle group are often at the peak of their intellectual powers, have enough experience to have been bloodied in battle without yet having tired of the war. Although they may be the hardest to recruit for the public interest group, the happy combination of an interesting case, a worthy client, and even a limited budget for fees and disbursements will sometimes suffice to recruit a top-flight practitioner in this group.

When working with a lawyer, a number of things are important to remember. First of all, recognize that a lawyer's time and advice are his stock in trade. Just as one would not walk into a department store, remove inventory from the shelves and walk out, do not "steal" your lawyer's inventory of time. Designate only one member of your group to deal with the lawyer so that he is not receiving phone calls from half a dozen people and having to repeat the same message to all of them; or worse still, receiving conflicting or inconsistent instructions. Make sure, when going to a meeting at his office, that all the necessary documents and papers are brought, including (for example) the notice of public hearing, relevant portions of the application, the group's intervention statement (if one has been filed), and so on. Also, do not expect the lawyer to be able to do things at the last minute. Hearing dates and appointments are often made weeks or months in advance to accommodate the timetables of a number of witnesses, other lawyers, board members or judges. Clients frequently suffer a rude awakening when they find that "their" lawyer is not simply sitting around in the office waiting for them to call. Hence, plan ahead. If it is known that a certain appearance will be required or even might be required by a certain date, advise the lawyer well in advance.

A lawyer's secretary is a resource whose skills should not be underestimated. While a legal secretary is not qualified to give legal advice, assistance in other forms can easily be provided. For example, a legal secretary can communicate with another lawyer or another legal secretary about administrative matters such as sending over papers or arranging dates, can communicate requests for information and can convey messages to the lawyer who may be tied up for several days in a hearing.

While it may be frustrating to have "your" lawyer fail to return calls for several days because of another hearing, recognize that cross-examination is often prepared (or repaired) far into the night while days are spent at the hearing. The intensity of the concentration required to deal with a mountain of facts in such a short time may simply preclude the mental energy to deal with anything else. The matter at hand usually requires total concentration. In such circumstances it is important for the client to be understanding. Just as you would not want your lawyer to be distracted from 100 percent concentration on your case, do not seek to impose a lower level of concentration on the problems of others with whom your group shares a lawyer. Even if your legal problem is the only one of importance to you, unless the lawyer is to be unemployed before and after your case, it cannot possibly be the only one of importance to him. So show some consideration.

As most litigation lawyers work very long hours, they have very little time to spend with their families. Hence they are particularly fearful of hysterical, inconsiderate clients. Avoid calling lawyers at home during the few hours they can spend with their families. Lawyers must, of necessity, recognize that there are more than eight hours in a day or five days in a week in which one can decently communicate with one's clients, especially if one has been tied up in hearings all day for several days in a row. But no one appreciates late-night telephone calls to discuss routine matters, or an hour-long phone call at suppertime, just as the lawyer or his or her spouse is busy cooking supper while feeding the infant twins. If such calls can possibly wait until the next business day, they should; where they cannot, the caller should be very brief and to the point.

In general, the relationship between a public interest group and its lawyer will be the happiest when each appreciates the peculiar problems and sensitivities of the other. The lawyer must recognize that the public interest group may be feeling anxious as a result of being treated by those in positions of power as weak, insignificant or of secondary importance; neglect by the lawyer enhances this insecurity. The public interest group must recognize that the lawyer is operating in a high-stress environment with pressures from other lawyers on all sides, as well as the normal financial, family and other personal problems which can often result from the strains of a litigation practice; overly anxious clients simply add more stress.

(b) Consultants

A distinction can be drawn between consultants and expert witnesses. The former provide advice and do not testify; the latter are expected to testify whether or not they also function as advisors.

The importance of consultants is often underestimated by tribunals because they are not seen to testify. Yet a limited budget may go farther through effective cross-examination and final argument assisted by a consultant than evidence which is prepared by an expert witness in haste because there is insufficient money to do the job properly. If enough can be accomplished in cross-examination and final argument, one might be wise to consider the comment of the senior counsel who said: "I worry far more about what my witnesses are likely to say under cross-examination than theirs."

If he is competent to give you good advice in the subject area of concern, a consultant's formal credentials are immaterial. This is not so for an expert witness, whose testimony will be given little, if any weight in the absence of extensive formal credentials.

Some consultants can provide assistance in the very important task of evaluating the general position taken by the other side, finding logical errors and assisting in preparing a sound position for intervention. While this broad approach may sound simple, it is not. There are many more experts who are skilled in the fine points of technical research and analysis than those competent to analyze policy options dispassionately.

At a more detailed level of analysis, consultants can be helpful in finding mathematical errors, flaws or eccentricities in method, alternatives not considered, and a whole host of technical questions and objections to the application under review. It is not uncommon for the applications of major corporations or government departments to contain conclusions resting upon erroneous calculations; a single method or time period of calculation which creates a distorted picture, the omission of important facts; or failure to consider what would happen if a number of assumptions proved to be invalid (or conversely, if factors assumed to have no effect materialized). A good consultant can often help in drafting questions in cross-examination which expose such flaws.

(c) Expert Witnesses

Effective expert witnesses are extremely difficult to find, and worth their weight in gold. Almost anyone with a PhD and a bit of courage might be willing to testify, but ineffective testimony can easily do more harm than good. On cross-examination, an inexperienced witness can often be forced to water down or even to repudiate what once was a boldly stated conclusion. The last thing a public interest group needs is to spend a large proportion of its very limited resources to pay a witness who is discredited and makes matters worse. Accordingly, it is good practice to find out from any expert witness being considered to be retained where and when he has testified previously. Then, contact staff members of those boards, as well as previous clients, to find out how well the witness is regarded. Shop around to see who is available, and then check out reputation and credentials carefully. Most witnesses exude confidence and are very reassuring. They will usually have a list of hearings at which they have appeared. In some cases that list will contain several disasters. Without checking, there is no way to know.

Some witnesses, who have spent most of their careers testifying for one client, should be avoided because they will appear to be too closely identified with that client. The best witness is one who has usually been considered good enough to be hired by a range of clients: applicants, interveners, regulatory agencies, government and public interest groups. Such a breadth of experience is also advantageous because an expert possessing it can explain, from a broader perspective, what part of one's case does not make sense and is doomed to failure.

An expert who disagrees with his client's prejudices, and says so, will be more valuable than one who merely remains silent and does what he is asked to do. All of us already feel strongly enough about our own prejudices to believe absolutely that we are right. What we need from an expert witness is objective, hard-headed, practical advice, not merely the emotional reassurance that comes from having one's biases reinforced.

The academic community produces a few of the best, but many of the worst expert witnesses to be found. The best are those with a broad range of clients, some practical experience in business or government on a full-time basis outside of university consulting, and the ability to explain complex theories simply and briefly. The worst of them may possess considerable theoretical knowledge, but are not very practical or comprehensible, and communicate poorly with anyone but their academic peers. In university examinations, getting the principle right may be more important than getting the right answer. With this background, the evidence of academics often contains careless arithmetic, grammatical, spelling and keyboarding errors — all suggesting sloppiness and, what may be worse, a tendency to solve problems by resorting to general theory without confirming whether the theory applies in the particular case. Often the regulatory process is too fact-and-number oriented to accept such an approach.

Academics are often attacked on cross-examination for their lack of practical experience, with questions such as: "Now Dr. Jones, how long have you worked for a railway?" An admission of no practical experience will usually result in the contention, in final argument, that little weight should be given to the evidence in comparison to that of the experienced, practical people who have been running the railway for all these years. The tribunal may not regard all of the witnesses of the applicant to be geniuses, but at least each is a known quantity, whose efforts have produced predictable (if unspectacular) results. Taking the untested advice of an unknown university professor involves unknown risks that regulators may be reluctant to accept.

A good academic witness will be aware that his evidence may be seen in this light, and will take pains to avoid appearing too academic. For such a witness, a good grasp of theory is just the beginning. The evidence will be prepared with accuracy and in detail, so that it can easily be plugged into a regulatory decision, rather than serving as another lecture to the tribunal. The evidence will be "packaged" so as to be eminently comprehensible and readable. Under ideal circumstances such a witness, working in close collaboration with an experienced, competent counsel, will produce a piece of testimony which is so good as to render cross-examination quixotic.

With all witnesses, whatever their background, great care must be taken to avoid becoming involved in inter-disciplinary ideological wars. For example, there is often an undeclared state of war between accountants and economists over the word "costs". Economists tend to view the evidence of accountants as distorting the "real" picture because accounting information is based on historical costs. As some of the costs on the books were incurred in the purchase of equipment a decade ago, undoubtedly they do not reflect a realistic estimate of what it would cost to replace that equipment today. Since accounting information is normally prepared for the purpose of informing shareholders of the financial situation of their company at a particular instant in time and in accordance with a set of generally accepted accounting conventions, it may not always be useful for regulatory purposes, one of which includes future pricing. Thus, to the regulatory economist, the accountant appears to be driving full speed ahead into the financial future while staring fixedly in the rear view mirror.

Yet tribunals have accountants on staff and, often, as sitting members. They see accounting costs, even with their limitations, as possessing a kind of certainty which only "actual" costs can possess, with the further advantage that costs used for rate-making purposes will closely approximate the books of account of the company.

Economists have a more dynamic, future-oriented view of costs. Where there is no actual out-of-pocket cost in the form of an expenditure, they are more willing to "impute" opportunity costs (and are usually better qualified to estimate them) than are accountants. This is said to produce a more realistic assessment of "real" costs, especially if one applies "discount rates" for the benefits one could obtain for investing the same amount of money in an alternative investment of approximately similar risk.

The author's own view is that, during a time of rapidly rising or falling inflation and interest rates, economists' techniques are, in principle more likely to reflect the real world than during times of relative stability. But when one applies these theories in practice, the results will not necessarily be any better. The problem of imputing costs which are not reflected in cash payments is a difficult one. The range of estimates as to how much to impute varies so widely and is often so artificial (e.g., the value sometimes imputed to a human life is based on jury awards in negligence cases) as to raise serious doubts as to where technique ends and merely subjective guesswork takes over. Usually, the types of costs to which numbers can be attached in any meaningful way is but a small fraction of the potential list of total costs and, even then, is not as readily checked against "generally accepted principles of economics", as there are none.

The foregoing example of accountants and economists can be repeated with engineers (some of whom are also heavily involved in both accounting and economics), financial analysts, biological versus physical scientists, and so on. The neophyte regulatory lawyer or public interest group advocate insufficiently aware of these differences in doctrine may be inadvertently persuaded to hire a member of one discipline whose criticism of the evidence of the opposing party is really based on little more than discipline-doctrinal differences. There is not much point in hiring an economist whose criticism, at bottom, comes down to little more than that the applicant's evidence was prepared by an accountant, or vice versa.

Even within the same discipline, there are different ways of doing the same thing. Again, a great deal of money can be wasted by hiring an expert, the gist of whose testimony is little more than "I would do it differently", when it really cannot be said that what the other person has done is somehow fundamentally wrong, or at least clearly inferior in some way to the suggested method.

A common failing of expert witnesses is to view the regulatory hearing as an opportunity to try to prove that they are more expert than the experts on the other side. Even if that is the case, demonstrating it may do nothing to help the client. To sustain technical brilliance under cross-examination, it will be necessary to resort to higher and higher levels of technical abstraction which will quickly lose the interest of the tribunal members. Regulators are not delighted to turn their hearing rooms into ego battlegrounds for experts. It is equally likely that board and staff members who may be less conspicuously brilliant than the witness may feel threatened or put down by such a display of intellectual fireworks. In short, a witness who attempts to make everyone his intellectual inferior is not likely to be popular.

To illustrate the importance of an expert witness being sensitive to the feelings of his audience, consider this anecdote told to the author by a member of a tribunal. A particular witness of some considerable intellectual capacity was seeking to explain his evidence so as to be comprehensible to a tribunal composed of lay people. He decided to do this by means of an analogy to a relatively simple situation which everyone would understand. He selected a tennis game, repeatedly inviting the tribunal to compare what he had done in his evidence to what they would do when serving, returning a serve, volleying, and so on. It was obvious that the witness was not only a tennis player but, more generally, a physical fitness enthusiast. To this tribunal member, who described himself as rather overweight and totally unfit, and detested anything to do with physical fitness, the continual reminder of his own physical state did nothing to endear the witness to him. It is sometimes surprising to learn that such strongly negative feelings can be created by what would appear to be only a mildly patronizing analogy.

6. TECHNIQUES FOR WORKING WITH EXPERTS

When using an expert to assist in preparing questions for cross-examination, it is important that the would-be cross-examiner also understands the questions and the anticipated answers. It is all too easy to fall into the trap of having the expert prepare what it is hoped will be the script, with the witness' answers to follow from the questions. Rarely will it ever work out this way in practice. If the questioner does not understand the purpose of each question, he will look very foolish when he does not know what to ask next if the witness gives an answer which obviously was not expected. Given that the witness being cross-examined is not likely to want to co-operate by making any damaging admissions, the number of potentially irrelevant and evasive answers that can be provided is almost infinite — certainly beyond anyone's ability to script.

Again, the danger arises that the expert preparing the script for cross-examination will, perhaps unconsciously, be trying to prove that he is a more knowledgeable expert than the one being cross-examined. The expert, however, will not be doing the cross-examination; hence the questions must work for whoever will. Moreover, unless the answer to each question is essential, the questions should probably not be asked.

A common mistake of neophyte advocates is simply to ask one's expert witness to prepare testimony, and then, to submit this. Unless one expert's evidence is checked by others (usually unaffordable to public interest groups), it will be prepared in isolation. This increases the likelihood of failure to detect errors, or to notice where parts of the evidence are incomprehensible. Checking by *someone* is essential.

Lawyers may feel an ethical concern about tampering with the evidence of a witness. This is a legitimate concern if the rewriting at the direction of the lawyer is carried to extremes. Certainly, in an ordinary court of law, a lawyer is not supposed to tell the witness what to say, to put words in his or her mouth. Similarly, for a lawyer to rewrite a witness's evidence to such a point that it is really no longer the witness's evidence but the lawyer's evidence would be unethical.

On the other hand, a regulatory tribunal is not a court of law, and the key concern is not really whether the witness is telling the truth. Rather, because an opinion is usually being offered, the key concern is what it is based on and whether or not it is comprehensible. Hence greater latitude must be allowed than in a court.

In the author's view, there is certainly nothing wrong with telling a witness that a particular paragraph is ambiguous or unclear in some respect, and should be clarified. This will merely prevent the evidence from being misunderstood, which will help rather than mislead the tribunal. Also, if there are obvious errors, such as the word "not" inadvertently left out, grammatical mistakes, typographical errors or mistakes in arithmetic, these can be pointed out to the witness. When we go beyond simple matters of clarification or the correction of mechanical errors, we are moving into a potentially more controversial area. Ultimately, of course, if the evidence is so bad as to be useless without complete rewriting, the witness should not be called.

As everyone will want to receive value for money from expert witnesses, they will ask to have the evidence changed so that it is useful. There is, however, a fine line between encouraging a witness to trim extraneous and irrelevant material or to add certain points not dealt with, and telling him what to say to the extent that the lawyer, rather than the witness, should have his name on the evidence. No one can say with precision where that line should be drawn; it is a matter of degree in each case.

7. COSTS OF EXPERTS

The cost of retaining experts varies enormously, although in general one tends to get what one pays for. Some witnesses who are quite inexpensive may know so little about the subject that they will, in effect, be paid for their education. An academic economist can sometimes be retained for as little as $400 a day.

Others can charge $1,000 a day or more. In the author's own experience, in one case, an "expensive" economist accomplished as much in two days of preparing evidence at $1,000 a day as many other economists charging half his rate might have accomplished in two weeks. Because he had so much of the necessary information at his fingertips and such a quick mind, he was also far more impressive in withstanding cross-examination than a less expensive expert would have been. On the other hand, some experts who could charge $1,000 a day do not because they are able to obtain financial support in other ways. For example, some of the personnel in "think tanks" are permitted to do a bit of outside consulting work, and usually charge fairly modest fees to community groups because financial security and a comfortable income is provided by their employer. Similarly, academic experts who do not have heavy office overhead to support can usually afford to work for less, and will do so. Finally, some experts will have (or can be persuaded to have) a special rate for public interest groups. It is understandable that their normal rates for government or business organizations would not reflect any charitable component. However, an expert who is interested in and sympathetic to some of the issues raised in the particular case, or who simply feels a sense of social duty to assist those who cannot afford to pay the full fee, will occasionally provide service to a public interest group at a relatively low rate.

6

An Introduction to Administrative Advocacy

1. BASIC PREPARATION

As part of the preparation for every case, it is absolutely essential to do three things:

1. *Read the Act* (or Acts, as the case may be) setting up the tribunal. If it seems incomprehensible on first reading, don't worry: understanding usually improves with repeated reading. Skim the key parts *several times* until they start to fall into place and the general scheme of it begins to emerge. It is not necessary to understand every detail. However, it is important to have a clear understanding of the specific powers exercised by the tribunal in relation to the case in which one is to participate, including an understanding of the criteria the tribunal may use in judging the application. If necessary, consult a legal specialist familiar with the legislation to explain the words or concepts which are unclear.

   A copy of the Act can usually be found in any law library, public library containing the statutes of Canada or of the province, the tribunal's own library or, in some cases, an office consolidation of the Act and regulations can be obtained from the Department of Supply and Services or provincial Queen's Printer.

2. *Become familiar with the procedures* employed by the tribunal (if these are written down anywhere). Write a letter to the secretary of the tribunal and ask for a copy of the Rules

of Procedure or, if there are none, some description of what
procedure the tribunal uses in its cases.
3. *Read previous cases*. If the tribunal has issued any written
reasons for its decisions in previous cases of a similar nature,
become familiar with them. The secretary of the tribunal may
be willing to provide a copy or advise where copies of relevant
decisions can be purchased. If the tribunal has a library, a
copy can usually be found there.

If a group is still unsure as to whether or not it can handle
a hearing without a lawyer, a realistic appraisal on the part of
group members of the following questions may help. First, how
long is the hearing expected to take? An answer to this question
can often be obtained by talking with officials of the tribunal
such as the secretary or counsel. What are the issues in the
hearing, how many of them is the group interested in, and can
these issues be separated from the others so that it is not necessary
to be present at all times? Can it be anticipated that procedural
difficulties will arise? What are the resources — both human
and monetary — of the group? Does it have members or staff
with the necessary advocacy skills? Are those persons able to
commit themselves to the hearing for the required length of time?
If there is uncertainty about whether the necessary skills or time
commitments are there, and if the group has the money, it may
as well retain a lawyer.

If the group does not have and cannot obtain the necessary
financial resources, and no one in the group can commit
themselves for the necessary time period, it must decide whether
or not any intervention is feasible. Unless an adequate division
of labour amongst the group members can be assured, the group
may be better off participating only by means of a written
statement. That way it will at least present the group's viewpoint,
and members of the group will not be left feeling that they did
a lot of work and had nothing to show for it because, despite
that work, they could not adequately prepare in the time available.

2. WORKING TOWARDS YOUR ULTIMATE GOAL

The former New York Yankees catcher, Yogi Berra, was known
for a number of witty remarks. One which is particularly relevant

to participants in public hearings is: "If you don't know where you're going, you may end up somewhere else."

To avoid giving the appearance of not knowing where you are going, the case must be planned backwards: from the end (the goal) to the beginning. Consider a comparison with designing a building. If each of the four walls are built, one after another, without planning beforehand where each of the other walls is going to go, the fourth wall may well not connect with the first one. Similarly, participation in a case before a tribunal is not likely to be very effective if each stage in the hearing is entered without having planned all the following ones.

As may be recalled from our earlier discussion of decisions and orders, the conclusion of a hearing is usually in the form of an order which is binding on all the parties (whether this is formally labeled a decision or an order is unimportant). Also, there are some tribunals, such as environmental assessment boards, which do not necessarily make binding decisions but make recommendations. Nevertheless, whether the final product is a decision, order or recommendation, that final result is the most that that tribunal can do. What is particularly disheartening is to discover that the tribunal cannot do what one hoped it could because it lacks the legal jurisdiction to do so. For example, a broadcasting intervener group was surprised and disappointed to learn that the CRTC could not order the Canadian Broadcasting Corporation (CBC) to change its programming in certain ways as this would require an amendment to the conditions of the CBC's licence, which the CRTC could not impose without the Corporation's consent. This again underlines the importance of reading the legislation carefully to find out what the tribunal can and cannot do.

A tribunal may have the legal power to do something but may have a strong and long-standing policy against it; hence, the importance of reading the previous decisions of the tribunal to understand its policies. For example, during the approximately 80 years of its existence, the Canadian Transport Commission refused to exercise its power to award costs to consumer groups. The National Energy Board never refuses a power export application on environmental grounds. The CRTC grants most, if not all, of the cable television rate increases requested.

The starting point of any planning for an intervention must

be with the order (or recommendation) sought. If a party does not know exactly what order it wants from the board, it might as well not be there. It is good practice to make sure the advocate knows precisely what the client wants by preparing a draft order in point form in simple numbered paragraphs. If it is uncertain whether the expectation of such an order is realistic, it may be worth preparing a number of alternatives, from the most desirable to the least acceptable. Even going through this exercise will be enlightening, and will have important benefits in planning strategy.[1]

Once the advocate has defined the order (or range of possible orders) sought, continuing to work backwards, one asks the rhetorical question: what conclusion must the board reach to justify granting this order? To illustrate by means of a very simple example, if the order sought is that the proposed electricity rate increase be disallowed in its entirety, then the board must conclude that the proposed rates would be excessive and that the present rates are entirely adequate. In the real world, of course, the situation is usually a bit more complex than this example and there may have to be several conclusions drawn to justify a single paragraph in an order. The more complex the order sought, the greater the number of conclusions the board will have to draw. Alternative orders further increase the number of necessary conclusions.

Next, one would work back from the conclusions. For any particular conclusion, again a rhetorical question: what arguments will be necessary to persuade the tribunal to reach this conclusion? To stay with our very simple example of the intervention in the rate increase application, to conclude that the present rates are fair, the board would have to be satisfied that these rates enable the company to recover its cost of capital so as to permit it to earn a fair rate of return for its shareholders. Hence, this is the argument one must be able to make.

So far, each of these steps has involved little more than the application of logic, in a step-by-step way, coupled with some basic knowledge of the policies and criteria usually used by these tribunals to reach their conclusions. At the next stage, however, the exercise becomes somewhat more difficult. It now becomes

---

1 For a full discussion of that issue, see Chapter 11 dealing with case strategies.

necessary to employ tactical judgment. To satisfy the board that any particular argument is correct it may suffice merely to state the argument. It may be so obvious, or so easily demonstrated by mere argument alone, that nothing more is needed. More often, mere assertion or argument alone will not suffice, and it may be necessary to rely on evidence. In our example, if the company seeks rates which will allow it to earn a rate of return of, let us say, 14 percent, and the argument is to be made that 12 percent would suffice, it has to be shown that 12 percent is the cost of capital and will enable shareholders to earn a fair rate of return. The tactical question then becomes: can the board be persuaded that 12 percent is the cost of capital merely by asserting it, or by arguing it from some general principles, or will it need evidence of this?

The answer to that question would depend upon a judgment as to how obviously correct the argument was. To examine the two extremes, if no one in Canada had ever been allowed a rate of return in excess of 12 percent, and if any argument made for 14 percent was manifestly ridiculous, that would probably be all one would need to say. At the other extreme, if a 14 percent rate of return was common and 12 percent unprecedented, it would take compelling evidence indeed to persuade the board to accept 12 percent. In the more probable case, which falls between these extremes, it is likely that some evidence would be necessary to demonstrate why, on the facts of the particular case at the given time, 12 percent is a better number than 14 percent.

Generally speaking, expert evidence will tend to be necessary when the dispute is about numbers, particularly about what point on a scale should be selected. Because the selection of such points inevitably involves a great deal of judgment and even some arbitrariness, expert evidence will often be critical. On the other hand, if there is no dispute about the numbers themselves but, rather, about what their significance is and what inference should be drawn from them, evidence may be unnecessary and even irritating to the tribunal. In environmental cases, for example, the question is often whether the predicted impacts of a particular project are acceptable in the public interest, or whether they are so severe as to be unjustifiable in comparison to the predicted benefits. While an environmental group may wish to challenge a proponent's estimates of both benefits and impacts, it may also be argued that, even if the proponent's numbers are taken at face value, the risks exceed the benefits. Judgments of this nature are essentially value judgments. *There is no expertise in value judgments.* Accordingly, calling an expert witness such as a biologist to say that the damage to the trees is less important than the economic benefits of the jobs created is likely to be unpersuasive. It may even offend the tribunal because the witness may be seen as attempting to usurp the tribunal's function to make the value judgment. When the opinion of an expert is entitled to no greater weight than the opinion of anyone else, such evidence should not be given.

Once it has been decided on what issues argument alone will suffice, it will then become possible to make up a list of the issues on which evidence will be necessary. It is important to note that, when it is said that evidence will be necessary, this does not mean to imply that all that evidence must be one's own. Quite often, most of the evidence will have been or will ultimately have to be provided by the other side. With the rate-of-return evidence in our example, unquestionably, the regulated company will have to present evidence as to its cost of capital. It may be possible to demonstrate in final argument, even without participating in cross-examination, that the evidence presented by the company is more consistent with a 12 percent than a 14 percent cost of capital. If this can be shown mathematically, provided that the calculations are all shown and are easy enough to follow, that may be the best way to do it. However, if the evidence is not very clear, or if the mathematics involves the employment of techniques which are controversial, it is probably necessary to bring in a witness who will testify to the correctness of the 12 percent.

As this example suggests, tactical decisions will have to be made fairly early on in the case (because of the lead times involved in retaining expert witnesses and allowing them to prepare adequately) as to what will be handled by argument alone, what by attacking the evidence of the other side in cross-examination, and what by the presentation of affirmative evidence of one's own.

If resources permit, it is preferable to bring in a competent witness on any issue in which the evidence is likely to be difficult and controversial. That is because it is unsafe to count upon cross-examination as one's only weapon to demonstrate the inadequacy of the opponent's evidence. Sometimes one may be lucky in cross-examination and succeed in so damaging the case of the other side that evidence will be unnecessary. Certainly, if no witness is affordable there is little choice but to try to do it that way. But usually even an experienced cross-examiner, when dealing with an experienced expert witness, is unlikely to sink the whole ship. More commonly, there will be some dents made on it, but that is all.

By now the planning process should have worked its way back from the order sought through the conclusions, argument and evidence, so that one can begin actively to plan the strategy for the case. Case strategies are discussed in depth in Chapter 11 but, before we conclude this chapter, it is important to highlight the crucial difference between evidence and argument.

3. THE CRUCIAL DIFFERENCE BETWEEN EVIDENCE AND ARGUMENT

Most non-lawyers (and many lawyers too) are afraid of being cross-examined. It may be frightening to be at the mercy of an experienced cross-examiner with a large budget and a small army of experts to help in preparing an infinite number of possible questions which must be answered immediately upon their being asked. On the other hand, it is also intimidating to cross-examine an expert witness in an area where the witness may have written several books and may have testified on average once a month for the past 20 years. Such a witness has, at one time or another, been asked virtually every question it is possible to ask and has had plenty of time to think of good answers. The delightful thing about argument, by way of contrast, is that *one cannot be cross-examined on one's final argument*. It is amazing how many potential advocates have been delighted to learn this. It has completely changed their view of hearings. Rather than expecting to be grilled in some sort of nightmare of a proceeding, they can then relax and recognize that in argument, one can say anything one wants without the intimidating process of cross-examination.

Of course, that should not be seen as an invitation to say

things which are irresponsible or foolish. The other side has final argument as well, during which it can attack what one has said. Usually, because an applicant or proponent has the burden of proof in a case, it will be given an opportunity for a final reply. If one's opponent gets the last word, it is important to be extra careful in what is said in final argument.

Citizens' groups have often fared rather badly in regulatory hearings because they have been unaware of the difference between evidence and argument. They have usually put forward as their evidence material which is essentially argumentative in its nature; that is, it consists largely of statements of value rather than statements of an evidentiary nature. For example, if a witness testifies on behalf of a native group that the harm likely to be done to the lifestyle of the native inhabitants of an area is excessive in comparison to the economic benefits of a proposed development, that will be very difficult to "defend". If the person is an anthropologist, he will be asked what is the source of his expertise in economics; if he is an economist, he will asked what he knows about native anthropology. Unless this is a unique expert in both disciplines, one or another part of the evidence, if not the conclusion, will probably be rejected. It will also be very difficult to answer basic questions such as "how do you know that is so" when the only possible answer is that that's the person's own value judgment.

Also, cross-examination is usually unlimited as to time. Final argument normally has a specific limit (such as one hour) or is expected by convention to be relatively brief. Thus, the damage which can be inflicted in cross-examination can go on for a day or more until the witness has been cut to pieces, whereas the rebuttal to the very same points made in argument cannot be sustained (while maintaining listener interest) for much longer than 10 or 15 minutes. Accordingly, *the cardinal rule should be to present as little evidence as is absolutely necessary.* If a particular statement can be made in final argument just as well as it can in evidence, obviously, since it cannot be attacked as viciously during argument as in evidence, it should be presented as argument.

Evidence is also normally much more expensive than final argument. It usually requires an expert witness with extensive credentials and the ability to prepare evidence which will withstand cross-examination. This requires recruiting the expert (which will probably necessitate following a lot of leads before a suitable and available witness is found), a major financial commitment and no guarantee that the witness will be believed in preference to the witness of an opponent. Final argument, at its least expensive, may mean little more than the cost of one person's time drafting a short speech.

This may make it appear as if no one should ever call evidence and that final argument will in all cases suffice. But that would be too easy. An intervention which relies entirely on final argument has its weaknesses too. First, the argument may not be very persuasive if unsupported by any special scientific or other expert evidence. The other side will have a lawyer who has the last word. That lawyer will be buttressed by the evidence of an expert who may be quite familiar to the board, having spent many hours, if not days or weeks, appearing before it. Board members will have had plenty of opportunity to develop a certain respect, and perhaps even affection for these hardworking witnesses.

Regulation is a human judgment process in which factors of subjectivity and personality inevitably have an important effect. However devastating a final argument appears to its presenter, if it occupies only one hour of a six-week public hearing there is not likely to be enough time to develop a great deal of sympathy for that point of view. Unless it can be demonstrated with irrefutable mathematics that the other side is plainly wrong, or unless there is good reason to believe that the tribunal has virtually decided against one's opponent and merely needs a token intervention to provide the basis for rejecting its proposal, final argument alone is not likely to have sufficient impact. Where, then, does this leave us?

Two important tactical factors must be recognized. First, because in most cases it will be necessary to deal with some evidence (either through one's own witness or by cross-examination) and some argument, it must be decided what is to be evidence and what is to be argument. Second, present no more evidence than is absolutely necessary. Present only the evidence without which final argument is likely to be unpersuasive.

If final argument is to be presented in writing, or is oral but may be supplemented by a written presentation, a lot of factual material (which would be inappropriate or boring to try to read aloud in final argument) can be presented in written form. Even if an expert has been asked to prepare a piece of testimony and it appears that some or all of it can be presented by an advocate in the form of final argument, then by all means present it during argument. The only qualification on this strategy is that if a highly technical 100 page final argument is given, that may well be perceived as an unfair way to avoid cross-examination. The evidence should not be so technical that it appears obvious that the presenter neither wrote it nor understands it, but is merely reading it aloud (if oral argument) or delivering it physically (if written).

7

Using the Rules Effectively

1. USING THE EXISTING RULES IMAGINATIVELY

Many non-lawyers are intimidated by the very idea of rules of procedure and practice, assuming that they will be very complicated. This assumption is reinforced because most tribunals seem to have a large number of rules which occupy numerous pages of typed or printed text. Nevertheless, appearances are deceiving. Most tribunals' rules are, in substance, quite simple and reflect basic common sense.

What makes the rules appear so lengthy is the necessity to describe in very full detail everything that is required to be done. For example, intervention statements are usually covered by a rule which specifies the size of paper on which they must be typed, that this typing must be double-spaced on one side of the page only, that the paragraphs should be numbered consecutively, and so on. None of this is very complicated, as is shown by the sample forms at the back of this book.

Obviously, in any public hearing there will have to be deadlines. As different events require different deadlines, there will be several rules dealing with these. After an application is filed, there will be a deadline for the submission of intervention statements. There may be a deadline for the submission of interrogatories (written questions requiring written replies), and another for interrogatory responses from the applicant. None of these rules will be difficult to understand. However, attention should be given to the definitions in the rules, usually found either within the rule itself or at the beginning or the end of all the rules in a special definition section. If a deadline is within "ten days", does that mean ten working days exclusive of weekends and holidays or just ten days? If the definition section does not say, find out from the tribunal how they have interpreted such provisions and, when in doubt, seek clarification from the tribunal or take the most prudent course and assume the least number of days that the rule might contemplate.

Once the rules have been read and understood in most ordinary cases it should not be very difficult to comply. Deadlines are usually reasonable so that they can be met. Most of the other rules have been tested for many years and found to work. If one has a particular problem with a rule it is probably for one of three reasons:

1. The meaning of the rule has been misunderstood to be worse than it is;
2. There is some special or unusual circumstance in this case which makes it difficult for the would-be participant to comply with the rule; or
3. The rule is badly drafted and needs to be revised.

Let's consider each of these in turn.

Very often rules are misunderstood due to lack of appreciation of what is their intention. For example, one of the most common causes of panic is the requirement found in many rules of procedure that "interventions must be filed within X days of notice of the application". This is commonly assumed to mean that all of the evidence of the intervener must be filed within X days. If that assumption is made it appears so discouraging that many people needlessly give up. In most cases, the rule does not intend that at all. All it requires is that a statement of the position of the intervener (sometimes called an intervention statement) must be filed in that time. That filing need be no more than two or three pages long. As a general principle, if a rule appears unreasonable and impossible, it is safe to assume the reader has misunderstood it and should seek clarification of what it really means.

In some cases a particular rule will apply to one situation even though it was drafted to cover another. In these circumstances the desired result is to achieve fairer treatment. This can be accomplished in a number of ways. Ideally, with the consent of the applicant (or whoever's consent one might need, depending upon the circumstances) a motion can be made[1] to the tribunal that the rule not be applied to the present situation in the way it is written. Alternatively, one can propose a new rule or principle to be applied.[2] Whichever of these steps is selected, certain basic principles should be borne in mind.

First, rules are not as rigid as statutes. A statute cannot be waived to meet a particular circumstance; only a legislature can change laws. However, rules of procedure are usually not legislation but regulations, and tribunals have the discretion, either expressly in their legislation or by necessary implication, to waive the operation of any rule if its application would not serve the ends of justice. This does not mean that the rules were meant to be broken or to be ignored merely because someone requests special consideration. There must be sound reasons for declining to apply the rule.

The single most common problem seems to be with time limits. Community groups often learn about a public hearing partway into the process, only to find that they have either missed the deadline for intervention altogether or have insufficient time to meet other deadlines. Alternatively, the hearing dates may be known in advance but the time it would take for the group to call a directors' meeting to develop a position may appear insufficient.

Generally, such problems evoke little sympathy from the tribunal, perhaps for sound reasons. Unless the public notice of an application is itself deficient, a group has a duty to keep its eyes and ears open if it wishes to participate in public hearings. If someone wants to play in the big leagues he must learn to play like a big league player. That means appointing someone in the group to keep track of such events as public hearings, and being sufficiently organized that when a hearing is approaching the group can prepare an intervention statement within conventional time limits. If the group cannot do even these basic things then perhaps the question should be asked whether the group is mature enough and well enough organized to participate effectively in any event.

---

1 Motions are discussed in detail in Chapter 13.
2 See also "Proposing New Rules", later in this chapter.

It does not take a great deal to entrust someone (such as the president or chair of the advocacy program) to carry out these tasks without requiring the consent of the whole board. If an organization has any long-standing interest in an issue, it will probably have a position that is well-known to its officers and senior members, even though it may never have been written down. If it has no such position and cannot even draft one within a few days, then it has no really coherent view of the issue and probably will not have a great deal to contribute. From the viewpoint of the tribunal, if a group cannot organize itself enough to set out a few paragraphs indicating the nature of its interest in a topic, then it does not seem unduly harsh to conclude that its interest in the subject-matter is insufficient to enable it to make a meaningful contribution.

On the other hand, in a truly major case in which the evidence may run to several volumes, it may well be that no person, however well organized, could analyze this data and prepare a coherent response in the time limit allowed by the rules. Presumably, it would not be very difficult, in those circumstances, to convince a tribunal of that and to ask it to change its deadline for the purpose of this hearing. Some tribunals even issue "hearing orders" for each particular hearing, under which they expressly amend their general rules or create new ones to meet the particular circumstances of the case. Someone unaware of this who reads only the general rules of procedure of a tribunal may needlessly panic. Again, the important point is: know the tribunal. The secretary can provide a copy of any applicable special hearing orders.

Whatever difficulty one may have with rules of procedure, an argument for special exemptions is unlikely to be effective without consideration of the position of the other side. Ask the question: if what we are seeking were to be granted, what would its effect be on all the other parties and, perhaps, on the tribunal itself? Would it cause anyone to waste money already spent? Would it necessitate unworkably tight deadlines for others further down the line? Would it set a new and undesirable precedent? The point of this mental exercise is to put oneself into the shoes of the tribunal faced with one's request. How would it feel, listening both to one's own argument and that which can be anticipated from the other parties? If the answer is "not very persuaded", then one's arguments had better be changed.

It should also be recognized that many tribunals see community groups as outsiders, amateurs and, frequently, as "crybabies". It seems that before such groups have even been permitted to participate in the hearing, they are complaining that they cannot get along with the same rules that everyone else has been living with for years. The first impression is that this group is going to be a lot of trouble throughout the case because it cannot play by the rules. In many cases this will be unavoidable. Consumer groups do not have the same resources as producer groups, nor environmentalists as polluters. Nevertheless, the constant plea for sympathy and special treatment wears thin very quickly, and should be used as infrequently as possible.

If the notice of the public hearing was inadequate it is better to complain directly about that than to say: "We cannot afford enough staff to find out when the hearing starts." If X days is insufficient to prepare interrogatories, explain the problem and put the matter positively: "We have retained Doctor Y as our expert advisor on this matter to prepare interrogatories for us. Unfortunately, due to earlier commitments he will be unavailable to assist us until next week. However, if the X-day deadline can be extended by five days, we can promise the Commission that with Doctor Y's help, we will be able to provide an excellent set of interrogatories which should be of considerable use to the Commission in eliciting evidence from the proponent which is not now on the record, thereby enabling the Commission to arrive at a much better decision." With that type of positive request, the intervener is not put in the position of begging for a special favour but, rather, is working with the Commission to develop a better hearing result. If the Commission asks itself, "what do we gain by granting this request?", the answer should be clear from the request itself. It may not appear to be an enormous benefit to the Commission to have yet another party present, with well-prepared interrogatories, but anything positive one can offer is better than nothing.

The third alternative we have noted is that the rule may be badly drafted. That usually occurs when a rule drafted for one purpose, perhaps some years ago, is inadequate to deal with a new circumstance. In that case it may be necessary to question the rule itself, at least insofar as it may be applicable to this case. Examples of this circumstance are rare, but they do exist. As one example in the author's experience, the CRTC had a rule among its broadcasting procedures under which a broadcaster could apply to exempt certain information from being disclosed on confidential grounds, as part of its application. The Commission treated such applications as if it had made a firm undertaking of confidentiality to the applicant. The problem this posed for interveners was that until the public hearing was announced, prospective interveners had no way of knowing that the main application had been filed, nor that the application for confidentiality had been filed with it. Thus, the interveners never had an opportunity to make a submission to oppose the latter. When this matter was raised before the CRTC, its answer was, in effect: "That's too bad; we received this information in confidence and there's nothing we can do about it." The matter was taken to the Federal Court of Appeal, which found that this application of the rule was unlawful because the Commission could not create a rule or interpret a rule so as to have the effect of precluding a meaningful public hearing. It is not normally necessary, however, to go to such lengths to challenge a rule.

Some tribunals do not have formal rules of procedure. In rare cases their procedures are simply unwritten. More usually, if they lack rules they do have something called "guidelines" or "procedures". These are, for all practical purposes, rules. They may not be drafted in the same legalistic language as the typical rules of procedure but, unquestionably, they are intended to constrain and organize what the participants may do.

Some tribunals make a fetish of "informality", pretending to be more accessible than those which they may refer to as "quasi-judicial". All tribunals have to have some basic rules, even unwritten ones, whatever they may choose to call them. Experience has shown that often those which claim to be most informal are, in practice, the most rigid. The desire to appear unconventionally informal can serve to mask a paternalistic authoritarianism which is every bit as rigid as those which openly acknowledge that they are using rules. Participants are better off knowing clearly what the rules of the game are (even if this does necessitate a bit of reading) than by the tribunal pretending that there are no rules thereby denying parties the ready knowledge as to what the unwritten rules are.

In practice, that vaunted informality usually translates to no more than a lack of opportunity for detailed oral questioning of an applicant or proponent and insufficient disclosure of written materials to permit interveners to prepare an effective case. This is excused on the ground that such techniques as interrogatories and cross-examination are "formalistic and legalistic" and would intimidate and discourage public participation. There is never any evidence offered in support of this assertion, and that is because all the evidence is to the contrary. Given that most of the factual information about a proposal is uniquely within the possession of the proponent, the latter has far more to fear from interrogatories than any intervener; likewise from cross-examination.

Alternatively, if the proponent is indifferent as to these procedures, it is the tribunal itself which lacks the confidence in its ability to be able to exercise its discretion properly to handle an overtly adversarial hearing. In that case, protecting interveners from the lawyers of the proponent may be little more than a socially acceptable excuse for refusing to hold a hearing with sufficient focus or depth to permit meaningful public participation. The experience of the Berger Inquiry, followed and imitated by numerous others, has demonstrated time and time again that it is quite convenient to split a hearing into community-style hearings without interrogatories and cross-examination, and technical hearings with them, so that interveners with varying needs can both be accommodated.

The refusal to accept that a public hearing is the public's hearing, rather than the board's hearing held in public, is the real reason for hearings which are largely meaningless exercises. Since it is most unlikely that a tribunal which employs such one-sided procedures will permit an intervener to accomplish anything meaningful at the hearing such hearings are better avoided altogether, taking one's complaints, instead, to the political level. When the rules of the game are all stacked against one side, so that there is little point in playing by the rules, if the tribunal refuses to make the rules more equal, one strong option is to refuse to play. In this modern age of public participation and consultation, the tribunal needs interveners more than they need the tribunal. Intervener groups have legitimacy whether or not they appear before a tribunal, but the tribunal has none if the public refuses to participate on the legitimate ground that its rules are unfair. One of the reasons why politicians set up tribunals is so that they may serve as "flak-catchers". If they stop catching the flak, while the politicians start to catch it, sooner or later pressure will be put on the tribunal to modify its behaviour; failing which, it will be closed down or reorganized.

2. PROPOSING NEW RULES

Quite often citizens' groups will not have problems with existing rules but, rather, with gaps in the rules. At other times the problem may not be a single rule but the combined effect of more than one rule. In any event, it may be in the group's interest that the effect of the rules be changed.

There are two ways in which a tribunal may be persuaded to change its rules: first, for the particular case at hand and, second, permanently. Let us consider each in turn.

If the forthcoming public hearing is the only one at which an intervener expects to appear, then it is unlikely that it would have any interest in a long-term change in a particular rule; even less so in a general revision of all the rules. In that case, rather than asking the tribunal to draft an entirely new rule and to pass it as one of its rules, which may require Cabinet approval, it may be persuaded simply to exercise its discretion to make an order waiving the operation of this rule, or applying it differently just for this case. But timing is crucial. Since it is unfair to change the rules of any game after some of the game has been played, the change must be proposed far enough ahead of time that it will not prejudice the other side. This is particularly true when the change affects a deadline on which other parties may plan and make arrangements which are costly, if not impossible to change.

Ideally, long before an intervener becomes involved with a tribunal's processes, its advocates will become aware of its rules and form an opinion as to which would need to be changed. If this does not happen, however, the closer the date at which the rule is to become operative, the more difficult it is to change it and the more compelling will have to be the reasons. Hence, apply for the change early. As has been mentioned, some tribunals issue hearing orders (or may be persuaded to issue one even if it has never done so before) if it is presented with persuasive arguments.

It is most important to remember that *just because there is no rule permitting a tribunal to do something does not mean that it cannot.* It can always create a rule for the purpose of the particular case. Again, remember the distinction between means and ends: the rules are the means to the end of a fair and efficient proceeding, not an end in themselves. Thus, if one can demonstrate that under the proposed rule the hearing will be better conducted and result in a better decision by means of a fairer process, in all likelihood that rule will be adopted.

For example, it may be that a tribunal has never allowed interrogatories in the past. It may have had a vague prejudice against them, but no rule prohibiting them. If it would be important in this case to file interrogatories, then carefully develop an argument as to why that would result in a better hearing. Examining interrogatory rules employed by other tribunals will enable the advocate to suggest an appropriate model to follow.

The only limitation on this advice is that the tribunal must have the statutory authority to make the rule proposed. Generally, the statute will be no problem, but there are special cases which must be considered. If the tribunal has no rule allowing for an award of costs to interveners one cannot simply ask the tribunal to create such a rule. Such a power must be granted expressly in the statute. If the tribunal is in favour of the proposed new rule but uncertain as to whether or not it has the jurisdiction, the tribunal may be asked to "state a case" to the court, if time permits. This is a procedure under which the tribunal asks the court for an opinion as to whether or not what is proposed would be within its jurisdiction. Many (but not all) tribunals have the power to state a case.

In some cases a tribunal, of its own initiative, will conduct a major and comprehensive review of its own procedures and practices. This represents a golden opportunity to modernize and reform those rules. However, such reviews are infrequent and tend to be used the least by those tribunals which need it the most. Nevertheless, it is usually easier to change a rule permanently (as opposed to merely waiving its operation) outside a particular hearing with its usually tight deadlines. Therefore, if the intervener expects to be appearing more than once before a tribunal, or if its anticipated appearance is some time away and the problem with one or more rules is already obvious, one should write to the chair of the tribunal to explain the difficulties with the rules (or the gaps in them) as presently drafted, and propose a new one (or several alternatives).

In many cases a tribunal will have some practice it is carrying on, such as having interveners speak in alphabetical order, which is not set out in the rules. In such a case it would be much more convenient to propose that the practice be changed without a formal recommendation that a whole new rule be created. All that is really being asked is: "This time, why don't we do it this way instead?" If the consent of the other parties is obtained and if it does not represent any great inconvenience to the tribunal the request will usually be accommodated. Without such consent, it becomes necessary to justify why what is being proposed should be imposed upon the other parties.

In general, the more familiar an advocate becomes with a tribunal's proceedings the better he will be at suggesting appropriate changes to its practices and rules. As well, it is helpful to be somewhat aware of the rules employed by other tribunals, to develop arguments based on useful comparisons. As few community groups would have the time to obtain this breadth of experience, a lawyer with a strong background in regulatory matters and administrative law can be invaluable, even in a short consultation.

8

Establishing and Protecting the Right to Participate Fully

1. INTRODUCTION

Establishing and protecting the right to become involved and participate in the procedures of an administrative tribunal often requires substantial forethought and careful judgment. This may not be a problem before tribunals which exist to resolve disputes between readily identifiable parties (e.g., labour relations, landlord/tenant, tax, welfare or unemployment insurance appeal tribunals). But in many administrative tribunals (such as the Competition Tribunal) it will be necessary for prospective participants to consider the nature and extent of the participation they should seek. This will require a judgment based on: (a) the identity of the prospective participant, the nature of the interest and the intended impact; (b) the governing statutes, rules and practices of the administrative tribunal; (c) case law on the rights of individuals to participate in administrative tribunal hearings and, to a lesser degree, in the courts.

There are three basic points to bear in mind. First, participation before an administrative tribunal is not an "all-or-nothing" determination. There may be levels of participation, ranging from simply a written submission of a position, through presentation of oral argument or calling a witnesses to full participation, including cross-examination. Furthermore, any participant may decide not to participate at all during the hearing of some of the issues while participating extensively on others.

Second, it is important to recognize that tribunals are, by their nature, fundamentally different from the courts. Accordingly, the law governing participation before tribunals is, and should be, different from participation before the courts. Rules also vary from tribunal to tribunal. Generally, the more a tribunal resembles a court, the stricter and more court-like will be its handling of would-be participants.

Finally, it is essential to know the law, rules and practices which govern the issue of participation in Canadian administrative tribunals. These owe nothing to the law and practices in the United States. The United States' *Administrative Procedure Act* and the institution of administrative law judges have no counterpart in Canada. As well, the United States law and literature frequently dwell on the necessity for public interest groups to have a proprietary or pecuniary interest in the outcome of a hearing before they will be granted standing to participate. Administrative tribunals in Canada do not impose the same barriers to public participation. Therefore, use of American materials (or even some Canadian materials which mistakenly rely heavily on American practice) can be misleading.

2. STANDING IN CANADIAN COURTS

Although administrative tribunals in Canada are not bound to follow the rules of standing that have been established for appearance in the courts, there is still good reason to be acquainted with this law. The rationale for the existence of administrative tribunals suggests that they should, if anything, be less formal and less restrictive in their practices than are the courts. Therefore it is logical to start with the assumption that anyone who has sufficient interest in a matter to be entitled to appear in court should also have enough interest to be entitled to participate before a tribunal. Furthermore, in recent years Canadian courts are becoming more reluctant to deny individuals the right to participate in a court trial if they intend to raise issues which can properly be determined by a court.

Courts have always had rules to determine standing (i.e., the right of an individual to bring a particular action). For many years the law for Canadian courts was that an individual could not challenge the validity of legislation or of an action of government or public officials unless specifically affected or exceptionally prejudiced, differently from other members of the general public.[1]

In the mid-1970s the Supreme Court of Canada decided two cases which made it clear that there were exceptions to the general rule. At the very least, the *Thorson*[2] and *McNeil*[3] cases decided that the courts have a *discretion* to allow a taxpayer to bring an action which questions the constitutional validity of legislation. The two cases can be read as having created an even larger exception to the general rule. For some years there had been significant disagreement about the exact extent of this exception.

Whatever the exact significance of the Thorson and McNeil cases, the Supreme Court's decision in *Minister of Justice of Canada v. Borowski*[4] goes even further in expanding the exceptions to the general rule. The judgment of Justice Martland, speaking for seven of the court's nine members, created a new test of standing, at least for individuals seeking to challenge legislation. After discussing the Thorson and McNeil decisions, Justice Martland said:[5]

> I interpret these cases as deciding that to establish status as a plaintiff in a suit seeking a declaration that legislation is invalid, if there is a serious issue as to its invalidity, a person need only to show that he is affected by it directly or that he has a genuine interest as a citizen in the validity of the legislation and that there is no other reasonable and effective manner in which the issue may be brought before the court.

It remains to be seen how this test will be applied, but it is an important change. It no longer requires that the individual be "affected" by the legislation (or the bureaucratic practice) challenged. It may be difficult to determine whether an individual "has a genuine interest as a citizen" and also that "there is no other reasonable and effective manner in which the issue may

---

1 *Smith v. A.G. Ontario*, [1924] S.C.R. 331, 42 C.C.C. 215, [1924] 3 D.L.R. 189.

2 *Thorson v. A.G. Canada*, [1975] 1 S.C.R. 138, 1 N.R. 225, 43 D.L.R. (3d) 1.

3 *McNeil v. N.S. Board of Censors*, [1976] 2 S.C.R. 265, 5 N.R. 43, 12 N.S.R. (2d) 85, 32 C.R.N.S. 376, 55 D.L.R. (3d) 632.

4 39 N.R. 331, [1982] 1 W.W.R. 97, 24 C.P.C. 62, 24 C.R. (3d) 352, 12 Sask. R. 420, 64 C.C.C. (3d) 97, 130 D.L.R. (3d) 588 (S.C.C.). This reasoning was extended beyond constitutional cases to challenges to the administration of laws themselves in *Finlay v. Canada (Min. of Finance)*, [1986] 2 S.C.R. 607, [1987] 1 W.W.R. 603, 23 Admin. L.R. 197, 17 C.P.C. (2d) 289, 71 N.R. 338, 33 D.L.R. (4th) 321, 8 C.H.R.R. D/3789.

5 *Borowski*, above, note 4 at 343 (N.R.).

be brought before the court". But, to the extent that the law of standing in Canadian courts may be of some guidance to administrative tribunals, this very liberal passage could prove to be of substantial assistance to an individual trying to establish participation rights.

3. STANDING IN TRIBUNALS

The decision as to who should be allowed to participate in an administrative tribunal's proceedings reflects two legitimate and competing interests: the need to encourage responsible and helpful participation by individuals with a genuine concern and the discouragement of the occasional nuisance intervention with nothing constructive to offer. Fortunately, Canadian tribunals have so far experienced very little irresponsible participation from individuals and, therefore, there is little excuse for tribunals to lean toward exclusion of individual participation. This may account for the fact that in practice, Canadian tribunals do not seem inclined to discourage participation.

The rule that administrative tribunals should not be bound by the same formalities as courts is well established. Also, the variation and range of tribunal formality has been recognized by the Supreme Court of Canada. In *Innisfil v. Vespra*,[6] Justice Estey, speaking for the court, said:

> The procedural format adopted by the administrative tribunal must adhere to the provisions of the parent statute of the board. The process of interpreting and applying statutory policy will be the dominant influence in the workings of such an administrative tribunal. Where the board proceeds in the discharge of its mandate to determine the rights of contending parties before it on the traditional basis wherein the onus falls upon the contender to introduce the facts and submissions upon which he will rely, the board technique will take on something of the appearance of a traditional court. Where, on the other hand, the board, by its legislative mandate or the nature of the subject matter assigned to its administration, is more concerned with community interests at large, and with technical policy aspects of a specialized subject, one cannot expect the tribunal to function in the manner of the traditional court. This is particularly so where the board membership is drawn partly or entirely from persons experienced or trained in the sector of activity consigned to the administrative supervision of the board.

---

6 [1981] 2 S.C.R. 145, 37 N.R. 43 at 64, 15 M.P.L.R. 250, 12 O.M.B.R. 129, 123 D.L.R. (3d) 530.

The degree of formality implicit in the tribunal's statutory mandate is reflected both in decisions about whether or not participation is allowed and, if it is, in the determination of the levels of participation to be permitted.

Sometimes a "parent statute", with or without other legislation, may stipulate when and to what extent individuals are entitled to participate. More frequently it is necessary to infer the legislative intent, because the legislation is not explicit. For example, in two cases the Federal Court of Appeal interpreted section 19 of the *Broadcasting Act*[7] as giving the public a "statutory right of presentation".

In the first of these, *Re Canadian Radio-Television & Telecommunications Comm. and London Cable TV Ltd.*;[8] the Federal Court of Appeal noted that the *Broadcasting Act* required a "public hearing" as a condition precedent to the granting of an amendment requested in an application by London Cable TV Limited. According to the reasons of Chief Justice Jackett, writing for the court:[9]

> ... at the very minimum, what the statute required, by requiring a "public hearing", was a hearing at which, subject to the procedural rules of the Commission and the inherent jurisdiction of the Commission and its own proceedings, every member of the public would have a status "to bring before" the Commission anything relevant to the subject matter of the hearing so as to ensure that, to the extent possible, everything that might appropriately be taken into consideration would be before the Commission, or its Executive Committee, when the application for the amendment was dealt with. To be such a public hearing, it would, in my view, have had to be arranged in such a way as to provide members of the public with a reasonable opportunity to know the subject matter of the hearing, and what it involved from the point of view of the public, in sufficient time to decide whether or not to exercise their statutory right of presentation and to prepare themselves for the task of presentation if they decided to make a presentation. In other words, what the statute contemplates, in my view, is a *meaningful* hearing that would be calculated to aid the Commission, or its Executive Committee, to reach a conclusion that reflects a consideration of the public interest as well as a consideration of the private interest of the licensee; it does not contemplate a public meeting at which members of the public are merely given an opportunity to "blow off steam". [Emphasis added]

7 R.S.C. 1970, c. B-11, [now section 10, R.S.C. 1985, c. B-9].
8 [1976] 2 F.C. 621, 13 N.R. 292, 29 C.P.R. (2d) 268, 67 D.L.R. (3d) 267 (C.A.). Leave to appeal refused (*sub nom. Cdn. Cablesystems (Ont.) Ltd. v. Consumers Assn. Can.*), [1977] 2 S.C.R. 720, 30 C.P.R. (2d) 76, 77 D.L.R. (3d) 641, 15 N.R. 111.
9 *Ibid.*, at 624-625.

If this judgment is read narrowly it may apply only if a public hearing is *required*. But if a tribunal is given discretion as to whether a public hearing should be held and it elects to hold one, the strong language of the *London Cable* case should still apply because there is no discretion to hold a meaningless hearing.

In the *London Cable* case the Federal Court of Appeal held that the interveners' participation did not necessarily include the right to cross-examination "in this case". But the interveners had, both before and during the hearings, requested access to certain "fundamental basic facts relevant to the proposed increase in rates" requested by the applicant company. Accordingly, in the words of the judgment,[10] the denial of access to this information

> . . . left members of the public, including the applicants, in a position where they knew that the licensee was asking leave to increase its charges to the public but where they had no means of forming a considered opinion as to whether such increase was justified by the circumstances and had no means, if they concluded that it was not, of preparing themselves to put forward their position at the hearing.

The court continued that this refusal by the Commission "to supply such basic information" meant that the Commission "failed to take a step that, in the circumstances of this case, was a condition precedent to the holding of a . . . 'public hearing'".

4. STANDING IN APPEALS AND JUDICIAL REVIEW

The second case occurred three years later, in 1979, when the Federal Court of Appeal again had occasion to consider the implications of section 19 (now section 10) of the *Broadcasting Act* and the CRTC rules. The essential question in *Canadian Broadcasting League v. Canadian Radio-Television & Communications Comm.*[11] was whether the Canadian Broadcasting League (CBL) had status to appeal a decision of the CRTC to the court. The CBL had qualified itself, under the CRTC rules, as an "intervener" and as a "party". It had been represented by counsel at the hearing and made submissions, including two

---

10 *Ibid.*, at 625.
11 [1980] 1 F.C. 396, 29 N.R. 383, 13 C.P.C. 331, 101 D.L.R. (3d) 669 (C.A.).

applications of a procedural nature; it sought disclosure of certain financial information, as well as permission to cross-examine a number of witnesses. The CRTC denied both of these applications. When the CBL applied to the Federal Court of Appeal for an order quashing the CRTC decision, the licensee argued that the CBL should be denied status to appeal because the right to an appeal required not only intervener status before the CRTC, but also a demonstration that the intervener was prejudicially affected in some manner greater than that of the general public, or had some proprietary or pecuniary interest in the outcome. The Federal Court of Appeal rejected the argument, relying on its finding in *London Cable* that the public had a "statutory right of presentation". The right of appeal was held to be "an extension of this access", the means by which "the public right of intervention" is made complete.

There may be a limit to the utility of the CBL judgment because the court also relied on the fact that the CBL had a "well-established role as an advocate of the consumer interest in broadcasting". The court refered to the CBL's 50-year history with "a well-identified role . . . as an organized contributor to public policy formulation in broadcasting". The court continued:[12]

> The record also shows that the CBL has played an active role as an intervenor in hearings of the CRTC. Its activities are supported in some measure by public funds. In my opinion this well-established role and assumed responsibility as a public interest advocate in the field of broadcasting gives it a sufficient interest not only for status before the CRTC but for status to appeal. That status is further reinforced in the present case because the grounds of appeal which the CBL seeks to assert raise issues as to whether it was deprived of procedural rights essential to the effective exercise of its statutory right of presentation.

This passage makes it clear that the identity of the party may be critical in determining procedural rights before an administrative tribunal, and that the courts may consider this identity in deciding whether the party has standing to challenge the conduct of the tribunal. Hence, what was held in relation to the Canadian Broadcasting League will not necessarily be held for every other group.

As a tactical matter, the message is clear: when seeking to

---

12 *Ibid.*, at 393.

intervene or to appeal, describe in considerable detail the history of the group and its accomplishments.

5. THE "RIGHT" TO CROSS-EXAMINE

Cross-examination is unquestionably one of the two most important tools available to the intervener (the interrogatory is the other). Although usually associated with lawyers, non-lawyers can learn the art fairly quickly, especially if they understand the substance of the evidence. Unfortunately, some tribunals refuse to allow cross-examination because they view their procedures as being too informal to accommodate this. That is a valid reason in tribunals in which the parties are approximately equal in strength and resources and no technical evidence is presented. As the complexity of evidence grows or the inequality between parties becomes more pronounced, the exclusion of cross-examination is increasingly unfair. A workable compromise can be achieved by holding two types of hearings, sometimes in the same case: community or informal hearings without technical evidence and without cross-examination, and formal hearings with technical evidence and cross-examination.

The right to cross-examine witnesses is alluded to in the *London Cable* and *Canadian Broadcasting League* cases, but there is no clear statement as to when such rights exist. The clearest, if somewhat complicated case on the right of cross-examination is the Supreme Court of Canada decision in *Innisfil v. Vespra*,[13] mentioned earlier (page 118) in this Chapter. The judgment discusses several issues, three relevant statutes and numerous authorities, only some of which shed light on the right of a participant to cross-examine. Nevertheless, an outline of the relevant portions of this case should be helpful in determining when there may be a right to cross-examine before an administrative tribunal.

The city of Barrie, Ontario, sought to annex part of the township of Innisfil, as well as parts of other townships. The townships intervened in Barrie's application before the Ontario Municipal Board, but were denied the right to cross-examine a witness on evidence of population projections submitted by the

---

13   Above, note 6.

provincial government. When the case reached the Supreme Court of Canada, that court found that the Ontario Municipal Board had a broad discretion to set its own procedures. Justice Estey stated:[14]

> The wording adopted by the Legislature in this provision is broad, and no limitations or qualifications are prescribed in the subsection or elsewhere on the nature or conduct of the hearing. The board must not, it is clear, adopt any procedure or follow any course that will in any way prevent or limit its enquiry into the "merits" of the application or "any objections" that "any person" may seek to place before the board. . . .
> The position accorded to the citizen of the community by the Legislature under the same statutes is the absolute and unqualified right to object to the application being granted in whole or in part. There is nothing in the statute which might be construed as authorizing the board, the Minister or the court to curtail the right of the people who bring "any objections" that any person may desire to bring to the attention of the board. . . .

The case later considers the importance of cross-examination[15] and concludes that "where the rights of the citizen are involved and the statute affords him the right to a full hearing, including a hearing of his demonstration of his rights", the citizen should not be denied the right to cross-examine unless there is "the clearest statutory curtailment of the citizen's right to meet the case made against him by cross-examination".

6. STRATEGIC CONSIDERATIONS

The practices followed by tribunals can be classified into two categories: those which allow interveners to participate fully and those which do not.

With tribunals in the first category, a public interest group would find no serious impediments to full participation caused by the tribunal itself. Following the rules will be all that is necessary. Thus, the only difficulty should be the initial effort of learning how to "play the game" within the rules. An experienced regulatory counsel can help to explain the working of the rules and make tactical suggestions to overcome specific problems. The board's own counsel or secretary, while not always willing to offer advice on the finer points of strategy, will usually

---

14 *Ibid.*, at 60-61 (N.R.).
15 *Ibid.*, at 63 (N.R.).

also be very helpful and will not charge for their time. If possible, it is also advisable to attend a hearing of that tribunal, to see how the rules are applied in practice. Finally, experience in one or two hearings will often greatly aid the transition from a neophyte intervener to an "old pro".

With the second kind of tribunal, which restricts the right to participate, serious difficulties are inevitable. No amount of experience before the tribunal will be helpful if its rules or practices preclude effective participation; the only way to change the situation is to persuade or compel the board to change its practices. There are three ways of doing this, listed in order of preference: persuasion, judicial coercion and political coercion.

Some tribunals can be persuaded to liberalize their practices on rational arguments alone: if not the first time, then perhaps by the second or third intervention. It is generally better to give the tribunal the benefit of the doubt than to adopt a posture of outrage at the very first appearance. Sometimes tribunal members will resist intervention simply because they have never seen interveners before or, if the occasional intervener has appeared, it was simply to grumble a bit and disappear again. It ought not to be assumed that the tribunal has a pro-industry attitude or, if it appears to have, that this is immutable. The author has seen tribunals initially oppose intervention, gradually warm up to it, and finally welcome it. There have also been others which have stubbornly resisted intervention only to have the chair and several members replaced by the minister or by a successor government. If the media relations portion of an intervention frustrated by regulator is properly handled, the resulting adverse publicity can put great pressure on the tribunal to reform its ways. We live in an age of public participation. The self-proclaimed omniscience of the regulatory bureaucracy is everywhere being questioned and the refusal to allow the public to have an effective presentation of its views is increasingly becoming the exception rather than the norm.

Unfortunately, there are still a few of the old style tribunals left. Whether because of inexperience or the arrogant viewpoint that the tribunal members know it all anyway, such tribunals cling to procedures which greatly restrict public participation. In particular, they often have restrictive rules with respect to disclosure of information (numerous excuses will be given why most of the relevant and useful information is confidential), interrogatories and cross-examination. The objective will be to limit the information available to interveners and, thus, to restrict their effectiveness, so that eventually would-be interveners will give up in frustration and go away. Then, if queried about its procedures for intervention, the tribunal will be able to claim that it has such procedures but that no one is interested in intervening, so they are simply unused. A protracted, frustrating battle is almost inevitable with a tribunal whose ultimate objective is to defeat entirely, or at least to restrict severely, any form of public interest intervention. The new Competition Tribunal, in its first case with interveners, was overruled by the Federal Court of Appeal for what was, in essence, a narrowly court-like view of the function of intervention.[16]

It is important for interveners to learn and understand the tribunal's existing rules so that they can be used to the full; new rules can also be proposed at any time.[17] At least then there is no excuse for excluding someone on the ground that he or she has not followed the rules.

There is another important principle of law which must be considered at this point, namely, that all parties to a hearing are to be treated equally.[18] Assuming that the rules allow someone who wishes to be an intervener to be a "party", and assuming that intervener status has been granted, it is possible to insist upon equal treatment with all other parties. In some cases this will be very useful, in others, it will be of no use at all because all parties are treated equally badly, that is, disclosure procedures are ineffective or non-existent and no oral questioning is allowed. This, of course, works to the prejudice only of interveners because most of the relevant information is in the possession of the applicant. Hence, the only way to have a significant impact is to persuade the board to change its procedures.

A few very restrictive boards (such as the Atomic Energy Control Board) do not even permit interventions, so that one

---

16 *American Airlines Inc. v. Competition Tribunal (Can.)* (1988), 33 Admin. L.R. 229, 89 N.R. 241, 54 D.L.R. (4th) 741, 23 C.P.R. (3d) 178 (Fed. C.A.), appeal to S.C.C. dismissed orally from the bench for the reasons given by the Federal Court of Appeal, March 2, 1989.
17 This has been discussed in Chapter 7 above.
18 See the discussion of this point in the A.G. *Manitoba* case examined in Supplement 1.

cannot even acquire a "party" status and the right to equality of treatment which flows from it. With such boards, any participation is virtually pointless. The Competition Tribunal has adopted the needlessly technical position that interveners are not parties, so that the right to be an intervener may not be of much value.

It is often thought that one has a "right" to intervene, or to cross-examine, but administrative law creates no such right unless a statute grants it. Moreover, if, as usual, statutes are silent on procedure, we fall back on the old cliché that "the tribunal is the master of its own procedure". Thus, unless the statute expressly or by necessary implication requires fairly liberal procedures, the tribunal can be as "closed" as it wants and it is unlikely that the courts will do anything about it.

If some form of public hearing is required (as with the CRTC), then there is a legal lever. The *London Cable* case[19] discussed earlier in this chapter was taken to court because the intervener, the Consumers' Association of Canada, had tried repeatedly to persuade the CRTC to permit greater disclosure, without success. When the matter was brought to the court the decision of the CRTC was struck down and it was forced to conduct the entire hearing over again, this time granting the disclosure. Additionally, the reasons for decision of the court became binding on the CRTC as a "precedent", thereby making it unnecessary to re-litigate the point in future cases. As well, other tribunals with similar statutes recognized that if a similar case was brought against them, they, too, would have their decision set aside.

A test case such as the *London Cable* case can be very important in its impact on the entire regulatory community. But test case targets must be selected carefully because if the case is lost, the tribunal's right to exclude or to deny permission to cross-examine will no longer be a matter of doubt but of certainty. As a result, the tribunal may become smug about its power.

The political route is the most uncertain of all, since politicians are reluctant to interfere with tribunals in the absence of some significant political advantage. While there may have been some considerable advantage in reforming, for example, the Canadian Transport Commission as part of a major thrust

---

19 Above, note 8.

towards transportation deregulation, a government is unlikely to waste precious legislative time merely to create the procedural right of cross-examination.

Discussions with the government department or minister responsible for a particular tribunal may be helpful. In some cases, without any legislative reform, a friendly chat between the minister and the chair of the tribunal may provoke more liberalization of access than an attack in the courts, which may cause potential allies to "circle the wagons" to protect the tribunal. If the minister refuses to become involved, that may be the time to consider the courts if there is a strong legal case to be made; or, if there is not, the media. It is not unheard of that a tribunal which is initially well-liked by the government falls out of favour over a period of a few years through repeated bad press and embarrassing questions on the floor of the legislature. The better organized and more credible the intervener, the greater its chance of this kind of success.

If there is an arguable case that one has a legal right, for example, to cross-examine, even if this is not a clear cut or unquestionable right, the tribunal should be pressed to permit it, but pressed tactfully. If the tribunal refuses, it is risky to threaten judicial review. This will merely appear to be impertinent, and will be more infuriating than helpful. A tactful way of doing the same thing is to ask the chair to refer the question to the Federal Court of Appeal (if it is a federal tribunal) for an authoritative judicial determination, or to the appropriate provincial Supreme Court, in other cases. Be prepared for the chair to refuse (they almost always do), but at least the message will have been delivered that there may be a legal case. If the tribunal refuses to refer the case and if a lawyer is ready to bring a judicial review application, it may sometimes be helpful to ask the chair to adjourn the hearing for a few days so that the issue may be brought before the court. If there is a really strong legal case, it may be that an intelligent opponent will even support the adjournment request, rather than run the risk of having the whole hearing set aside at the end and having to do it again. This is rare, however, as the tribunal and the applicant usually wish to run as quickly as possible toward the conclusion of the hearing, and face any legal problems later, should they arise. Hence, a request for an adjournment for purposes of judicial review will usually be refused. Then the tribunal's hearing and the judicial hearing will probably be held simultaneously, necessitating the use of legal counsel at each of these if appearance at the tribunal is to be uninterrupted.

Nevertheless, there have been numerous cases in which a court has been willing to grant a judicial review application on an emergency basis on 48 hours notice or even less. Thus, upon a refusal to adjourn the hearing before the tribunal while the legal issue is heard by the court, one may be able to appear in court within a day or two and obtain a decision from the bench prohibiting the tribunal from proceeding further without allowing the party to cross-examine. (Cross-examination is used as an example only; the same arguments apply with respect to the refusal to permit intervention, or any other procedural aspect of participation.)

If a party wins this judicial review application the tribunal initially may be somewhat resentful, but shortly will treat the intervener with a new-found respect. Even if the application fails, the intervener has demonstrated a willingness to fight for what it perceives to be its rights, and, if it had a good case and commences an appeal of the court decision immediately, the tribunal and the applicant will see the potential for a future victory dangling over their heads. Swift, decisive action taken by an experienced lawyer with a reputation for toughness may help obtain some sort of accommodation with the tribunal even before the appeal is heard or, if not, will provide ammunition for a further appeal to the minister.

But even if an intervener is not anxious to bring an application for judicial review, when appearing before the tribunal its counsel should firmly and clearly request, at every appropriate point in the hearing, permission to cross-examine particular witnesses (unless it is known that the tribunal's practice is to permit it in any case). Thus, if there is any doubt, the intervention statement should contain a request to cross-examine. If that is refused, the request should be made again orally as a preliminary motion at the pre-hearing conference. If no answer is given, there should be a telegram sent to the chair a week or two before the opening of the hearing requesting a decision on one's application for cross-examination. If the response is negative, the application should be presented again, orally, at the opening of public hearing.

If the chair again refuses at the public hearing to grant this procedural request, and if the intervener does not wish to, or for any reason cannot, make an application to the courts, then consider seriously whether there is any point in participating further. By acquiescing in the procedure of a tribunal which allows little opportunity for meaningful participation, one is implicitly endorsing the procedure and encouraging the tribunal to continue it. There does not seem to be much point in deluding oneself into believing that a serious contribution can be made if the procedural opportunity to do so is unavailable. It also gives the impression that all the pressure for a different procedure was merely posturing, and that the tribunal was right to have refused.

The real test of the integrity of an advocacy group occurs when effective access procedures have been denied and the group has been funded by government to assist its advocacy efforts. Does it then spend the money simply because it is available, and hope for the best? Does it delude itself or rationalize by asserting that its mere presence is helpful, however, restricted its advocacy may be? Or does it turn the money back to the government on the ground that it will not waste public funds and allow itself to be used in this manner? The decision is not an easy one.

9

Winning the Battle for Information

1. NOTICE

One of the major problems with public hearings has been to find out what is happening before it is too late. Public hearings are usually advertised through notices in the Canada Gazette or the official gazette of the provinces. Neither of these have widespread readership. There are sometimes small advertisements in local newspapers which are also likely to escape notice. Direct mailings from tribunals tend to be the best way of keeping interested persons informed, since anyone on tribunal mailing lists will automatically be informed of hearings without effort on their part. Usually, all one has to do is ask to be put on the mailing list and, in some cases, pay a small annual charge.

It is often possible to predict that an application is about to be filed simply by reading the business pages of the better newspapers. For example, because one cannot build an inter-provincial pipeline without permission from the National Energy Board, when the first news story appears stating that a pipeline company is planning to build its pipeline through one's backyard, it is reasonable to anticipate an application to the National Energy Board. A letter should be sent to the Board promptly expressing interest in the matter and requesting notification as soon as the application is filed. Similarly, reports of interviews with business journalists or speeches to annual meetings by presidents of public utilities companies often precede an application to the appropriate board for an increase in rates.

What can be done if someone learns, by one means or another, of a hearing which is going on, or, worse yet, has already been completed, which might affect his or her group's interests? If the hearing is still on it may still be possible to be allowed to present evidence, or otherwise to participate, even if the deadline for interventions has passed: check with the board secretary or simply attend on the next hearing date and ask for permission to be heard, if not immediately, then at some future time.

If permission to participate is denied or if the hearing has already finished, it may be wise to check to see what notice was given. Tribunals must, both by common law and by many statutory provisions, give "reasonable" notice — reasonable in the sense that it is timely, widely disseminated, and the content conveys the real intentions of the giver and enables the recipient to know the case he or she has to meet.

The test of whether notice is in a particular case reasonable is an objective one: was the notice adequate from the point of view of a reasonable person? Thus, if notice is given to, for example, all persons in an area by means of a newspaper advertisement, it must be clear to a person reading the advertisement whether or not they are affected by the hearing. If a person was legally entitled to notice but did not receive it (through no fault of his or her own), it may be possible to re-open the hearing, at least to allow him or her to make some submissions.

2. INTERROGATORIES/DISCOVERY

Under crushing case-load pressures, courts of law have developed "discoveries", which are formal opportunities for parties to discover what will be the evidence of others, before the trial. In courts there are three forms of pre-trial discovery: questioning under oath (before a simultaneous reporter, not a judge), exchanges of documents and written questions (called interrogatories) sent by one party to another. Tribunals, to date, usually allow only interrogatories (a few permit discovery of documents and the Competition Tribunal's rules allow questioning under oath).

The purpose of discovery is to reduce the time spent at an oral hearing. Since all parties and the decision-maker must be present at the public hearing, public hearing time is expensive and, accordingly, the more that can be done between the parties before the public hearing, the better. The concept of discovery before tribunals is also part of the growing philosophy of openness in hearings — to ambush parties at the hearing with unanticipated evidence is unfair and leads to adjournments, which are costly and waste a great deal of time. For these reasons, relatively full disclosure before hearings is now considered the norm in courts of law, at least in civil cases and, increasingly, in criminal cases as well; a few of the more progressive tribunals are not far behind the courts.

Unfortunately, many tribunals have not kept pace with these developments. Most of them permit no pre-hearing discovery of any kind. As a result, everything must be done at the public hearing (which explains much of the delay which has come to be called "regulatory lag"). Such tribunals may assume that the application will be complete, or that their staff, through deficiency letters, can get all of the necessary evidence before the public. Others rather patronizingly assume that since the tribunal is conducting the hearing and must decide the case, it is essential only that it be aware of such evidence of the applicant that it considers important. As for the interveners, they can fend for themselves or call their own evidence, if they have any.

In many cases, intervention before such a tribunal will tend to be a frustrating waste of time until it can be persuaded to improve its discovery procedures. This may require some modification of the tribunal's perception of its role from what might be called the "proprietary model" of the public hearing ("This is our public hearing in which you may, if you are lucky, be permitted to participate") to a more "participatory model" ("This is the public's hearing, and all participants are to be given a fair opportunity to controvert the evidence of those with opposing interests").

The most basic tribunal discovery procedure is "production and inspection of documents". This permits interveners to seek production of (i.e., an opportunity to see or copy) any document which is not part of the application but which is referred to in it. Given such a rule, the incentive is to avoid referring to any document since this will preclude anyone from knowing about it and, therefore, from seeking production of it. Of course, the applicant may refer to it orally at the public hearing, if asked where such and such a number came from, but its production at that time would probably be too late to benefit the intervener.

Applications will sometimes refer to a large number of lengthy documents. If the intervener seeks production of all of these, in the absence of a specific rule as to what form the production must take the applicant will simply invite the intervener to attend at its office to read them. This might involve someone peering over the intervener's shoulder as he or she reads through piles of incomprehensible documents and laboriously takes handwritten notes, since all of it cannot possibly be remembered. Unless the tribunal orders the applicant to provide a photocopy of these documents, the applicant has no duty to do so, or even to permit the intervener to make a copy at his own expense. All in all, production and inspection of documents is a procedure of limited use in most regulatory hearings, which may explain why it is so infrequently used. In fact, its existence is somewhat of an historical anachronism, probably borrowed from early discovery procedures of courts of law. While the production and inspection of documents is of some use in certain kinds of civil litigation, it is by no means the exclusive discovery technique available in the courts. It can hardly serve that purpose for tribunals.

Interrogatories are written questions to the other side. Unfortunately, the recipient will often play the game of trying to give as little information as possible. This should be anticipated and counteracted by making interrogatories difficult to resist by being as specific as possible. It is better to send ten short, simple interrogatories than one long and complicated one. Also, each interrogatory should be numbered and dated so that it can be referred to accurately as the replies come in.

Fairly common interrogatories include: requests for financial statements of the company, parents and subsidiaries for the past five years with projections of certain items one year ahead; requests for detailed information about the capital structure of the company, if not provided in the financial statements; data about quality of service; information about company policies, practices and philosophies not found in annual reports; detailed breakouts of expenditures by type of service, or region if not provided in the application; organization chart of the company's senior officers and their functions; number of employees employed in various functions; etc.

Because the applicant needs sufficient time to prepare replies, interrogatories must be sent out as soon as possible to provide the maximum lead time.

Interrogatories can be a more useful procedure than production and inspection of documents, provided that the interrogatory process is properly timed and well policed by the tribunal. For the interrogatory procedure to be effective, any relevant question put to the applicant in writing must be required to be answered fully and promptly. When there are many interveners, this can place a great deal of stress on the staff and consultants available to the applicant. Nevertheless, unless sufficient time is allowed for adequate interrogatory responses, and unless complete, thorough and informative answers are compelled, the interrogatory process can quickly deteriorate and become a sham.

One abuse is to submit applications full of rather banal information and public relations statements, designed more for the press on the opening day than to permit serious scrutiny. The pre-hearing stage then becomes a game of hide-and-seek between the applicant and the interveners, the latter trying to ferret out the evidence necessary to discern the justification for the application, the former attempting to provide just enough information to avoid the appearance of stonewalling, but not enough of substance to be of use to its adversaries. In effect, the substance of the application — to the extent that it has any substance — is written during the interrogatory process.

Two other common abuses are overblown claims of confidentiality as the reason for declining to supply the information sought, and the unwarranted assertion that the information sought is irrelevant and immaterial. A most irritating game is the paper chase, where an intervener is referred to one interrogatory as the response to another one, which in turn refers to a further interrogatory and so on, the last reply finally referring the reader back to the applicant's original evidence, or refusing to answer on the grounds of relevance or confidentiality. It is also not uncommon to provide, for example, an answer with two numbers and a percentage rather than three numbers (where it is obvious that the purpose of the question is to do a ratio and proportion calculation), or other such combinations which frustrate the intervener's ability to test the applicant's calculations.

All of these games are designed to wear down the opposition and use up time. While it is not impossible for tribunals to deal with these effectively, they may themselves lose patience with refereeing numerous interrogatory disputes, and give up on policing the abuses. Once a public hearing has already been scheduled or, in the case of interrogatories submitted during the public hearing, is well under way, tribunals seem most reluctant to bring the whole process to a halt simply to get an answer to a few interrogatories. Most applicants know this. A healthy dose of objections, evasion or simple non-answering will often at least reduce the number of areas in which the application may be attacked by means of useful interrogatory responses. While the tribunal may ultimately compel replies to some interrogatories, the intervener's success ratio is by no means 100 per cent and at least delays and costs have been imposed on interveners who are already at a great disadvantage due to the disparity in access to resources and information. Unless the tribunal is sensitive to such abuse of its processes, is unintimidated by the applicant, and insists on full and proper responses however long it takes, the interrogatory process can be reduced in its effectiveness.

Assuming that one eventually obtains a useful reply, it may be used in several ways. The intervener's own witness can incorporate the numbers into his or her evidence; or the entire interrogatory can be introduced as an exhibit, either through an intervener's witnesses or in the cross-examination of one of the applicant's witnesses, whichever timing is the most effective. However, unless the interrogatory is in one way or another introduced into evidence, it cannot be cited in argument.

If there are a number of co-operative interveners they will often exchange interrogatories and replies. Nevertheless, one should not, without consent, introduce as an exhibit an interrogatory response prepared for another intervener.

3. OTHER USEFUL SOURCES

There are a number of other sources of useful information.

If one's opponent is a large public company whose shares are listed on a United States stock exchange, it will have a legal requirement to make filings with the United States Securities and Exchange Commission (SEC). Because United States securities law requires much more information to be disclosed than does Canadian law, one can learn a great deal that way. There are Canadian agents (such as Infoglobe, a service of the *Globe & Mail*) who will obtain these documents for a modest fee. They advertise regularly in the business sections of newspapers.

As one dramatic example of the information that can be obtained in this way, several years ago Bell Canada insisted on confidentiality for any and all information concerning its contract with the government of Saudi Arabia, claiming that such confidentiality was a term of the contract and that the whole contract would be jeopardized if disclosure were made. The Canadian Radio-Television and Telecommunications Commission (CRTC) substantially accepted this argument, and refused to order the disclosure. Shortly thereafter it was discovered that much of the information sought had been filed with the SEC in the United States and therefore was public information and was obtained from that source. Needless to say, for some time thereafter, the company did not have a great deal of credibility in its claims for confidentiality.

Another important source of information is the evidence in other cases before the same regulatory tribunal, or other tribunals regulating the same activity. To stay with public utilities, United States regulators such as the Federal Communications Commission or the state public utilities boards regularly demand very full disclosure of information and, apparently, this has not injured competition in the United States. Quite often, merely showing Canadian tribunals the depth and quality of information routinely available in the United States is enough to make them drool.

Similarly, some boards in Canada are better than others in ordering disclosure. Finding precedents in other provinces can be helpful.

Sometimes a surprising amount of good information will come

from fairly mundane sources. Company presidents who may cry doom and gloom in front of a regulatory tribunal when seeking a rate increase will present a much more optimistic picture of the future in a speech to shareholders at the annual meeting or to a group of financial analysts. Stockbrokers can often provide copies of such speeches. Even Statistics Canada, whose data is usually both too aggregated and too late to be of much use for public hearing purposes, can be helpful. If long-term sales and profit trends in an industry have been improving, and that is not the case for the company involved in the particular case, it may suggest weak management rather than the need for higher rates.

Dealing with Crown corporations can be a special problem. They are very secretive because they are frequently so inefficient in their operations and so committed to overstaffing and over-building that, if the truth were known, the government would be severely embarrassed. In some cases such corporations are completely unregulated, despite their monopoly status: for example, Hydro-Quebec. In others, for example Ontario Hydro, there is the public misconception of regulation through the Ontario Energy Board (OEB), yet the OEB has no decision-making power regarding Ontario Hydro and can only make recommendations, which Ontario Hydro can and does ignore. For such corporations it may be necessary to study the evidence submitted over the years to various legislative committees, or to dig into government spending estimates from the provincial treasurer. It may also be helpful to have a friendly member of an opposition party present a written question to the minister through the normal legislative process. If all else fails, there may be no alternative but to write an open letter to the minister and have it published in a newspaper. If the information sought is the kind that should obviously be provided, perhaps the newspaper will even write a supportive editorial. This can sometimes be suggested in a meeting with the appropriate member of the editorial board of that newspaper.

There are also two libraries one should consider. First, most tribunals have their own libraries which often contain all sorts of useful information from past hearings and various bits of data collected from here and there. The Crown corporation or even private corporation may have its own firm library, to which one may be granted access.

The information may be buried somewhere, and the task may be like looking for a needle in a haystack, but persistence may lead to success.

10

Extending Resources

Much of this book has been written on the assumption that those who seek to participate in tribunal hearings have resources sufficient at least to retain some professionals to work with them. This chapter is based on the opposite assumption.

Groups with very limited or virtually non-existent advocacy budgets can still participate. The best way would be to obtain funding from the government. That is not because financial self-sufficiency is not important; usually it is preferable to maintain the independence which comes from having one's own money rather than relying upon government. However, tribunal hearings tend to be called on relatively short notice, and serious participation in them is rather expensive. In all likelihood it will be impossible to raise sufficient money to participate effectively prior to the hearing.

Some government departments do provide funding for public participation. For example, the Federal Environmental Assessment Review Organization (FEARO) has obtained funding for participants in major environmental hearings. Some commissions of inquiry (such as the Grange Commission examining the baby deaths at Toronto's Hospital for Sick Children, which funded the parents) have some kind of limited funding and, if they are not initially aware of the need for this, can usually be persuaded to seek funding if pressed.

A few ongoing tribunals, notably provincial public utilities boards, the Ontario Energy Board and the Canadian Radio-Television and Telecommunications Commission (CRTC), while unable to provide funding, can at least make costs awards. These are usually after the fact but, despite this, it is sometimes possible to persuade competent lawyers and expert witnesses to work on the hearing with the express understanding that they will only be paid if the tribunal awards costs. That is not as great a risk as it sounds, because it will usually be well known what the practice of the tribunal is. A tribunal which regularly awards full costs will only fail to do so if the work done by the representatives of the intervener was not of a quality sufficient to justify requiring the customers of the utility to pay for it. With costs awards, even those groups which otherwise could afford to participate only in a minimal and half-hearted way can make a serious and effective intervention.

Unfortunately, most tribunals do not have the power to award costs. While it is strongly recommended that every effort be made to lobby for legislative change, in the meantime, limited resources must be extended in other ways. One of the main resources is the staff of the tribunal itself.

Some tribunals, particularly the one-time inquiry, may be persuaded to call an expert witness as its own witness, at the suggestion of an intervener group. That is just as good as the intervener calling this witness, since an honest witness would say the same thing regardless of whose witness he is, and there is the great advantage that the intervener does not have to pay the bill. As an alternative, during the Beaufort Sea environmental assessment hearings held by FEARO, consultants hired to advise the panel were also made available, without any charge, to any of the participants who wanted advice and assistance from them. Ongoing tribunals will have staff economists, engineers or other experts who can be of assistance. While these people are too busy to do all of the intervener's work they can at least point in the right direction, help to articulate better the intervener's concerns and suggest appropriate decisions of the board, evidence in previous cases and textbooks or other background reading. Similarly, the tribunal's lawyers can assist in understanding and complying with the rules of procedure. To a group that has some reasonable amount of expertise, even this limited assistance can be useful.

Most non-business groups extend their resources by using volunteers. These can be both a benefit and a curse. A hardworking, knowledgeable volunteer can be worth his or her weight in gold; a lazy or unskilled one can be an embarrassment, especially because it is very difficult to fire a volunteer.

If a hearing will be a relatively short one, perhaps only of one or two days, it is sometimes possible to persuade an economist or lawyer to donate that amount of time in an interesting case. Usually, university professors tend to be more sympathetic to donating time to a public interest group than their professional colleagues in full-time commercial practice. However, quite surprisingly, the author has found that the most experienced and successful lawyers — those who could bill for 366 days a year if that were possible — are often the most willing to donate a day or two if they can be made to feel excited about the case. This will usually be either because they have some sympathy for the cause or because the case itself is an unusual and interesting one; or, preferably, for both reasons. Even large, seemingly forbidding corporate law firms usually have one or two lawyers willing to help on occasion. The trick is to find out who. Again, usually a professor at the university will know the practitioners in the field who can help.

In some provinces legal aid can be obtained for appearances before tribunals, particularly those which significantly effect the rights of individuals, such as workers' compensation or immigration. Unfortunately, a few provinces still restrict legal aid to criminal cases only. Where civil legal aid is covered, legal services may be delivered either in the form of a certificate usable with a lawyer in private practice, or through some sort of clinic. While it is usually difficult to get a certificate to appear before an administrative tribunal, except in cases such as immigration, there are often legal aid clinics which can provide these services to citizens' groups. Two well-known Ontario examples include the Canadian Environmental Law Association and the Advocacy Resource Centre for the Handicapped (ARCH). Manitoba legal aid has a public interest law centre which assists clients who appear before, for example, the Public Utilities Board. Quebec also provides direct assistance through several of its clinics. Note that once such a clinic takes on a case, it not only provides legal assistance but also expert witnesses and consultants.

One problem which frequently arises is the coordination of the efforts of volunteers and professionals. Sometimes two members of a volunteer group, unknown to each other, will approach two different lawyers to ask for assistance, and both will succeed. That is, until the two lawyers find out that they have both been recruited to work on the same case, which may well result in both resigning. Another problem arises when the volunteers are unwilling to delegate full authority for the case to a staff lawyer or to an outside counsel or expert so that instructions, which come from a committee of volunteers, become hard to obtain. Professionals, who are accustomed to being treated with respect by their clients, equate this kind of dithering not with democracy but with lack of trust, and are likely to resign. The appropriate principle would seem to be that once someone competent has been found the lawyer should be left alone to conduct the case as he or she sees fit.

It is not always necessary to have a professional as the spokesperson for the group. On the contrary, it is sometimes desirable to use the professional merely to train the volunteers, and to let the volunteers conduct the hearing themselves. Nevertheless, it must be recognized that some hearings are simply so complex that no volunteer who is not also a professional and has sufficient time to prepare adequately, could do a competent job. In that case, for volunteers unassisted to dabble in such hearings is as dangerous as do-it-yourself brain surgery.

Some groups, unfortunately, have a strong ideological bias against professionals and a corresponding overestimate of the potential contribution of volunteers. Such groups replace the tyranny of the professional by the tyranny of the amateur. That is not to say that professionals have all the answers or should be allowed to make the key policy decisions. However, given the competition from the proliferation of public interest groups which are active today, and the extensive opposition they receive from a variety of applicants or proponents in both private and public sectors, it makes sense to present the best possible case. That can only be done when both volunteers and professionals are used in a rational way, recognizing the strengths and limitations of each.

It is not necessary to abdicate all authority to professionals; they have no expertise in making the value judgments which underlie policy positions. However, it is also pointless for amateurs in one field, however professional they may be in another, to pretend that they are more expert than a real expert. That is why the most satisfactory working relationships seem to arise when the professionals are properly instructed by the volunteers as to what their policy positions are, and then left alone to execute their instructions on the basis of those positions.

11

Case Strategies

Far too few advocates recognize the necessity of developing an overall strategy for each case. Rather, what tends to happen is that the strategy is implicit or unconscious, based on the assumption that the advocates know what to say. Sometimes that may be true, but often it is not.

Many ongoing tribunals (such as the Canadian Radio-Television and Telecommunications Commission (CRTC) or the National Energy Board (NEB) at the federal level, or the public utilities boards in the various provinces and territories) tend to have frequent hearings which involve almost all the same parties. The same lawyers and the same witnesses appear in front of the same commissioners year after year. The atmosphere may become like that of a club. When a new consumer group appears for the first time, its presence may be seen as disruptive and its representatives as outsiders. This is especially so if the traditional interveners are large industrial customers which use the hearings to try to pressure the regulated company and regulator into giving them special discounted rates unavailable to ordinary consumers. It would be rather optimistic to believe that all this can be changed by a single intervention, particularly if it consists of nothing more than filing a brief. Even a full-scale intervention, vigorously pursued by experts, is unlikely to correct all the rate privileges of the past, because it would create too many powerful losers too quickly. Hence, we come to the first and most important principle of intervention: the benefits of participation are cumulative. To intervene successfully one must intervene regularly. Not only does this develop the skills of the advocates but, also, it helps to build the reputation and the importance of the intervener group with the tribunal's members and staff. If it is known that the intervener is not going to go away after this hearing, but will be back again and again, the tribunal will be much more likely to feel that it has to accommodate the intervener. Then, although there may be some ambivalent feelings about this, the new group gradually becomes a member of the club.

The awareness that an intervener may have to appear before the same tribunal several cases in a row will have important implications for its case strategy. It will require development of an overall, long-term litigation strategy for the group. (This is not to use "litigation" in the narrow sense of taking cases in court.) The development of a tribunal litigation strategy begins with the articulation of the general goals or objects of the organization. Then, when particular issues arise, someone in the organization should commit to writing what the organization's objectives are in relation to that issue. Are they primarily to educate the public, to change public opinion? If so, cases undertaken for the supposed publicity value are often crushingly disappointing. For the money spent in taking a case before a regulatory tribunal (or for that matter, before a court of law) one could purchase several newspaper advertisements, which have the advantage that the message or content is determined by the purchaser rather than by the tribunal. In other words, litigation is an expensive and ineffective way to engage in a public relations campaign unless it is realistic to expect that the case will be won. (In a limited sense, "won" includes a case which is lost in court but reveals such a shocking set of facts that the government is forced to change the law. Such cases, however, are exceedingly rare and citizens' groups are forever disappointed at how much it takes to shock government into action.)

Is the organization's objective to influence the tribunal to adopt a particular policy? If so, this requires regular intervention. An important consequence of regular intervention is the necessity of limiting public relations and media campaigns. That is because tribunals resent "trying the case in the newspapers" and there is little point in alienating them if you are seeking favourable rulings. Hence, one of the consequences of going "the legal route" may be a reduction in the organization's effective capacity to go "the media route."

Since cumulative intervention is intended to create growing credibility with the regulator, it also limits the freedom to criticize regulators for all but the most serious mistakes. If someone appeals every decision of a tribunal that does not go the way he would like, particularly if he loses appeals repeatedly, the tribunal will cease to take him seriously. This does not mean that no matter what a tribunal does it must simply be accepted stoically. But one must pick the targets for appeal carefully and win at least some of the time. There is no advantage in gaining a reputation as a sore loser.

Repeated intervention also makes it important to maintain consistent policy positions from hearing to hearing. That is another reason why these policy positions should be the intervener's own, not those of hired experts who may change from one case to another. There are almost as many schools of thought among expert witnesses as there are witnesses. If a new witness is presented each time, offering a new theory of the intervener's position, the board will never know where the group's views are coming from and what they really believe. The rapid staff turnover experienced by some groups, when coupled with a tendency to ignore what is in the files, may result in radical shifts of position within a very short time period, without any explanation for the change.

Given this need for consistency, one must be especially careful in espousing any new or changed position because one may be stuck with it for several years or forced to face the embarrassment of abandoning it. Policy positions should be selected the same way as shoes: they must be comfortable and wear well.

To look at this in the context of the overall litigation strategy, there are often several different routes along which a particular position may be advanced. Depending on the facts, one possibility may be an ordinary civil action in a court of law. Another may be a private prosecution for a criminal offence, or a breach of a statute (such as one regulating pollution). Another option may be a complaint to a provincial ombudsman or human rights commission; these have the advantage that the expense of the investigation and subsequent proceedings, if any, are borne by the government rather than by the individual or group. The point of mentioning these alternative strategies is to encourage recognition that *merely because someone is holding a public hearing does not mean that one must participate.* Conversely, merely because no one is holding a public hearing should not discourage a group from initiating one, where appropriate, by making an application to a tribunal. One is *not limited to intervening in the applications of others.* Many tribunals allow groups to seize the initiative and apply; for example, for consumers to apply for a decrease in the rates of a company with excessive rates.

It is too easy to assume that one knows what one wants without having examined the options. The process of forcing oneself to go through the discipline of preparing a formal strategy statement, setting out the long-term objectives of litigation activity, followed by the short-term objective in the particular case, helps to keep clear the relationship between means and ends. It also has the advantage that if facts have changed since the last case, or if one's appreciation of the issues has changed, one will not continue down well worn paths leading in the wrong direction.

So far we have been considering case strategies in general terms. Some specific examples of hypothetical strategy statements are set out below to illustrate better what these might be.

1. The purpose of intervention in this case is to discourage the tribunal from reaching the overly broad conclusion desired by the applicant, which would have negative impacts on our position in a forthcoming case.
2. The purpose of participation in this case is not to persuade the board of anything, but merely to collect trend data for the next case, to help to determine what further data will be needed for the next case, and to attempt to preclude the board from arriving at any positions which will injure us in the next case.
3. Our strategy in this case is to encourage the board to recognize and accept as an issue that . . . , so that in future cases we may obtain favourable orders on this issue.
4. The applicant in this case has asked for a rate increase; our strategy is to persuade the board that not only is a rate increase unnecessary but that a rate decrease should be ordered.
5. As an alternative to the above strategy, that although some

of the rate increase is justified, it should be much smaller than requested.

Setting out the basic position to be taken in the case is only the first part in designing the strategy. Part of the strategy statement is to decide how that position is to be presented. Should the approach be a head-on, frontal attack cross-examining every witness and bringing in one's own? Or is there some fatal flaw in the case of the other side which makes much of this unnecessary? This depends very much on the type of case and the quality of the evidence.

Public utilities are generally very good in preparing and presenting their cases, perhaps because the tribunals are ongoing and the same kind of evidence, updated for each case, is repeated every time. Environmental impact statements, on the other hand, tend to be very poorly prepared. They are usually presented by an applicant which does not appear regularly before the tribunal (it may rarely have a project significant enough to require environmental assessment) and, in some cases, the inquiry itself is a one-time tribunal. Although the evidence will usually be voluminous, it may be very thin in substance or may have major gaps.

Given the very limited resources of most citizens' groups, their case strategies will have to depend on a carefully focused approach, more like a rifle than a shotgun. This usually starts with the recognition that the chain of logic used by one's adversary is only as strong as its weakest link. Therefore, it is unnecessary to try to break each link. Rather than becoming preoccupied with all of the evidence and calling in experts to deal with all of it (or giving up because an all out attack would be too expensive), the first step is to break down the position of the other party into a series of logical propositions. When these are carefully analyzed, it is often found that there is a readily discernible gap in the chain of logic, and that the proposed conclusion does not necessarily follow. What is missing is usually more important than what is there. If that is so, one can zero in on the gap and attack it, leaving the bulk of the case alone.

Unquestionably, finding the fatal flaw is both the least expensive and most effective advocacy tactic: it is like pulling down a whole house of cards by removing a single card. It is amazing how many applications contain such flaws. Unfortunately, they are not easy to detect; if they were, the authors of the application would have noticed them before, or at least concealed them better. Only when the submissions of the other side are read repeatedly, and discussed with others, do these flaws suddenly seem to pop out and become apparent as if by magic. A brief description of some of these follows.

Perhaps the most frequent, but also the most subtle is the tautological argument — an argument that is true of necessity and, therefore, trite — for example, a statement equivalent to "the man walked around with his head on". Obviously, if he had been decapitated, he would no longer be walking around. As a relatively recent illustration of this, in an application by Bell Canada for "rate rebalancing" before the CRTC, the company introduced certain mathematical models to forecast the "macro-economic impact" of rate rebalancing on the Canadian economy. These purported to show a slight improvement in the rate of inflation, the rate of unemployment and the size of the economy if "rate rebalancing" was approved. That would suggest that the proposed rate restructuring would be good for the economy and, therefore, should be approved. However, one of the features of all of these modelling exercises is that they necessitate making certain assumptions.

In this case, the forecaster was instructed to assume, in making the forecast, that the rate proposal would result in an improvement in economic efficiency because the phone company would be moving from a less efficient to a more efficient rate structure. Yet once that assumption is made the improvements to unemployment, inflation and gross national expenditure follow of necessity because that's what an improvement in economic efficiency does. If, instead, it had been assumed that the proposed rate structure was less efficient than the current one, there would have been a corresponding increase in unemployment, increase in inflation and decrease in gross national expenditure. Clearly, the impact on the economy shown by this model was entirely produced by one's initial assumption. It did not prove anything about "rate rebalancing" but only about the consequences of the assumption of the person employing the model. These kinds of model results are tautological.

One could have brought in another expert in modelling to

examine the thousands of equations employed in the model to determine whether or not it was a good model. Tens of thousands of dollars later the conclusion probably would have been that it was. Yet this would have been a colossal waste of resources. Had the strategy been to bring in an equally good modelling expert and to develop one's own model, it also would not have been successful, probably because the result would have been much the same if the initial assumption was similar. Thus, if the advocate is aware of this basic feature of models, the fatal flaw in this case, tautology, is fairly easy to detect. Only a few basic questions in cross-examination or in an interrogatory were necessary to verify this. The appropriate strategy for this portion of this case would have been to demonstrate that the forecasted benefits for the economy were meaningless because they assumed what it was that they were supposed to prove.

In environmental assessment cases the environmental impact statement (EIS) is often based on a comparison between what would happen if the project proceeded without mitigation measures and what the situation would be like if certain mitigation measures were employed. Usually this will show that there will be less environmental impact with mitigation than without. Of course, there would be even less environmental impact, or none at all, if the project did not proceed. As well, there may be other ways of constructing the project which, although more expensive than the chosen method, would result in less environmental damage than even the chosen method, with mitigation. The fatal flaw in such an EIS is its assumption that the project will proceed as proposed, when that is the very question that has to be determined. A good EIS will canvass several alternatives, and a truly excellent one will look at the "null option", the status quo. A case strategy for dealing with an inadequate EIS might be worded as follows: "To demonstrate that the EIS is deficient in that it fails to canvass reasonable alternatives with which the tribunal could compare the proposed project." Notice, again, that this strategy does not require an extensive understanding of the fine points of the evidence because, as is so often the case, it focuses on the importance of what is missing from the EIS rather than merely what is in it.

Once a case strategy has been designed, one can then look

at the specific techniques to be used to achieve it. Tactical considerations such as whether to call evidence or whether to confine oneself to argument, and the appropriate balance between these two, follow logically from the overall case strategy. Likewise, the decision as to whether to cross-examine or to call one's own evidence, or to do both, becomes a lot easier in the context of an overall strategy.

Finally, it is important to preserve flexibility. If it begins to appear as if the initial strategy was wrong, one should consciously rethink it and, if necessary, revise it. If it turns out that resources are insufficient to achieve the selected strategy (perhaps because the initial strategy was too ambitious) it may have to be revised to something smaller but more achievable. On the other hand, if more and more flaws in the others side's case begin to emerge as the evidence unfolds, it may be desirable to expand the strategy to include other types of attack. That way, one will not fail to obtain maximum tactical advantage of the weaknesses in the other side's case.

12

Opening Statements and Final Argument

In some respects a case before a regulatory tribunal is like a highly structured and lengthy debate: there is the opening statement, the evidence and the final summation.

1. OPENING STATEMENTS

A few tribunals do not allow opening statements, others discourage them; but the majority take no strong position one way or the other, leaving it to the parties. Some tribunals regard opening statements as largely unnecessary because they believe they already know what the positions are from the intervention statements. It is the author's practice always to present an opening statement, despite the intervention statement, if a board will permit. This cannot, however, be a mere repetition of the intervention statement; it must say something new.

The best way to encourage a board to listen to one's opening statement is to resist using that opportunity for routine posturing. Instead, try to say something unexpected. If one must say something predictable, say it in an unpredictable way. For example, although the intervention statement may have been devoted to areas of disagreement in order to set out a position, the opening statement might begin with areas of agreement so as to underline what contentious issues remain. Or, if the interrogatory process had been unsatisfactory, thus necessitating more extensive cross-examination than might otherwise have been the case, the opening statement could outline the inadequacy of the information available from the applicant, preparing the tribunal for what is to come.

In general terms, the opening statement should set out what the party intends to prove, whether through evidence or argument. It should be indicated who the witnesses will be and what will be the nature of their testimony. Finally, it is important to state what order the party will be asking the tribunal to make, and on the basis of what conclusions. (If the reader has paid close attention to the preceding chapter on case strategies, it should now be clear why a really good opening statement cannot be made without having a well-developed case strategy.)

In some cases the absence of a right to make an opening statement on the first day of the hearing will work severe prejudice to the interveners. In a case which is expected to take more than one day, if the applicant commences its evidence on opening day, very often it will do so in the presence of newspaper, radio and television reporters sent by their editors to cover the hearings. Of course, these reporters will want a brief story of the first day's events, and then, typically, will be gone. The first day's events — indeed usually the first hour's — will be the sum total of the media coverage of most public hearings. Unless all parties are permitted to make opening statements at the beginning of the hearing only the applicant's side of the story is likely to be told in the media.

Nor is this media imbalance necessarily remedied by an intervener offering to slip out of the hearing room to do an interview. Since interviews during hearings may be frowned upon, one can jeopardize goodwill with the tribunal by granting such an interview. The applicant may even attack the intervener in front of the tribunal by asserting that its participation in the case is merely as a publicity stunt. The applicant will imply rather ingenuously that the reason why its opening statement was reported was because it was presented at the hearing but that it did not give any interviews; and that the intervener's turn to open its case will come when it presents its evidence. Of course, by then the media will have long since lost interest in the story and will not come back, several days or weeks later, each time a new intervener presents its case.

Tribunals may be quite naive about this point unless it is

explained to them. Then they may be offended by the importance placed on publicity, as if this implies that they would be influenced by publicity rather than restricting their attention to the evidence and argument presented at the hearing. This becomes especially difficult if the applicant is rather clever about it and, instead of presenting an opening statement, has its first witness, typically the president of the company or some senior officer, appear as a "policy witness" to deliver what is, in effect, its opening statement as if it were merely part of the evidence.

Media stories are important: they influence the opinions of both the general public and politicians; and tribunal members are sensitive to both. The best way to prevent the applicant from stealing all of the media attention on opening day is to give everyone an equal opportunity to make an opening statement.

The time to bring one's request to make an opening statement to the tribunal's attention is not on opening day, which may surprise everyone, but well before then, preferably at a pre-hearing conference. Seek permission to present an opening statement before the applicant presents its evidence. If that request is refused, then, to increase the pressure, renew the request during the preliminary motions on opening day, in the presence of the media, pointing out the unfair advantage a refusal of this request would give to the applicant.

Opening statements have another advantage which, for reasons of tact, one should never say to a tribunal but which should be kept firmly in mind. To try to save time, some tribunal members, like some judges, will insist that they have read every word of the papers filed (or that they will do so by the end of the case). The author has learned from bitter experience, on several occasions, that such assertions are not to be believed. Despite having the best intentions, there is probably a lot they will not read. There is a substantial probability that one or more members of a tribunal with an expert staff will not even have read the intervention statements; indeed, there is a tendency in some tribunals for the members not to read most of the memoranda of evidence and any written final argument, but to rely on the oral portion of the hearing and on summaries and briefing notes from staff for the rest. Hence, about the only way to ensure that the members of the tribunal will really grasp one's position early in the case is to speak to them directly when they are sitting in their chairs and cannot walk off the hearing platform. One of the major advantages of a ten minute opening statement is that at least for ten minutes the members of the tribunal will have no choice but to listen, and, thus, to become familiar with the key points of one's case.

In one case in the author's experience, a judge of the Supreme Court of Canada introduced the appeal by advising counsel that he had read all of the materials, thus eliminating the need for counsel to summarize them. Five minutes later, the judge asked the question:

> 'Counsel, would your client be satisfied if the tribunal whose decision you are appealing had, instead of making an order for X, made an order for Y?"

It was then necessary to remind him tactfully that in fact the order had been for Y, and that was the reason the client was appealing. Obviously, the materials had not been read very attentively.

Another story is commonly told that a judge opened a hearing on a motion by saying to the lawyer:

> "Counsel, I want you to know that I have read all of the papers that you have filed in this matter, so it will not be necessary for you to repeat anything in them. Just come to the point immediately and tell me what it is that you want."

Counsel's reply was:

> "It is interesting that you should say that, M'Lord, as I have not yet filed any papers in this case."

In a tribunal which hears the same applicants, case after case, and has months in which to consider the applicant's evidence before the public hearing opens, the applicant has an enormous advantage over any single intervener, even one that has the resources to intervene repeatedly. Accordingly, asking that opening statements be permitted, orally rather than in writing, is an important equalizer. For the same reason, counsel should try to insist that final argument — or at least part of it — be presented orally as well. That is the only way to make sure that "he who decides" will actually hear.

2. THE RELATIONSHIP BETWEEN OPENING STATEMENTS AND FINAL ARGUMENT

The relationship between opening statements and final argument is very important. Recall the advice usually given to debaters: "Say what you are going to say, say it, and say what you have said". If an opening statement outlines what will be said during the case, then that should be a fair description of the evidence and argument actually to be presented. Accordingly, when it comes to final argument, it should be similar to the opening statement. The only way to ensure this is to write the outline of the final argument at the same time as writing the opening statement. This, obviously, has important planning implications.

As has been mentioned in previous chapters, the proper way to plan and construct a case is working from the end, backwards. That means outlining the order sought, then the conclusions the tribunal is to be asked to reach, and then the evidence one is going to have to present to justify those conclusions. Ideally, if the case is successfully presented as planned, the opening statement should be very close to the final argument.

It is always possible, of course, that the evidence will take an unexpected turn and that one will be forced to change the draft final argument. In those circumstances it is better to admit that something new has been learned during the case and to present a final argument based on the evidence, than to try to ignore damage the case may have suffered by pretending nothing has happened. But whether or not interveners are permitted to make opening statements, the final argument, at least in outline form, should be written before the case begins.

3. FINAL ARGUMENT

(a) Style

What should the final argument be like? That depends very much on two factors: Who the tribunal is and who the advocate is. Some tribunal members only want to hear facts, facts and more facts. Anything that is not a number or a statistic seems like irrelevant rhetoric to them. Others feel that they can read the evidence for themselves; what they want is analysis, interpretation and context within which to view those facts. Perhaps the majority of tribunal members want a balanced mixture of both.

There was one revealing instance in the author's experience in which, long after a case had been decided, the chairman of that hearing panel was reminiscing to the author about why he had decided it the way he had.

> "Your argument was very good," he said, "in that it summarized for us in a useful way both the facts and the law, as well as the relevant policy considerations. However, your opponent's argument was absolutely brilliant. He was more like a real lawyer."

In the particular case, counsel for the other side had a very limited understanding of the highly technical evidence and no patience to acquire more. His final argument had been a spontaneous mixture of comedy, table-thumping denunciations, rhetoric and hyperbole: a real performance. It was perfectly designed to that particular chairman's concept of what a "real" lawyer's argument should be — like a television lawyer's emotional presentation to a jury. Obviously, that lawyer was not only a good actor, he really knew his tribunal.

This example illustrates both aspects: what to say and how to say it. These depend upon both the nature of the tribunal and the nature of the presenter of final argument. The table-thumping style, once so popular among courtroom advocates, has now largely fallen into disfavour except for the purpose of occasionally providing a bit of comic relief. Most tribunal advocates today would be quite uncomfortable with presenting a highly emotional argument, even if it is done tongue-in-cheek as a bit of an act. If the tribunal does not see through the act and is not amused, it may reject it as merely theatrical and devoid of substance. On the other hand, if the members do see through it, there is the risk that they will not be amused or entertained but will feel that their intelligence is being insulted. Hence, the emotional presentation — unless it comes from a lone individual representing only himself or herself — is likely to be a high risk strategy which few people can pull off successfully.

Perhaps the best advice one can give as to final argument is one which would fit most styles of delivery and most tribunals most of the time. First, there are the obvious virtues: thoroughness, accuracy, brevity and imagination. But beyond such clichés, the best final arguments, the ones which would score close to 100 per cent if they were being marked as an examination, are those which most closely reflect the ultimate judgment produced by the tribunal. Hence, write the final argument so that the tribunal can, ideally, simply adopt it as its reasons for decision. To do this successfully one must be "thou-oriented" rather than "I-oriented". Or, in the modern jargon of computers, final argument should be "user-friendly". Obviously, it helps to know who the "user" is, which means reading many of the previous decisions of that tribunal, and studying the personalities and preferences of the particular tribunal members sitting on the case.

"*Don't tell them what your problem is, solve theirs.*" Solve theirs cleverly and you can also solve your own. Too often the essence of a final argument can be reduced to a syllogism of this sort: we have a problem; they are causing it; make them stop it. But if the board acquiesces to this request, it may cause problems for others: the applicant, other interveners, the government, or even absent persons. This creates problems for the board; hence, it may prefer the *status quo*. A better approach than a cry for help is an offer to help to the tribunal, a problem-solving approach. This can be expressed as a syllogism of this form. You have a problem in choosing between how much weight to give to policy objective X [the other side's proposal] and policy objective Y [the advocate's proposal]; we can help you to achieve the best balance, which is as follows . . . ; therefore, the best decision you can make in this case is . . . .

The standard advice given to law students is: "If the law is against you, argue the facts; if the facts are against you, argue the law". To translate this to the tribunal context (where legal controversies are usually not involved): "If the policy is against you, argue the facts; if the facts are against you, argue the policy". Obviously, this can only be done if one knows the policies as well as understands the facts.

(b) Determining the Context

Perhaps the most important single thing to recognize is that both the facts and the policies have no life of their own, no meaning in and of themselves. Rather, what makes them meaningful is the context in which they operate. In this sense, *context is everything*. *Facts* derive their relevance from *the context* of *the issues* in which they are placed; *statements of issues* are seen as adequate or inadequate depending upon whether they incorporate what seem to be *the important facts*. So, there is both a factual context and an issue context, and the two are interrelated.

The significance of this to a particular case before a tribunal is that usually the applicant will try to define, and thus to control, the context: to define the issues and to emphasize those facts which help it to achieve its objectives. Very often, a clever applicant will design and present its case to the tribunal with the issues defined in such a way that there is virtually no way anyone else can beat the applicant on that definition. It then becomes necessary to force a change in the context: expand the scope of the issues or redefine them so as to wage the war on a more neutral ground.

(c) Typical Applicant's Arguments and Responses

(i) *The inevitability imperative*

In environmental cases, typically, the proponent will argue that some form of development of the type it is proposing is inevitable/essential in the national interest and must be permitted, so that the only relevant issue remaining is what kind of development it should be. The argument will then be made that the proposed project is better than some hypothetical alternative which the applicant or someone else could propose and, therefore, should be permitted.

Comparing the applicant's proposed project with its proposed alternatives is usually a no-win situation for an opponent. Undoubtedly the applicant will design the alternatives to be so unacceptable that any rational person would choose the favoured option. The only way to attack the proposal successfully is to change the context: to question the inevitability of the development, and then to argue that even if some development is to be allowed, there are better alternatives than the "straw men" put forward by the proponent.

This may seem very elementary, but it is remarkable how

frequently those proposing almost any change to the status quo, whether it affects the environment, the railways, telephone rate restructuring, energy, the merger of two major corporations de-indexation of pension benefits, extended patent protection for pharmaceutical companies — virtually any highly controversial economic initiative — will "sell" it on the ground that "you may not like it but it is not nearly as bad as the alternatives" and, in any case, "something very much like it is inevitable". Perhaps the best response to the tyranny of the self-fulfilling prophesy of inevitability comes from Alan Borovoy, the astute counsel of the Canadian Civil Liberties Association, who is fond of saying "Do not force my groin onto the horns of a non-existent dilemma."

(ii) The continental imperative

Turning from environment to public utilities, the argument commonly made is that what is proposed is happening in the United States and, since markets are becoming increasingly continental, if not global, regulators must acknowledge these forces. This is another species of the "inevitable" argument, which both denies the existence of freedom of choice and, in many cases, makes unverified assertions or incorrect assumptions about the true situation in the United States.

For example, we hear the argument that telephone rates are moving closer to costs throughout North America and, therefore, for Canadians to fail to lower long-distance rates results in placing Canadian companies at a competitive disadvantage. On a closer examination of the facts, we would recognize that there are a whole host of assumptions here which are simply untrue.

First, for the average Canadian business, telephone costs represent less than 2 percent of total operating costs. Unless our rates are many times higher than rates in the United States, this is not likely to make a significant difference to our competitive position. Moreover, it assumes that many, if not most Canadian businesses compete with companies in the U.S. That is also simply untrue. With the exception of a handful of large exporters, mostly in the natural resources and primary manufacturing industries, most Canadian companies have as their customers and competitors other Canadian companies and do not compete directly with American companies.

Also, it is a myth that United States rates are closer to costs than Canadian rates, because no one can measure authoritatively and objectively what any particular telephone service costs. Since most of the same equipment is used commonly for all services (including the telephone set, the internal wiring, the external wiring and large parts of the switching equipment which comprise the core of the switched network), the allocation of costs to any particular service is purely arbitrary. Hence, so is the conclusion that the service "costs" any particular amount. Indeed, the very definition of a "service" as "local" or "long-distance" is itself arbitrary given that the boundary between an extended area for local calling and adjacent suburbs which are treated as long-distance are set in accordance with criteria which are highly discretionary. This is especially true given that the cost of telephone transmission (in an age of satellites and microwave systems rather than land-lines) is no longer very distance sensitive.

Telephone companies, like other regulated entities, try to use "costs" like a magic black box which they control and from which they produce numbers intended to be treated as irrefutable facts. In practice, these seemingly "hard numbers" cited with such authority are the results of a mechanical application by the computer of one of a variety of rather arbitrary costing methods, each of which can yield widely varying results. Indeed, the selection of the costing method itself usually determines the outcome. To put the matter another way, any skilled economist or accountant who works in this field can boast to the client "Tell me what you want something to appear to cost and I will give you the costing method which produces that result."

(iii) The cost imperative

Apart from the method of costing, the only relevance of costing itself lies in the policy argument that one person should not pay for another's service. To permit such cross-subsidization is bad economics because:

1. It sends the wrong price signal to consumers, inducing one consumer to consume too much of a service and the other too little;

2. It causes the utility to misallocate resources by providing too much of one service and too little of another;
3. It causes society to misallocate its resources because some customers will spend too much on this utility's service, leaving less money to spend on other goods and services, and vice-versa; and
4. It is unfair because it amounts to a transfer of income from one consumer to another.

In practice, to identify all these negative economic consequences presupposes that we know what things cost in some objective, meaningful way (which is usually untrue). Even if we could, in theory, calculate the cost of everything meaningfully, to eliminate cross-subsidization as a policy assumes that economic efficiency is the only goal of regulation. Too little attention has been paid to the absurdity of this assumption.

That may be the way economic texts see the situation, but regulation is by no means the exclusive property of economic text writers. In fact, most legislation establishing the mandate of rate-setting tribunals says nothing about economic efficiency, either explicitly or implicitly. Usually, it merely says that rates must be "reasonable and just", leaving it to the regulator to determine what these words mean. Even when such legislation expressly deals with price discrimination, it does not state that all price discrimination is bad, merely that the regulator should preclude "unjust" discrimination or "undue" preference. Such language only begs the question: what do these value judgments mean?

Any utility's rate structure is rife with cross-subsidies — inevitably and perpetually; hence the rigid application of this economic theory makes no sense. Consider, for example, a typical utility which divides its customers into rate groups based on the amount of usage. Assume a hypothetical rate group with 100 customers, each being charged the same amount per unit of gas, electricity or telephone service, with rates justified on the basis that the average cost incurred by the system to serve customers in this rate group is approximately the same. If we are dealing with a gas pipeline, some of the customers may have had their drops (the pipe from their house to the pipe running along their street) installed in 1959, others in 1989. The cost of service to customers who joined the system recently will be much higher than those served by pipes installed when costs were much lower. If rates are to be based on costs, should we not charge each customer on the basis of when the drop to that house was installed? If the drop is replaced, should we not suddenly raise the customer's rates to recover the higher cost? No utility prices in this individual way, so all of them ignore such cross-subsidization.

Similarly, with telephone service, if A's home is near the switching exchange but B's home is three miles away, it will cost more to string a wire down to B's house than to A's. Because their rates are averaged, A can argue that he is paying too much and B is paying too little. A's argument would be that A is subsidizing B. On the other hand, if A is more talkative than B, so that A's average phone call is 15 minutes whereas B's is five minutes, A will more likely be the cause of the company having to install more switching capacity, and will be imposing more costs on the system than B. So B can argue that it is really he who is paying too much and A who is paying too little. Now the subsidy would appear to be reversed. Yet if B, despite his brevity, makes more of his calls during the peak (9 a.m. to 5 p.m.) calling hours, while A makes his in the off-peak, it may not make a difference that A's calls are longer because additional facilities will only need to be added to meet the peak load demand, when the equipment is utilized beyond capacity, rather than the off-peak, when there will be considerable unused capacity. So A can, on this ground, re-assert that it is really he who is paying too much.

What these simple illustrations show is that it is not very easy to determine who causes what cost to any utility system and, to a large extent, *the apparent costliness of any particular service will be dependent upon which costs one chooses to measure and which one chooses to ignore.* No utility measures all costs; often the unmeasured costs — which are simply ignored — may well exceed the measured ones. Telephone utilities, to stay with our example, ignore both the time of day at which local calls are made and the level of usage of lines on local calls. Accordingly, a customer (such as a typical business customer) which uses its line virtually entirely during business hours (the system peak), and keeps its lines busy on average perhaps four hours a day, would not be charged a rate which reflected the cost difference in that time or level of usage versus that of a residential customer which used its line in the off-peak for an average of only one hour a day. Hence the cliché that rates should reflect costs is meaningless; they are at best a crude approximation of some of the costs of a broad customer class.

These examples also illustrate the fact that ultimately, the only truly fair rate system would be one in which each customer is given his own rates, based entirely upon his own costs. Since most utilities have millions of customers, this is clearly impractical. It would cost far more to determine what a particular customer's service costs (by doing a special cost of service study for that customer) than most customers would provide in revenue over an entire lifetime. Hence, all utility rate-making is based on averaging over broad customer classes. To return to our gas pipeline example, all customers on a given block (or area) are allocated the same (average) cost for their drop regardless of when it was installed or (within certain limits) how long the pipe is.

On the basis of probabilities, one can say that approximately half the customers in any rate group will be above average, the other half below, in terms of the costs they impose on the system. Thus, *by the very definition of "average", roughly half the customers in a rate group will always be subsidizing the other half*, to a greater or lesser extent.

Large business users, who are usually placed in relatively small rate groups, if they are at one end of a particular group, often argue that they should be moved to the next lowest rate group because their usage characteristics more closely resemble the other group and, as a result, their rates should be lowered. Of course, if that customer were allowed to move into the lower group, the next customer would be the last customer at the lower end of the group, and would say that it, too, was on the wrong side of the average and was subsidizing everyone else in the group who was on the receiving side. If one customer after another were allowed to move into the next lower group, two effects would be noticed. First, the average cost of the customers remaining in the group would steadily rise and so, the rates for the remaining customers would have to rise. Second, in the rate group to which these customers were transferring, the newly re-classified customers would be on the benefitting side of the average, causing complaints from customers at the lower cost end. These customers would ask to move into still lower rate groups. If this game were allowed to proceed unchecked, eventually everyone would end up in one huge, very low-priced rate group and the utility would become bankrupt.

Over time, these moves, and revenue-saving counter-moves by the utility, lead to a proliferation of rate groups, a growing complexity of rate structures (which become virtually incomprehensible to all but a handful of experts who understand their implications) and a marked tendency for the weakest customers, the residential consumers (who have neither the time to understand the complexities of the rate structure nor the resources to play these regulatory games) to be left paying larger and larger shares of the costs of the system. By that stage, costing is no longer a method for ensuring that customers pay the correct rates (if it ever could be that) but merely another elite weapon in the perpetual struggle to obtain a larger share of society's resources at a lower price.

In a system in which numerous cross-subsidies are unmeasured and inevitable, there is no economic theory which justifies eliminating a particular one without examining and eliminating all of them. In fact, *reducing one cross-subsidy in isolation may result in making the total system less fair*, as it may increase the total cross-subsidy to customers who are already, on balance, benefitting from more cross-subsidies than they are paying.

For example, it is very often argued that residential customers have been obtaining a free ride or special benefit at the expense of industrial customers who have been subsidizing them, but that this free ride must now end or at least be reduced: rising national and international competition is creating global pressures which must cause rates to move more closely towards costs. But which costs are measured and which are ignored? This is determined by the cost of service studies (if any) which may have been done from time to time (usually infrequently, as they are rather expensive). Cost of service studies are done or not done in response to particular pressures from customers, regulators or, after a while, are necessitated by the obsolescence of earlier studies. The techniques of costing used in these studies are determined by the corporate/regulatory culture of the particular utility and the tribunal by which it is regulated, as well as by the long-term pressures of the dominant customers. Since it is the pressure of the largest customers which induces the utility to measure certain costs, while ignoring others, it is often easy to make a cross-subsidy appear or disappear.

Tribunals will often need to be reminded, in final argument, that what they may have taken for granted for so many years, in the absence of any residential consumer intervention, has led them to have adopted a rather distorted picture of the universe. The preoccupation with costs — usually defined in a narrow, skewed way — has impoverished the dialogue as to what goals rates are supposed to serve. The current fashion towards moving to "cost-based rates" has caused regulators to ignore both the inevitable arbitrariness of most utilities' costing and the value judgments implicit in "undue" discrimination.

The concept of undueness is an important element of regulatory policy which is conveniently ignored by the cost fetishists. Public utilities are usually granted or have territorial monopolies, which is a privilege contingent upon them providing service to anyone within the service area. The service area will include some very lucrative points (for example, for Bell Canada, the Montreal-Toronto-Ottawa triangle) as well as some unprofitable remote areas. Nevertheless, so long as on average the company earns sufficient revenues to cover its costs and to provide a fair profit for its shareholders, the company is financially indifferent to whether a particular customer group is profitable or unprofitable to serve. In response to the argument — "We don't want to provide service to that group at that rate any longer because it is too unprofitable" — must come the response — "Because your overall earnings are adequate, your value judgment as to which customers are too unprofitable (i.e., pay rates unduly discriminatory against other customers) is irrelevant; that is a judgment only the regulator can make."

It has been stated repeatedly that there is no expertise in value judgments. The fact that any rate discrimination is taking place may (or may not) be clear from the evidence regarding costs; but the level at which this discrimination becomes "undue" is a value judgment in which the utility's witnesses have no greater expertise than any passerby on the street.

An effective final argument against the cost imperative type of argument will challenge the fundamental assumptions of the opponent by examining the context within which those assumptions hold true or do not. The usual argument that residential rates must go up to reflect their costs assumes, but should require proof, that:

1. There is a recent cost of service study which measures the costs imposed on the system by the various rate groups.
2. All relevant costs (e.g., time of day, season, extent of usage) are included in the study;
3. All specifically identifiable costs are correctly measured and allocated;
4. All joint and common costs are appropriately allocated if possible (note we do not say "correctly" because there is no correct way; the "if possible" qualification is necessary because if too large a proportion of costs — e.g., more than one third — are joint or common, any allocation may be arbitrary);
5. That other cross-subsidies in the system either do not exist or are relatively insignificant;
6. That other cross-subsidies which exist do not offset the alleged cross-subsidy which is sought to be eliminated;
7. That the failure to eliminate this cross-subsidy would amount to the perpetuation of an "unjust" preference or "undue" discrimination in accordance with some widely accepted societal norm;
8. That the elimination of the cross-subsidy would not cause other, worse evils (such as forcing low-income customers to give up the service, there by undermining universality of service; or increasing cross-subsidies to other users; or reducing disproportionately the demand for other goods and services throughout the economy).

One or even two of these assumptions can usually be supported with evidence, although with difficulty. Supporting all of them is virtually unheard of.

(iv) *The social welfare imperative*

Frequently, in final argument, we will hear applicants employ terms like "it's good economics" or "our position is supported by economic theory". But economic theory is not monolithic, and what is usually being alluded to is only one theory, most often called the Paretian theory (after Pareto) that society is better off if its aggregate wealth is increased; even if the number of losers may vastly outnumber the winners. What this view of economics does not tell us is whether these results will be more just — a question economics cannot answer, but which must be determined by regulators if rates are to be "just and reasonable", as the statute usually requires.

The problem of the distributive effects of any particular change is well illustrated by the hypothetical case of a society which has only two persons in it, a billionaire and a pauper. At the beginning of the year, the billionaire has his billions and the pauper has only five dollars to his name. Through a number of transactions between the two and with members of other societies, at the end of the year the billionaire has acquired an additional hundred dollars in wealth; the pauper has lost a dollar, so his net worth is down to four dollars. According to Paretian economic theory, that society is better off because its aggregate wealth has been increased (by $100 — $1 or $99). But one of the members of society has had an insignificantly small percentage increase in wealth while the other has lost 20 percent of his. It seems unrealistic to argue that such a society is truly better off.

This example does not prove that economics is wrong or irrelevant, but it does demonstrate that it would be wrong to use Paretian economic theory as the sole or perhaps even the principal basis for making judgments about what is just and reasonable. This is perhaps the best response to a final argument which appears to be strong in economic theory but not in common sense. For example, in 1987 Bell Canada proposed to the Canadian Radio-Television and Telecommunications Commission (CRTC) that local charges should increase by $1.25 a month as the first stage of a five-stage "rate rebalancing" process. Since 80 percent of long-distance calls are made by approximately 20 percent of telephone customers, mostly large corporations and governments, Bell conceded that some 82 percent of residential users and even 61 percent of business users would be losers under its proposal. With each successive stage of rate rebalancing, which could ultimately result in a doubling of local rates, the ratio of losers to winners would rise from approximately 4:1 to almost 100 percent. Hence our simple example of the pauper and the billionaire is not so far-fetched. As is so often the case, a handful of large users will be helped by a change which would hurt the vast majority of customers. What should be required to be shown, then, is not merely that Paretian economic theory supports the proposed change, but that the ultimate impact will be *more just* than the status quo.

It is impossible to provide a complete list of every potential type of final argument one might ever be called upon to make, or even to provide broad general categories in a comprehensive way. This chapter has tried to illustrate some of the more usual types of arguments made in the most common types of hearings. The purpose has been to show that it is usually necessary to *broaden the context*, to *expand the focus* of the examination before the tribunal, and to *include values which are important* to the client but either unimportant or unhelpful to his opponents.

This advice, however, should not be carried too far. It will take a sophisticated final argument to persuade a tribunal that has, over the years, become lulled into treating contentious theories of economics as if they were the law of gravity that such theories should not be applied in this case. This certainly cannot be done in an emotional way, with the assertion that rates should not go up because "We can't afford to pay them" or that the increased pollution should not be permitted simply because it would mess up the environment. If an adversary is proposing a norm which one wishes to attack and to replace with another norm, the latter must also be a recognized societal norm justified with reference to some form of authority or reason. In the words of that famous Canadian fundraising song: "Tears Are Not Enough."

(d) Content

The content of the final argument will be very heavily influenced by the extent to which it is oral or written. Even if final argument is to be oral there is usually nothing to preclude a written submission to supplement it as well, provided that copies are given to other parties. If final argument is exclusively in writing it is still important at least to ask to have an oral component, however short. Even half an hour is better than no opportunity for eye contact with the tribunal while making the final argument.

During oral final argument, everyone will be bored if it is primarily citation of numerous statistics and detailed references to technical exhibits. These should be in a written supplement to be handed out, and simply referred to orally: "The evidence for this is found in the written supplement at point 15." The oral final argument should be smooth and coherent rather than chopped up with technical references.

The argument should begin with an introduction, listing the points to be made. For example:

> "The proposed project should not be allowed to proceed for three reasons — a ...; b ...; and c .... Each of these will be discussed in turn."

This also makes it clear at the outset precisely what it is that the party wants the tribunal to do. If one does not indicate the order sought at the outset, one risks giving the impression that the argument will be a long litany of complaints, or perhaps an expression of concerns in search of a conclusion. Imagine how embarrassing it would be if a member of the tribunal interrupted, near the end of the argument, and said: "That's all very interesting counsel, but what do you want us to do about it?"

Once it has been indicated clearly what order the tribunal is being asked to make, it will then be listening for what logically follows: *how* should it be done and *why* should *that* be done.

The "how" part should be obvious or relatively easy in most cases, as the content of the order should flow from the powers of the tribunal. In some cases, if the legislation is very complicated, or if what is sought may be difficult to achieve legally within the Act, it may be desirable to obtain an opinion from someone thoroughly familiar with how the Act has been interpreted.

The "why" part should usually be the largest part of the argument. Its roots must be firmly planted in the legislation establishing the tribunal, although it is not always necessary to refer to it explicitly. It should also take account of existing policies of the tribunal or traditional ways of interpreting that legislation. Although tribunals are not strictly bound by their own previous decisions as if they were precedents in a court of law, a tribunal will not change its mind on important questions of policy unless compelling reasons are shown. If one is asking for a change in policy a persuasive justification will be needed to show why the status quo is wrong and why one's proposal is the best solution; conversely, if the other side is seeking to upset the status quo, that should be emphasized together with reasons why the existing policy is preferable.

The reason given for almost anything will have to be supported by facts. In many cases these facts are found in the transcript or in the memoranda of evidence submitted by various witnesses. An important reference to the evidence of a particular party should not merely be a paraphrase, the accuracy of which can be attacked. It should be supported by a specific reference to the transcript (as in: volume 10, page 2550, lines 12 to 16) or the exhibit by number and page (as in: exhibit Bell 15, p. 12). That way the tribunal can, after counsel has finished speaking, satisfy itself that the evidence has been summarized correctly. If the statement by the witness was particularly eloquent or important, and if time permits, quote it directly and then give the citation.

It is amazing how vividly parties at the hearing will remember important concessions made by witnesses during cross-examination. It is also amazing how frequently the tribunal, rendered numb by days or perhaps weeks of cross-examination, failed even to notice. Hence the importance of quotation.

It happens in many hearings that a comment is made in final argument to the effect that, of course, it will be recalled that the witness admitted X, only to receive startled expressions and raised eyebrows from the tribunal; clearly this comes as a surprise to them. If the speaker is alert to these responses, and is carefully observing the faces of the tribunal members, even if one is well prepared with transcript indexes and references, a surprise reaction can permit an immediate shift in presentation. Rather than continuing with the argument as planned, the alert advocate will quickly refer the tribunal to the appropriate place in the transcript and, if it is an important reference, will read the quotation out loud so that the tribunal members can hear it for themselves. This kind of interaction with the tribunal highlights both the importance of oral argument itself and of remaining flexible in it so as to be sensitive and responsive to reactions from the hearing panel.

Some advocates provide a summary of the evidence and then go on to draw conclusions from it. Others argue points of policy using the evidence as illustrations. Whichever way it is presented, the argument is not complete unless the tribunal can both follow the logic and be satisfied that it is supported by the evidence. Therefore, it is unproductive to waste a lot of time discussing the personality of this or that witness of the other party (except in those rare cases in which credibility is really the issue). Generally, it is better to attack arguments than to attack personalities.

Since very few applications for anything are totally proved, or even totally supported by evidence, it may be more productive to dwell on what it missing than to keep attacking what was produced. Hence it is a desirable practice to set out in a series of short, logical propositions what it was that one's adversary had to prove, and then, to highlight the gaps or weaknesses. It is usually much easier to show that the other person's case was not proved than to show that it was disproved or proved to be wrong. A finding of "not proved" is all it takes to win.

Finally, it must be emphasized for anyone representing a citizen's group that a balanced final argument should make as many concessions as possible without giving away the case. That is for two reasons. First, the typical citizen's group —representing consumers, the environment, native people or some other under-represented interest — will usually be seen to be negative in its approach, "against" everything. The more concessions made, the more difficult it becomes to be tarred with that brush. Second, such interveners usually oppose some sort of "establishment" organization with a lot of economic and political clout. Since the regulatory process is subordinate to the political process, the economic and political clout of a proponent or applicant is usually rather important to the tribunal. Again, the more that can be conceded, the narrower will be the issue over which this important corporation or governmental agency is being opposed.

It is frequently observed that tribunals tend, after time, to be — or at least to appear to be — "captured" by the very people they are supposed to regulate. This is not only from fear of political reprisals but also because, if anyone listens to the same arguments from the same parties over and over again, there is a tendency for skepticism to be worn down and, ultimately, for the tribunal to accept them. After a few years even the most independently minded tribunal member can become "captured" through repetition and familiarity. For these reasons it is often unwise for an intervener to attempt to attack the arguments of the other side head on.

As will be recalled from the various "imperatives" discussed earlier in this chapter, major applicants are very good at packaging their arguments in some high-sounding principle with which it is impossible to disagree. Then, for the tribunal to turn down that application may appear to be repudiating that principle. For example, it is difficult to reject an application which will bring about greater international competitiveness for one of Canada's few "world-class high-tech" industries, or one which will allegedly create 1,500 new jobs in a depressed area. The effective opponents of these arguments will recognize the pressure the tribunal will be under to capitulate. Lord Acton once said "Nationalism is the last refuge of the scoundrel." There are a lot of scoundrelly final arguments to be heard, in which the applicant wraps himself in the Maple Leaf flag in order to sell what may be really a very bad proposal. The effective intervener's final argument must acknowledge that these values are important. Unquestionably, it is important to improve our international competitiveness in high-tech industries, or to create new jobs. But the tribunal can safely turn down the proposal if it will not really achieve that end, or if the costs of doing it are too high. Hence the tactical objective must be *to separate the facts of the proposal from the worthy ideal behind which it hides.*

The final argument must contain some praise of the worthy ideal, and then a careful separation of the proposed project or application from it. Typically, the argument might be that it is not necessary to do what the proponent is proposing in order to achieve that objective. Or, one might argue that the proposal would actually defeat rather than enhance that objective. Or, that the price to be paid for achieving that objective is too high in terms of the loss it would create in other socially desirable objectives. This way the advocate explicitly acknowledges the tribunal's need to respect the value professed by the applicant, without accepting the applicant's proposed implementation.

The end of the final argument should summarize the points made. Then, like any good sales representative at the end of a presentation, ask for the order.

13

Motions and Objections

A motion is a request that a tribunal do something of a procedural nature. The list of possible motions is virtually infinite, but the most common would be: a request that the tribunal compel the applicants to provide disclosure, e.g., more detailed information than is contained in an interrogatory; an application for an adjournment; and a request that a certain witness be called to testify, or be recalled.

Before asking a board to order something the request should first be made by means of a telephone call or letter to the lawyer for the other side. (It is considered improper for a lawyer to contact another lawyer's client directly without clearing it with the lawyer). If the other party refuses to agree to the request within a reasonable time, then it should be stressed that unless the request is fulfilled by a certain date, a motion will be made to the board. For self-protection, make notes of any telephone conversations with the opposing lawyer, including the date, time and content of the conversation. Then, when the motion is presented, one can tell the board that the request was made on a particular date, and denied.

Since motions may be either contested or on consent, before making a motion it is usually desirable to find out whether other parties agree. The tribunal always retains its power to make a decision whichever way it sees fit, of course, but it is unlikely to reject a motion made on consent.

The daily proceedings before a board should be interrupted as little as possible. Normally, at the opening day of the public hearing, the chair will ask whether there are any "preliminary matters to be dealt with". This is the time to make any motions. If the chair forgets to open the session this way, and invites a party to call evidence before an intended motion can be made, one must immediately, but politely, interrupt and suggest that before the evidence is heard there is a preliminary matter. This is not considered rude and, indeed, may be essential. Then the chair will either allow the motion to be presented immediately or will set another time for it to be heard.

Motions may be presented orally or in writing, depending upon which is more appropriate or as the rules of the tribunal may require. The procedure used on motions parallels that of the hearing itself. A motion is a mini-hearing within a hearing, whether done in writing or orally. The party making the motion must set out, either orally or in writing, clearly and concisely, what order is sought and why. In support of this motion the party may present such arguments of law, procedure or policy as desired, and may, in rare cases, even call evidence through witnesses if necessary. The opposing party will have a similar opportunity to explain why the motion should not be granted, and then the mover will have an opportunity to make a final reply.

The most common (and often, from an intervener's perspective, the most important) type of motion is a motion to request further information. Many tribunals have rules allowing for interrogatories or applications for the production and inspection of documents. Even if the one before which one is appearing does not, all is not lost. If the tribunal's rules allow motions of any sort (or even if they do not), one can always make some sort of formal request to obtain disclosure. Since every tribunal has broad discretion over its own procedure, it would be worth preparing a list of the documents or other information desired and attaching these as an exhibit to a standard-form notice of motion, or even to a simple letter. There is at least the possibility that the other side will comply with the request, either because it is willing to release the information or because it seems not worth the trouble to resist.

If the other side does not comply, one should try to set down the motion for oral argument before the tribunal immediately, well in advance of the hearing of the case itself. Alternatively, and perhaps most conveniently in view of the tight timing of the majority of hearings, if the necessary information is not obtained prior to the hearing, a motion should be made at the *opening* of the hearing itself.

It may well be that the rejection of a such motion, particularly one which seeks more information, would render participation in the balance of the hearing to be futile. If a critical piece of information is denied, there may be a legal remedy in the courts.

Since much of what takes place is a battle for information it is important to anticipate what motions will have to be made, and to plan their strategy beforehand. If it appears as if meaningful participation in a case will become impossible, *i.e.*, a critical motion may be rejected, consider retaining a lawyer on "stand-by" to bring an application in court to compel disclosure of the information as soon as the motion is denied.

Another choice is to leave the hearing. This should not be done as a theatrical display of bad temper for not getting one's own way. But, if the evidence needed to make an important argument is denied and there is no point in continuing, one might as well leave as sit in the hearing room without the real likelihood of affecting the outcome but, by one's very presence, lending dignity and credibility to the process. There is no law that says that anyone must continue to participate in a process which seems unfair and unreasonable.

A particular species of motion normally heard during cross-examination is an objection. Counsel who called the witness may object to the witness being asked a question on one of several grounds (e.g., that the question is irrelevant, unfair to the witness, unanswerable in the way in which it has been put, has already been answered by the witness, and so on). Other counsel may object to leading questions (those which suggest an answer) from the lawyer who called the witness.

It is important to know during cross-examination of one's witness when to object, and how; also, when one's own cross-examination is being objected to, how to fight the objections. Some counsel will rarely object, feeling that if someone is being unfair, the tribunal will recognize it and look unfavourably upon the whole exchange. This depends on how sensitive the tribunal is to what may be unfair to witnesses, how zealous it is in protecting them and, also, how formal it is. Some tribunals will allow almost anything, even outright rudeness to a witness, unless there is an objection. All but the most formal tribunals will be offended by frequent objections of a technical nature, but most will allow a well-founded objection to be sustained. Typically, objections will tend to be upheld, for example, when:

1. A witness has been asked the same question in different ways several times and has already answered it once. This repetition constitutes *badgering* or *harassing* the witness. (However, if the witness has been evasive or refused to answer the question properly, the objection will not be sustained.) It is also badgering to interrupt the witness unfairly, to refuse to allow completion of an answer that fairly replies to the question asked. (But it is proper to interrupt if the witness has clearly misunderstood the question and is in the process of answering a different question.)
2. The question is too hypothetical, or is asked in such equivocal form that the answer will be of no value. While hypothetical questions are permitted, up to a limit, if the answer to the proposed question could be nothing more than conjecture on the witness' part, which the witness has already indicated, and if the questioner persists, an objection may be sustained.
3. The relevance of the question to the issues in the case is doubtful. Objections on the basis of relevance tend to be increasingly successful later in the day or toward the end of a long hearing when everyone is weary. Earlier in the case, before the issues are clear, the tribunal may be less ready to cut off a line of questioning which may potentially open up new territory. If an objection is raised on the grounds of relevance, and if that line of questioning is designed for some purpose which will in time become apparent, one should indicate this to the board and ask for its indulgence in allowing a few more questions. But having done this, the cross-examiner had better deliver.
4. A line of questioning being pursued repeats that of a previous cross-examiner. Even though the present cross-examiner may not have been in the hearing room when that cross-examination was taking place, upon objection the tribunal will probably rule that entire line of questioning out of order, referring the questioner to the transcript instead. Of course,

this may create a problem in that when the transcript of the earlier questioning is finally read it may be found that this was not the line of questioning intended at all. By then it will probably be too late, as the witness will have been discharged and may have gone home, perhaps to another city. It is most unlikely then that the board will order him or her recalled to answer three or four questions — which highlights the need to keep abreast of what is happening by reading the transcript if one cannot be at the hearing.

5. A witness seeks to introduce an exhibit which is inadmissible according to the rules of evidence or, for some general reason of fairness, ought not to be introduced or introduced in the manner attempted by the other party. While tribunals do not adhere strictly to rules of evidence (they have no legal requirement to do so), it must be remembered that such rules were developed to provide procedural fairness and will often be invoked to exclude evidence which the tribunal considers unfair. For example, if a document was not supplied to a party following a proper application for the production and inspection of documents, the first party, if the other side now seeks to introduce this document, can object.

6. The cross-examiner, while quoting the witness' own earlier evidence (or some other evidence) to the witness, quoted it incorrectly or out of context.

The manner in which an objection must be made is fairly simple: stand up immediately (even if this means interrupting) and say: "Mr. Chairman, I am very sorry to interrupt, but I have an objection to make." Then, in as few words as possible, indicate what the objection is and present the arguments in favour of it. Normally, the other side will be allowed to respond and the mover will be allowed a final reply.

The possibility of objections during any public hearing is another reason for interveners to ensure that they do not have the same person acting as both witness and lawyer. It is awkward for a witness himself to object, because he can give the board the impression that he simply does not want to answer the question. That is why it is important to have a second person playing the role of the witness' lawyer (even though that person may not be a lawyer). Therefore, even if an intervener has neither an expert witness nor a lawyer, it should choose from its available staff or volunteers whoever would be the best in each role, and separate the roles.

It should be noted that it is also possible to object to a *ruling the tribunal makes*, although this must be done with great tact. For example, if a party wished to introduce an exhibit and, without there being any objection from the other side, the tribunal decided not to admit it, assuming that this evidence is critical to one's case, one should object to the tribunal's ruling and put this objection on the record. This can be done very simply by saying: "Mr. Chairman, I have heard your ruling, I understand it, and I must follow it. However, I must indicate for the record, with respect, that I object to this ruling on the ground that the evidence being excluded is relevant, important to our case and should be admitted."

Although it is generally regarded as bad practice, a few lawyers use the tactic of making deliberately distracting objections at strategic points in time. For example, if a lawyer's witness is floundering under heavy fire, a well-timed objection can lead to a ten-minute debate about the law of evidence which will give the witness time to regain his or her composure and may, if successful, demoralize the cross-examiner temporarily. If a cross-examiner is having a hard time in dragging out some important evidence from an evasive or circuitous witness and (as is usually the case) the tribunal does not intervene to help, the opponent's objection that the questioner is being repetitious and badgering may add to the pressure to give up questioning. If the lawyer on the other side seems to be interrupting frequently, unless these objections are valid (which should encourage one to re-think one's cross-examination), the strategy may be to make the questioner nervous. This means he is probably hot on the trail of something good, and should persist.

There is a general rule against interrupting cross-examination for anything but the most serious reason. If one has beaten back one or two objections already, it may then be proper for the cross-examiner to object to the frequent and unjustifiable interruptions. If that objection is sustained, one's opponent will have to stop obstructing. Although boards are not as strict in this respect as are courts, it is better to *object only for serious reasons* than to appear as trying to obstruct the legitimate cross-examination of one's witness.

14

Cross-examination — Preparation of Strategy for Cross-examiners

Cross-examination is such an important subject that this manual devotes four chapters to it. In all four, for the sake of convenience, the cross-examiner will sometimes be referred to as "counsel" or "lawyer". This does not imply that only lawyers can cross-examine. On the contrary, many non-lawyers who understand the substance of a subject very well can, with a bit of training, learn how to cross-examine better than many lawyers.

Cross-examination is the most difficult and probably the most important advocacy technique. It is usually assumed that lawyers have some special training in this, but anyone who has spent any time in courtrooms or tribunal hearing rooms will know that this is not always the case. Cross-examination techniques and skills are not formally taught anywhere — neither in law schools nor in bar admission courses (with the possible exception of a limited-enrollment trial practice seminar in one or two law schools). A non-lawyer need not be intimidated from cross-examining on the assumption that it is so highly specialized an art that one could never learn how to do it. *Competent cross-examination can be done by any fairly alert person. But it does require practice and considerable planning.*

Cross-examination consists of a series of short questions posed to a witness by representatives of an adversary party. It is intended to test the soundness of the evidence by giving the cross-examiner an opportunity to try to make the witness retract, modify or qualify the testimony. Unlike examination-in-chief, which is narrative in format and which excludes leading questions, most of the questions in cross-examination are leading questions which suggest a "yes" or "no" answer. Some of the questions are for pure information (such as, "Why did you do this?"), but these tend to be rare because they are open-ended and the answers unpredictable.

The inexperienced cross-examiner usually tries to confront the witness by asking questions which are really short speeches with which he expects the witness will agree. Usually the witness disagrees, the questioner is startled, and questions become more argumentative. After a short while these will be disallowed by the tribunal. The neophyte questioner usually feels crushed by this unanticipated lack of success, feeling that the witness is dishonest and the tribunal biased for not giving him a fair chance. The root of the problem is the questioner's failure to recognize the appropriate place of evidence and argument. The purpose of cross-examination is not to argue with the witness but to test the witness' evidence. One will not likely succeed in setting out one's own position through seeking agreement with it by the opponent's witnesses; if they agreed, they wouldn't be testifying for an opponent.

As many cases are lost through cross-examination that is unsuccessful or inconclusive as are won because of it. Television dramas frequently portray successful lawyers (usually in criminal cases) obtaining startling confessions with a stunningly brilliant series of questions. In the real world, unfortunately, an opponent's witness is not bound by any written script. As will be seen from section 5, "Games Witnesses Play", in Chapter 16, there are many ways in which clever witnesses can avoid giving damaging answers. It takes a lot of careful planning, a good understanding of the subject-matter and a forceful personality to cross-examine effectively. In the real world of expert witnesses (as distinguished from the movies and television), there are serious limits to what can be accomplished through cross-examination even by the most brilliant cross-examiner.

It is impossible to develop a meaningful strategy for the cross-examination of a witness without having a reasonably well-defined strategy for the entire case. This can best be done by working backwards from the desired result.

First, decide what arguments to use to persuade the tribunal to give your group the order sought (and perhaps, to deny others the orders they seek, if these orders are mutually exclusive). Then consider what evidence will be needed to make each argument persuasive. (It should not be assumed that any of this evidence can be extracted through cross-examination. Most witnesses who make a successful career of testifying in such cases are far too glib to be caught having to make devastating admissions or concessions.) Cross-examination of an expert witness is a poor substitute for calling one's own witness. Ideally, have available to call one or more expert witnesses to cover every important issue in the case.

There is a further difficulty inherent in advocacy before boards: what is a relevant issue? A court of law makes decisions on legal questions defined through pleadings, but a board, usually required to decide matters "in the public interest", will have a much more difficult task of defining issues. Almost everything may be seen as a regulatory issue by the participants before some tribunals and, perhaps, even by the regulators themselves. (The latter may have an interest in permitting the hearings to go on seemingly endlessly, such as a desire to persuade Treasury Board that more staff and commissioners must be appointed. Some tribunals, which may have very few cases brought to them each year, or may regulate only one or two companies, may feel that they can better justify their existence by encouraging lengthy hearings. Of course they blame the delay on the long-windedness of lawyers and not on their own lack of control of the process.) Once the issues in the case have been defined, at least in the lawyer's own mind, and a list of the necessary evidence developed, one can then decide whether it is necessary to cross-examine particular witnesses.

It is not always necessary to cross-examine every witness. In many circumstances it will be desirable not to cross-examine a witness but, instead, to attack the evidence in final argument when the witness is not there to defend it. Indeed, it can be stated quite categorically that no witness should be cross-examined unless what is sought to be achieved by cross-examining cannot be accomplished in final argument. If there are weaknesses in the witness's logic, why confront the witness, only to provide the opportunity to fill in the gaps? Rather, make the attack in argument.

It is difficult to cross-examine properly, however, without having clear objectives. There are really only four things one can accomplish in cross-examination, all of them "negative" to the witness:

1. By drawing the witness out, get him to exaggerate or overstate his evidence;
2. Get the witness to change his evidence in some material aspect;
3. Get the witness to agree to a new version of the evidence — yours;
4. Show the witness to be unreliable (if he is so). (But, if you are alleging a contradiction in his evidence, make sure that the two statements really are incompatible; if you are seeking to show a difference, be sure that the difference is really significant.)

The four objectives of cross-examination indicated above can be achieved in a variety of ways, limited only by the imagination.

An important thing to remember about cross-examination is that *you often don't have to cross-examine*, even if you are very good at it. *Never cross-examine without having a specific purpose in mind*: it will show. There is a substantial risk in any cross-examination that all that will be done is to make the witness look better. The "let-me-at-him" impulse should not be yielded to, in the absence of other more rational reasons to cross-examine. The blood to be spilled may be your own.

When one cross-examines a witness, by implication, one is flattering him. If his evidence is going to be dismissed in your final argument as being merely fatuous or inconsequential, it may be counterproductive to treat the witness' evidence as being important enough to attack in cross-examination. Once the cross-examiner's credibility with the tribunal has been established, perhaps one of the most effective ways to minimize a witness' testimony is simply to rise when the turn to cross-examine comes and say that one does not believe that any questions are necessary. At the very least, the witness will have been prevented from making a number of self-serving speeches. On the other hand, if it is felt that something positive to one's client's case can be established by cross-examination, then by all means cross-examine.

There is an old cliché of cross-examination: never ask a

question unless you know what the answer is going to be. Of course, counsel will rarely be so fortunate as to get the precise answer sought from an expert witness, so there will need to be several alternative "game plans" worked out. Ultimately, cross-examination planning should look like some sort of flow chart indicating where to go and the different combinations of ways to get there, depending on what answers the witness gives. Even with this planning, counsel will quite often be surprised by the clever answers given and will have to think fast. With an answer which leaves the questioner with absolutely no idea of where to go next (which sometimes happens), one might try to drop the line of questioning altogether and come back to it again after some more preparation during a recess, lunch break, or ideally, overnight.

If a witness has made some important errors in calculation which have the effect of changing his conclusions, why try to humiliate him during cross-examination? This may allow him the opportunity to repair the damage in some way. Arithmetic errors can be demonstrated just as effectively and with great surprise in final argument.

If the witness makes any mistake which is major and obvious, it is unnecessary to ask him to admit it. Only if the error is subtle, or complex to demonstrate, is it necessary to have the witness acknowledge it. Even then, the decision to cross-examine that witness does not imply that every part of the evidence must be questioned. The test of what to question and what to leave alone should be: what will be lost if I do not cross-examine on this point?

As should by now be clear, the author's preference is minimalism in cross-examination, during which control of what is happening is shared with the witness, with maximum emphasis on final argument, over which the witness has no control. This is especially important if the witness' evidence does not prove what it purports to. The exception would be when the opportunity for oral final argument is non-existent or inadequate. Since written final argument has little dramatic impact and, in many cases, will only be skimmed quickly (if at all), it cannot be relied upon as the only tool to attack a witness' evidence. In that situation the oral aspect of cross-examination becomes much more important. Where there is adequate time for oral argument, the key tactical consideration should be a realistic forecast as to whether the intended cross-examination is likely to improve one's position for final argument over what it would be without it. If cross-examination only makes the witness look better, it has backfired; if it is inconclusive, it was a waste of time.

Often it will appear to the observer that the cross-examiner asked a few relatively innocuous questions and ended what seemed to be an uneventful cross-examination. Then, in final argument, the answers to those questions are suddenly made very meaningful either by the context in which those answers are placed or by the use that is made of them in comparison to other evidence presented by the cross-examiner's own witness. Hence, we should look at what types of questions can be asked, and for what purposes.

The first kind of question would be one seeking to obtain more information. For example, what method was used to do a certain calculation, or what the equation was. None of this needs to be aggressive, as these are simply questions of clarification.

A second category of questions is the 'what if' variety. Sensitivity analysis ("what if inflation is 1 percent higher") is the best example, but there are others. One popular technique is to determine what the result would be if the witness employed a different method. This is sometimes done by submitting one or more pages to the witness, through counsel (preferably in advance if the calculations are anything but very simple) setting out the alternative method and asking the witness to fill in the blanks for the numbers that are not already available to the cross-examiner or that the cross-examiner does not wish to assume to be of a certain value. Then the witness is asked to complete the calculation. Of course, the witness will also have the opportunity to state whether in his opinion this alternative method is correct and appropriate.

Leaving aside objections as to method, in many cases the computer program and data base of the applicant will present the only possibility of having certain calculations made. For example, if the objective is to find out what the total revenues would be if rates different from the proposed rates were introduced, that would be virtually impossible for an outsider to calculate in the absence of a considerable amount of information about the numbers of customers in various customer classes and their likely responses to the proposed changes in price. Ideally, this kind of complex calculation should be requested in inter- rogatories, as it may take time to do the work. If it is asked in cross-examination, the questioner may be stuck with having to wait for a week for the answer, by which time the witness may be gone. If the questioner had the foresight to ask for the calculation via interrogatories, the response is then usually available in time to serve as the basis for cross-examination.

Other kinds of 'what if' questions involve asking the witness to make different assumptions than the ones employed in preparing the evidence, or to give different weight to the factors used in arriving at the conclusion than the witness did.

A third kind of question merely seeks agreement of the witness on things which are relatively uncontroversial. Thus, the witness may agree that there is more than one possible way to calculate what he did, or may acknowledge that the witness you will be calling is a credible expert in the field. Indeed, if there was some special reason why the method used was different from that of counsel's expert, it may be possible to persuade him to agree that were it not for that special reason (which can be dealt with later) he might well have used the same method. He may concede that the method he employed involves a considerable amount of subjective judgment and is by no means merely mathematical or objective. He may also admit that his answers would have been improved had his budget for research been larger and the time frame within which to prepare the research extended. These kinds of questions, if well thought out, can obtain answers which may be important concessions, without being at all adversarial or confrontational. Thus, they tend to be relatively low-risk areas of cross-examination.

Once it is decided that a witness will be cross-examined, the entire cross-examination for that witness should be planned. Rather than taking the witness' evidence at page one and going through it to the last page, the sequence of questioning should be determined by both topic and tone. There are two important strategic rules to be considered. First, ask all the friendly questions in the beginning. If an aggressively adversarial tone is adopted at the outset, the expert witness will respond with guarded hostility and friendly concessions will be unobtainable. Second, if there is a more confrontational portion of the cross-examination, within it, present the best material first. That way the tribunal's attention is caught and maintained early on. If, instead, one starts with minor matters and hopes to build momentum, the tribunal may run out of patience before the important questions are reached. As well, if the strongest points are made early in the cross-examination the witness is much more likely to be respectful for the rest of it.

So much for the overall strategy. Let us turn now to the questions.

15

Cross-examination — Preparation of Questions

There are two general approaches to preparing questions for cross-examination: the first is to organize the questions into discrete topics and to move from topic to topic. The second is to mix up the questions regardless of topic. Each has its advantages and disadvantages.

1. QUESTIONING BY TOPIC

Questioning by topic has the advantage that the tribunal can see very clearly where the cross-examination is going. This gives the appearance of having planned carefully and being well-organized. It also makes it much easier for the cross-examiner to prepare final argument.

The major disadvantage is that to a clever witness (and unfortunately, most of them are), it will be obvious where the cross-examiner is headed. This means the witness will play along for a while without resistance, but just when the questions start to get too close for comfort, he will begin to play games, which will make it very difficult to get the answer to any really important questions. Despite this, some cross-examiners have sufficiently forceful personalities, and are sufficiently patient in closing escape routes that eventually the witness will have no choice but to provide the answer sought, to avoid appearing evasive and dishonest. Yet this process can resemble wrestling with an octopus, in which one has to pin down one's opponent tentacle by tentacle. It is tiresome and very time-consuming. It is also rather boring, so the tribunal will probably "tune out" for large parts of it. When a concession or admission is finally extracted, its significance will often be lost on the tribunal.

In this respect, tribunals tend to behave quite differently from courts of law. A judge sensing that a witness is playing games with the cross-examiner will be quite stern in insisting that the questions be answered fully and fairly. The witness will be told bluntly to cease the petty quibbling and obfuscation if his evidence is to be believed. Tribunals, however, are rarely so interventionist. Outside Quebec, which has a tradition of appointing judges to tribunals, few tribunal members have had any judicial experience; even those who are lawyers have not usually practised before the courts. Unlike judges, who would intervene actively to enforce appropriate rules of conduct during cross-examination, tribunal members either just sit there counting the hours or discreetly read or write other things, occasionally looking up to demonstrate that they are paying at least some attention. It is virtually impossible to concentrate totally, day after day, through long, boring answers and questions which seek to clarify them but elicit even longer and more boring answers. That is why it so often happens that important concessions can be made by a witness without the tribunal even noticing. Such concessions must be emphasized during final argument.

2. THE RANDOM METHOD

The other method of questioning is to write out one's questions on cards and then to shuffle the deck. This results in questions seeming to come in random order, with no clear pattern.

The advantage of this method is that the witness never knows where the cross-examiner is going, and is always kept off guard. As there are never enough questions all in a row on the same topic to indicate precisely where the witness is being pushed, the witness has no clear conception of where to resist. With the witness off-guard and somewhat unnerved, his mind will be racing to anticipate where the questions are going and to control the damage by providing the "right" answer. Apparently simple questions will result in long pauses and consultation with advisors or assistants, while the witness thinks through all the possible answers to the question and the implications of each for future questions he might be asked, or past questions to which the answer has already been given. "Am I being consistent? And what will be asked next?" the witness will think. These long pauses do not show up on the transcript, but certainly will be noticeable to the tribunal. It will be obvious to the tribunal that the witness has been forced to be very careful, which engenders respect.

If the witness asks "Where are you going with this question?", if the question has been properly drafted, the cross-examiner has no obligation to indicate to the witness how it is intended to use the answer. A fair response would be "The question is a perfectly straightforward one. Do you not know the answer?" If the question is straightforward, the witness will appear evasive if he refuses to answer.

The two disadvantages of this method are the increased work in preparing final argument and the trouble the tribunal will have in following the questioning. When all questions are presented in sequence by topic, final argument can be prepared almost automatically. When the questioner has "shuffled the deck", he has to organize it again so as to arrange the questions and answers by topic. This takes longer and requires a good indexing system. Nevertheless, if that is the only way to get any worthwhile concessions out of a witness, it may be the best way.

If the tribunal is having difficulty following, they will either tune out or perhaps ask what the cross-examiner is doing. But even if the members listen attentively, it will be as difficult for them to understand what the questioner is trying to achieve as it is for the witness. Since very few tribunal members have had any experience cross-examining, they will not recognize the technique or its purpose, and may begin to press the cross-examiner impatiently with questions like "I don't understand what you are doing, where are you going with these seemingly purposeless questions?" This would appear to support the witness's position, and may make it difficult to continue in this way. Yet, if this is the only way one has prepared, one may have no choice but to proceed or terminate cross-examination altogether. Hence, a back-up copy of the questions, arranged in an obvious sequence, may be prudent. In the circumstances, all one can do is ask for the tribunal's patience, with the promise that this will all become clear during final argument. If they agree, that is a promise one had better keep.

When this second technique works well, it is quite spectacular. The tribunal members will have watched the questioning with some degree of concern whether anything useful would come of it. When the cross-examiner, in final argument, puts all the pieces together in order, and develops a context around it, it can seem like a minor miracle.

3. PANELS

Some tribunals allow witnesses to appear in groups, called panels. These may include people drawn from several different disciplines or different departments of a company so as to provide a comprehensive position. Panels help eliminate the situations in which one witness says to the cross-examiner that the answer to that question should be given by another witness, and when that witness appears, says that the first witness misunderstood the question and that it is really within that witness' domain. If everyone is on the panel together, this kind of falling into the chasm between witnesses does not arise. One would think that this would make panels desirable from the standpoint of the cross-examiner but, usually, that is not the case.

Even with a single witness it is difficult to get straight answers to straight questions but, at least to some extent, one can pin down an answer eventually. With a panel there is an unfortunate tendency to "gang up" on the cross-examiner. If a really tough question is asked, one member will, perhaps by pre-arranged signal, fill time with technical-sounding irrelevance for a few minutes while another thinks of what the answer should be. The second member then contributes the answer. If the third member of the panel thinks that the answer given concedes too much, he then puts in his own "two-bits worth", which somewhat contradicts what the second speaker said. Despite significant differences in content or emphasis, the first and second speakers will then agree with the third. Thus, all too often the answer to any question is seemingly interminable, and the record is left in a state of ambiguity as to what the collective answer really was.

Trying to clarify the confusion may be more trouble than

it's worth. If the contradiction is pointed out, the witnesses will insist that one has misunderstood the answer or, in any event, will insist on "clarifying" matters for another 20 minutes, to no real purpose. If one tries to use only a small part of this answer in final argument, counsel for the other side will complain that it has been quoted out of context and will pick some other part of the answer which gives a different impression and thus undermines the desired conclusion.

The only good defence against this technique is an alert tribunal which is aware of what is going on. A few tribunals now insist that the question be answered by the person on the panel to whom it is asked. Therefore, find out in advance who is going to be on the panel and what the specialty of each witness is, and preface each question by saying: "This is a question for the economist, Dr. Jones." Then, if one of the other witnesses tries to chime in, interrupt immediately by saying rather curtly that the requested answer has been given by Dr. Jones and there is no interest in anyone else's answer (assuming the answer was a useful one). If Dr. Jones' answer didn't help, then accept answers from others or, if none is offered, ask if anyone has anything to add.

If the tribunal before which one will be appearing does not require panel members to answer questions put to them individually, it is always something one can propose to the tribunal by means of a motion. Alternatively, one can simply assert when starting to cross-examine that one will be putting questions to this or that witness and that one would like only that witness to answer them.

Just because an opponent chooses to call a "gang" of witnesses does not mean that a cross-examiner has to permit them to "gang up" on him. If the witness to whom a question is asked does not know the answer, or if he can genuinely demonstrate that the question is more appropriately answered by someone on the panel with a different specialty, then one may have to take an answer from the other witness. Otherwise, the question should be answered by the person to whom it is asked. If the cross-examiner knows the personalities of the witnesses and their specialties, he should be able to prepare in such a way that questions are related to the specific witness of his choice.

4. DRAFTING QUESTIONS

The major mistake inexperienced cross-examiners make is to ask questions which are too long and complicated. Multi-part questions may be all right in examinations at school, where one can answer "all of the above" or "b and c", but that is not cross-examination.

Questions seeking basic information (e.g., "How did you do this calculation?") should generally be asked during the inter-rogatory process, in writing. If the tribunal does not have such a process, or one forgot to do so with this question, it may be possible to obtain the answer by asking the witness' lawyer to provide a written answer. Generally, it is not a good idea to clutter up cross-examination with too many basic questions of clari-fication. Since the answer to these questions is likely to be uncontroversial yet time-consuming to present orally, an alert tribunal will wonder why the questioner did not simply write a letter to the other side.

Most questions asked in cross-examination should seek a negative or affirmative reply. The usual opening words should be "Would you agree that...?" or "Is it true that...?" If the question requires some preliminary explanation in order to be comprehensible, this preamble should not form part of the question. Rather, the cross-examiner should state that he is going to provide a bit of background and then will ask a question. After providing the background, the question should be introduced this way: "Now, having explained all that by way of introduction, my question to you is this:...?" In that way, if the witness asks the cross-examiner to repeat the question, one does not have to repeat the entire background material, or risk having some slight difference in the way it is asked the second time. Even the slightest difference in wording permits the witness to protest that the second time it was a different question, and to ask which question it is that one now wants answered.

In the process of arguing with the witness about what the question means, it is very easy to lose sight of the purpose for which the question was asked. In the end, although one may ultimately get an answer to a question as reworded as a result of discussion with the witness, this may no longer suit one's original purpose. That is why the reader is referred to the sample question sheet shown on page 198.

This type of sheet, when used with others set out later in this chapter, can help the cross-examiner to remain organized throughout the case and, also, to determine whether the purpose of a particular question or line of questions has been achieved. Because drafting questions is a difficult and time-consuming exercise which one would not wish to repeat unnecessarily, these sheets should be kept for future use in other cases.

At the top of the page one inserts the name of the case, the witness being cross-examined, the name of the client group and the date. The cross-examination will probably require several sheets of paper, hence, in the upper right hand corner each page should be numbered as page 1 of 10, page 2 of 10, etc. Below the page number is room for reference to transcripts by volume, page and line. This is filled out when the transcript is received, so that it can be cross-referenced to the questions and the purpose of the questions. This cross-referencing makes it much easier to prepare final argument. To the left of the reference of transcript is the space for answer sheet numbers, which are explained later in this chapter.

The left-hand column is headed "Purpose of Questions". Here should be written the purpose for which the questions on that page or subsequent pages is asked. For example: "To demonstrate that the witness' answer that nuclear plants are more efficient than fossil fuel plants in generating electricity is highly dependent upon interest rates".

The second column headed "Ref", is for references. This enables the questioner to list beside the purpose what pages of exhibits or transcripts the witness should be referred to as the source of the question. Typically, a question to a witness might begin with "Dr. Smith, I'd like you to refer to Exhibit 112 at page 42 and also Transcript Volume 10 at page 2000."

In the right-hand column one writes the question to be asked and the expected answer, the latter usually being "yes" or "no". Depending on its wording, the question might require a complex answer, as in: "Dr. Smith, employing your model, how much would the cost of a nuclear plant increase over its expected 40-year lifetime if the average interest rate in the period was not eight percent, as you assumed, but nine percent?" Alternatively, a better form of question might be "Do you agree that, on the basis of your model, an average interest rate of nine percent (rather than eight percent), compounded over its life expectancy of

SAMPLE QUESTION SHEET

Case:	Client:	Page ____ of ____
Witness:	Date:	Ans. Sheet # Trans ____ ** V____ P: ____ L: ____

Purpose of Questions	Ref.*	Question & Expected Answer

*Reference to Exhibit or Evidence page numbers here

** V. = volume
P. = page
L. = line

40 years, would cause the cost of a nuclear plant to increase by approximately 20 percent?" Here, the answer would clearly have to be "yes" or "no".

In using these sheets, one would simply not turn over the page until the purpose set out in the first column had been accomplished. This may sound elementary but it is important because witnesses will often quibble with the question or will fail to answer it directly, and the questioner will not notice that the purpose has not been achieved. In response to the latter example, Dr. Smith may say that the answer depends upon a whole host of factors, in response to which the cross-examiner will have to say "Again Dr. Smith, on the basis of your model and that one change in interest rates, I am asking you to agree to approximately 20 percent higher. Do you agree or, if not, what is your best estimate?" If he ducks the question once more, try again until eventually you get a clear answer. If that question proves troublesome, and if there is some genuine issue as to whether it is worded properly, one should reword it and ask it in some different form. Here, having the *purpose* of the question directly in front of the cross-examiner will be useful.

If the witness is still uncooperative it may be necessary to point out to the tribunal that the question made perfect sense, that it was clear and unambiguous, and that the witness is being uncooperative. An effective chairperson will, in the circumstances, turn to the witness and insist that the question be answered properly. Others will simply leave the cross-examiner to his own devices. There is no greater letdown than seeking an order from a tribunal that the witness answer the question only to discover that the chair simply lacks the intestinal fortitude, or the knowledge, of how to do this!

If the tribunal tends to be passive and to avoid confrontation, all one can do is comment adversely on the witness' refusal to be cooperative and pass on to the next line of questioning, reserving for final argument the comment that the witness was very defensive during cross-examination, and citing instances. It might also be worth a sharp rebuke to the witness such as "Dr. Smith, if you aren't prepared to defend your evidence by answering questions fairly put to you in cross-examination, then you shouldn't be appearing here as a witness before this board and asking it to take your evidence seriously." And then sit down.

As another alternative, one can press on with that line of questioning with a comment to the effect that: "Mr. Brown, I know that you are the president of a large and important company and, within that company, are accustomed to having your way with your subordinates. However, when you appear before this tribunal you do so as an ordinary witness just like everyone else, and you have to play by the rules just like everyone else. If you find it beneath your dignity to have anyone question you, you can always send one of your subordinates here to be cross-examined. But you have testified and your refusal to answer questions makes a mockery of the whole process and demonstrates a lack of respect for the tribunal. So you have a choice: either withdraw your evidence on the basis that you are unable to defend it or defend your evidence by making a serious attempt to answer any proper question put to you. Now here, again, is my question . . . ".

At this point, the witness' lawyer will probably leap to his defence. The question will be attacked as unanswerable in the form in which it was asked, vague, improper, etc. If that is correct, the cross-examiner has unquestionably lost the battle. But if the question was carefully worded and perfectly proper, all one should need to do is say so firmly and ask for a ruling that the question be answered. Sometimes the chair will seek a face-saving compromise and will reword the question. Beware of this in case the question is not correctly worded to elicit the desired answer. If it is well worded the cross-examiner will soon have the answer and, hopefully, will not need to go through this altercation again; if it is not, the cross-examiner should repeat his version of the question and respectfully explain the difference.

Even if the chair does not rule in one's favour that is no reason to be discouraged. The tribunal may well be irritated by the arrogance of the witness, or the over-protectiveness of his lawyer, even if it does not have the courage to confront them. At this point there is little choice but to go on to the next question and to hope for better results.

If the witness continues to be uncooperative, as is so often the case, one can simply look out the window, ignore the irrelevant answer and repeat the question. If one does this two or three times with each question, eventually the witness will get the message that the cross-examiner is prepared to be as tenacious as he is and that sooner or later, however passive the tribunal appears, it too will become frustrated with what is both a time-consuming and unproductive process. If the questioner is firm, chances are good that the witness will give in first, on the basis that if the tribunal becomes unhappy it will probably be unhappy with both the questioner and the witness and, as the witness' client needs a positive order from the tribunal, it needs its goodwill.

A questioner can help the process along somewhat by summarizing lengthy and irrelevant answers of the witness with "In other words, the answer to my question is 'yes'." After this is done a few times, the witness will catch on to the fact that the questioner is going to insist on getting a clear "yes" or "no" answer, and will not be distracted with an obscure speech.

Not all answers will be short enough or simple enough to be written on the sample question sheet. Accordingly, it is useful

SAMPLE ANSWER SHEET

Case: _____ Client: _____		Page _____ of _____
Witness: _____ Date: _____ Time _____		Q. Sheet # _____
Purp. #: _____ Q # _____ Trans$_V$____ P: ____ L: ____		

(Notes re new Questions or Final Argument here)	(Answers here)

SAMPLE ARGUMENT SUMMARY SHEET

Case: _____ Client: _____		Page ____ of ____
Witness: _____		

Purpose of Questions	Argument	Reference			
		Ex.	Tr.	Q.	A.

to have an answer sheet as well, of the type shown on page 201. As will be seen from the top of the answer sheet, in the right-hand corner, there is a place for cross-indexing with the question sheet number and, in the bottom row of the top box, the purpose number, the question number and the transcript references. In the bottom right-hand box one writes in the answers in very quick summary form. During recesses or coffee breaks, or sometimes even by pausing between questions, the bottom left-hand box can be used to indicate the need for further new questions or points for final argument. Thus, one can decide, on the spot, whether to attack an answer in final argument (which one might mark with a red ink asterisk) or whether to ask a follow-up question now or later in the cross-examination (when the witness may have forgotten this particular answer).

Finally, there is the argument summary sheet, shown on page 201. These should be made out each night after the cross-examination, whether based on one's own cross-examination or that of other questioners. In the left-hand column under purpose of argument, insert the conclusion it is hoped the tribunal will reach. Then, in the argument column, set out in summary form a few words which indicate what the argument is, and under the reference column at the right side of the page, the appropriate reference by exhibit number and page, or transcript volume, page and line. Where the argument is based on one's own cross-examination these will be very easy to lift from the question and answer sheets, which can also be referenced by number under the Q and A columns on the right hand side of the page.

While it is not essential that precisely these forms be employed, it is important that the argument be prepared each night systematically, and the transcript indexed, so that a coherent final argument can be assembled quickly. With computers with hard disk drives it may be easy to put the transcripts into computer memory using optical character readers. Some court reporters now make available diskettes as well as or instead of hard copy, and these can also be inserted into memory and indexed. Whatever the technique used, the linkages between the exhibits in evidence, the transcripts, the interrogatories and final argument should be maintained throughout the case.

16

Cross-examination — Games Witnesses Play and Counter-strategies

1. INTRODUCTION

This chapter and the next critically examine the tricks used by witnesses to confuse lawyers cross-examining them, and vice-versa.

Many view cross-examination as the epitome of the worst aspects of the lawyer's trade: the tendency to twist words, to distort meanings, to take arguments out of context and, generally, to try to confuse and browbeat the witness. There certainly is some truth in that perception. Accordingly, within the limits of space, some of the more commonly used lawyer's tricks will be exposed.

Little can be done, however, to protect the witness who presents evidence that is, at bottom, weak. It takes no clever lawyer's tricks to show that. If the witness is testifying as to matters beyond his professional qualifications, stretching his data to conclusions it cannot support, making unverified assumptions, arithmetical errors and so on, a skilled questioner will destroy the evidence rather quickly. Hence the need, almost compulsively, for the prudent witness to go over his evidence again and again, number by number, word by word, clarifying ambiguities, toning down over-statements, and making the whole piece as "attack-proof" as possible.

Some of the lawyer's games identified in the next chapter may seem transparent, and one may question their potential effectiveness. However, they are often used successfully by lawyers to give an unaware tribunal the impression that a witness whose evidence is basically sound has made an admission repudiating his whole position when in fact this is not the case. These games are often dependent upon getting the witness to admit something relatively trivial and building a whole framework on that admission, never allowing the witness to explain or the tribunal to see how flimsy it all is. In final argument, the witness is made to *appear* to have admitted a mistake, or to *appear* to have withdrawn or watered down his earlier conclusions, even though that is not the case.

Like those of witnesses, many of the cross-examiner's techniques depend for their effectiveness on the fact that the process of cross-examination in a long hearing is often so tedious that the tribunal will not listen very closely to the precise wording of every question and answer. Accordingly, it will tend to be left with rather general, sometimes superficial, impressions. The clever cross-examiner often exploits this soporific quality of hearings. For example, one popular trick is to ask a witness whether, in preparing the evidence, the report of a certain Royal Commission or Task Force, or the famous text written by Professor Bloggs was read. The answers, usually, will be in the negative. The list of what has not been read will always be a lot longer than the list of what has been read, especially if one carefully selects works of marginal relevance. Through a combination of incredulous and scornful acting gestures, the cross-examiner can leave the impression that the witness has not done even the basic reading necessary to present informed testimony in the case.

Before we consider attacking the memorandum of evidence presented by the witness, it should be noted that *what the witness does not say is often more important than what the witness does say*. Frequently, a good witness, careful to retain long-term credibility with the board, will provide evidence ingeniously hedged with one or two qualifications which, when looked at closely, reveal that the witness is really not saying very much at all. Unfortunately, a tribunal that is insufficiently alert or has a tendency to be sympathetic to the party who called the witness may draw all kinds of incorrect inferences from this evidence.

For example, evidence may be presented to try to demonstrate that the productivity of a company is improving. Without attacking this evidence, it may be important to draw to the tribunal's attention that the evidence does not say that the company is efficient, or even efficient relative to other similar companies. The numbers merely indicate that the company is becoming more efficient *than it once was.* If this company's efficiency is starting at a very low base, it may well be that despite improvements, the company is still rather inefficient and has a long way to go. In these circumstances, at least make sure the tribunal realizes that the witness is not saying that the company is efficient. A good witness will readily concede such limitations.

Second, without in any way attacking the witness, it should be possible to get a good, honest witness to agree that the evidence is based on a particular view of the facts. Many of the statements made are true *only* in the narrow context in which they are made, that is to say, if several (usually unarticulated) assumptions hold, or if we accept certain definitions or conditions. For example, a financial witness predicting the cost of capital of a company may base it on profit forecasts made by the company and assumed to be correct. If any of the assumptions on which the evidence is based are shown to be wrong, or changed even slightly, the expert evidence may have to be substantially altered or may even be rendered useless.

One of the most common tactics of neophyte cross-examiners (and often the least successful) is the attempt to impeach the credibility of the expert witness. Unless a cross-examiner is very confident of easy success, why try to break down or bully a professional? The most successful cross-examiners are usually cordial, straightforward and simple in their approach; they project neither frustration or aggression, nor a saccharine sweetness to mask their hostility. They are just getting their job done.

A great deal of careful planning and preparation has to go into cross-examination unless one is thoroughly experienced at cross-examining and very familiar with the subject matter of the evidence. There is nothing more embarrassing than having 20 or 30 people waiting while an unprepared cross-examiner fumbles with a pile of disorganized paper, wording and re-wording clumsy questions disallowed by the tribunal or objected to by counsel for the witness. There is usually time to write out every question in advance, especially when written evidence is prefiled; if not, at least the key questions should be carefully worded and written out.

2. WHAT IS MISSING

In preparing for cross-examination one must understand the manner in which the witness' evidence-in-chief will be prepared. An experienced witness will present as little evidence as possible, while drawing as many conclusions as the evidence permits. Obviously, the less evidence presented the less there is for cross-examiners to attack. The art is to present all the conclusions needed to make the case, using no more evidence than necessary to convince the tribunal that the conclusions are based on solid homework. It can safely be assumed that there is a lot more evidence in the background which has not been brought forward. It is also reasonable to assume that this evidence is not as favourable to the witness' position as the evidence presented. Some of this can be discovered through interrogatories or by asking during cross-examination when and how the evidence was prepared.

3. "FRIENDLY" CROSS-EXAMINATION

While lawyers for two clients with overlapping or similar interests are not permitted by legal ethics to concoct a friendly cross-examination, it does not take much ingenuity to know where a client's self-interest lies. It is not uncommon for an expert witness to approach counsel to say that if he were to ask a particular question, the response would probably be "yes, because . . .". Indeed, the two clients' experts may know each other and may well have discussed the cross-examination. Although a few tribunals consider it improper to permit "friendly" cross-examination, many allow it, and with some justification.

Friendly cross-examination may appear shocking to lawyers who have not practised before such boards, but it should be remembered that unlike the situation in the courts, where plaintiffs and defendants rarely sue each other more than once, in the regulatory arena persons who today are adversaries may be allies tomorrow. Even in the same hearing, if at some point in the hearing it appears that the tribunal is likely to license only one party, two or more initially competing applicants may join together to form a consortium. While this area of regulatory practice has its ethical problems for lawyers, an awareness of the tactical implications is important, regardless of which party counsel represents.

4. KEEPING TRACK OF THE ANSWERS

In any major administrative hearing keeping track of who said what and when can soon become a major problem. It is vital during the course of the hearing that someone spend the hours necessary to do this job properly.

The author's practice is to prepare cross-examination on forms divided into columns headed "purpose", "reference" and "questions and answers" (see sample forms on pages 198 and 201).

The first column is used to describe the purpose of this particular portion of this witness' cross-examination. With this purpose clearly in front of the cross-examiner, however confusing and technical the answers the witness may give, one is less likely to be led astray, to invent inappropriate unanticipated questions to follow-up unexpected answers, or to lose sight of the basic purpose. Second, in the reference column beside each question, insert the number and page of all exhibits or transcript volumes to which the witness should be referred. This avoids the awkward shuffling of papers which would otherwise result. Third, write out every question of any difficulty in the question column, and include in parentheses definitions of any important terms in case the witness confronts the questioner with such a request. Finally, in the right side of the question and answer column, note the kind of answer anticipated (usually "yes", or "no", although sometimes there may be several possible qualifications). Depending upon which of these answers the witness provides, different groups of prepared questions may follow. Therefore, for each anticipated answer, have an arrow pointing back to the question column, showing different questions or lines of questioning to be followed if that particular answer is given. Also, of course, there is the possibility that the answer is none of the ones anticipated, or is much more complex than simply "yes" or "no". For these answers one can use a separate answer sheet.

One of the major benefits of this kind of preparation is that counsel may well discover, while writing out the expected answers, that none of them is of much use. This helps to recognize that the question itself is probably unnecessary or badly worded.

As in a chess game, it may be necessary to plan several moves ahead. Ideally, with the last question in a series of questions, the witness is left with no choice but to provide the answer that counsel is seeking. To achieve this ideal is difficult, and will require careful planning so that unacceptable alternatives are eliminated with earlier questions. It may be necessary to design several alternative game plans so that the failure of one is not fatal. Because the number of permutations and combinations of "If he says this, I must ask him that" is very large, it is not practical to write out dozens of alternatives. Rather, counsel must have a good working understanding of the chain of logic along which he wishes to lead the witness, so that if the witness goes astray, counsel can lead him back to one of perhaps two or three basic alternative plans. The purpose/question/answer sheet (see sample form on page 198) is a useful technique for keeping track of these.

It is important to index every new daily transcript, every day. Failure to do this for even a few days can put one too far behind to catch up. It is virtually impossible to prepare final argument efficiently without indexed transcripts, as every argument which requires transcript references would take hours to prepare.

Transcripts can be indexed manually. A proper job of indexing by subject and speaker, with a minimum of marginal notes, takes about an hour per 100 pages or roughly two hours per daily volume. To do the same job with a personal computer will take about one-third of this time. It requires an IBM or clone using the MS/DOS operating system and the appropriate indexing software (such as Summation, from Litigation Support Services Inc. in Toronto). To get the transcript into computer form one can either buy a diskette from the court reporters (if they can provide one that is ASCII compatible — not all of them are) or use an optical character reader (OCR) to get the pages into diskette form. These machines are still expensive to buy or rent, so the best bet is to persuade the tribunal to require the court reporters to provide PC compatible diskettes.

Our memories tend to play tricks on us. Often a cross-examiner thinks that a witness gave a certain answer but, upon checking the transcript, finds either that the witness did not quite say that, or that so many other things were also said that the words which provoked such joy upon first hearing them are buried. Only with a close examination of the day's transcripts each night can it be known whether to re-ask certain questions the next day, if that is possible, or to arrange for reply evidence from one's own expert.

Any important errors in the transcript should be corrected promptly. Advise the court reporters (they usually want a letter to confirm an oral request) of the error.

This discipline of summarizing transcripts nightly has the advantage of forcing the cross-examiner to focus on what was obtained from the previous day's transcript while the memory of it is still fresh. When the evidence phase ends and the hearing moves rapidly to final argument, transcript summaries and indices will provide the basis for a coherent, integrated presentation. To try to do all this at the end, from memory, would be extremely difficult.

5. GAMES WITNESSES PLAY

(a) The Professional Witness

Witnesses can be classified into two general categories: professional witnesses (who are regularly retained to appear before the same tribunal or the same types of tribunals) and other witnesses such as company employees or academics who testify relatively infrequently. Counsel may have to cross-examine a witness who, in the three preceding years, has testified in some 15 telephone rate cases. Such a witness would clearly be a professional witness, who has to be approached differently from, let us say, the applicant's vice-president of finance, who might testify once every year or two.

The company expert witness may know as much about economics or engineering as the professional witness but, as a witness, he is likely to be much more amateurish. He is also likely to be more intellectually honest. Although this may be less true of the non-technical "policy" witnesses of some highly regulated companies (who may spend enough time at hearings as to be virtually professional witnesses), generally speaking, the company employee may not show the same aggressive striving to concede nothing. The professional witness typically earns the majority of his income from a few clients, appearing before two or three types of regulatory agencies; he is only as secure as his performance in the last hearing. If his credibility is lost, so is his income. Hence he will tend to seek to protect himself in a variety of ways, some of them, unfortunately, a little intellectually dishonest.

(b) Tricks in Preparing Evidence, and Counter-strategies

(i) Ingenious understatements

Testimony will often be very carefully drafted to say very little to but appear to be saying a lot more. This exploits the natural tendency of the reader to draw inferences and, thus, to conclude what the witness wished even if that conclusion goes beyond what can be supported by the evidence. The witness is safe so long as he only implies, but does not draw the conclusion himself. For example, he will conclude: "Therefore, Option 3 merits the board's serious consideration." The board will tend to infer that this amounts to a recommendation of Option 3. Yet the witness is merely suggesting that the board consider it: what the evidence says is literally what it means and nothing more. This can be made clear by asking the witness whether the recommendation is for consideration or for adoption.

(ii) Undisclosed alternative methods

Almost anything which can be calculated can be calculated using more than one acceptable method. Although one method may appear to be superior to others in a particular application, if that is what the witness has concluded he should have so indicated in his evidence; a description of the alternative methods and their results should have been set out, together with the witness' reasons for selecting the preferred method. Yet a witness will often fail to disclose that there are several other methods of calculation (some of which he may actually have used in an earlier draft, but not mentioned) which can produce widely varying results — sometimes leading to a different or even totally opposite conclusion.

If only a single method of calculation is shown, it might be worth asking the witness whether the method used is the only possible method. Usually the answer will be negative. Then, ask for a list of every other known method. Each time the witness stops, ask whether he is sure that there are no other methods, as this might induce him to continue with the list. Eventually, if counsel understands the quantitative implications of each of the different methods, he can ask the witness to redo his calculations using some of the other methods, and to disclose the results and conclusions which would follow from each. If, as is sometimes the case, the witness has selected the method which leads to the best result for the client, counsel can discuss the witness' bias and lack of candour in final argument.

(iii) Hidden assumptions

Assumptions without any empirical basis may be used merely because they lead to the desired conclusion. The witness should be asked to spell out what his assumptions are and be pressed repeatedly to make his list exhaustive, as there are often unarticulated premises of which the witness himself may have been unaware. Counsel might help by asking, for example: "Haven't you also assumed that the rate of change is constant? And that inflation will not rise above five percent on the average in the next decade?" When a healthy list of assumptions has been provided, counsel can ask whether the witness has verified empirically the validity of each of these. For most (if not all) of them, the answer will often be negative. (It can then be stated in final argument that the witness' evidence was excessively dependent on unverified assumptions and was, at bottom, just a bunch of guesswork.)

(iv) Sensitivity analysis

Counsel should consider asking the witness to perform a sensitivity analysis — that is, to recompute assuming a certain increase or decrease in each of the original assumptions. For example, assume inflation not at four percent but at each of five percent, six percent, and seven percent. This will enable the board to determine the extent to which the conclusion is sensitive to variations in the assumptions. If a three-percentage point increase in inflation, for example, causes the cost estimate to quadruple over the life of the project, this might indicate extreme sensitivity. By knowing the sensitivity of the conclusion to changes in the values in each assumption, the board is in a better position to decide what weight to place on the conclusion.

Computer "spreadsheet" programmes are now widely available and commonly used. Hence, providing answers to such questions can be relatively easy and quick. If the evidence provides details of the calculation, counsel can pre-test his questions by using a spreadsheet himself.

(v) Hypothetical sentences and other semantic games

Assumptions are not always easy to identify, as they are often hidden in clever semantic disguises. Thus, the witness might say: "As the karfogie valve oscillates in phase with the resonator circuit, it follows that . . .". "As" is used here to mean "if", or "whenever". Actually, it may rarely or never happen, as the witness might well have to admit if pressed.

Alternatively, the witness might say: "Given that the marginal cost of capital rises more rapidly than the average cost of capital, it follows that . . .". Given by whom? Even if the assertion is an invariable economic truth, or if it is based on the writing or research of a famous and unquestionable authority, it should be so labelled by the witness, as the reader of the evidence should be given the opportunity to verify whether the application of that truth or writing is valid in the context.

One common device for concealing assumptions is to put the statement in a subtle, hypothetical form: "If we acknowledge that customers of my client's trucking company ship parcels of an average weight of 50 pounds, then it is clear that . . .". Note that the witness has said, "If" we acknowledge. But must we? Is he really saying anything different from "if we assume"? Presumably, if we do not so assume or acknowledge, the conclusion does not follow. The alert counsel who spots such statements might ask the witness whether he is saying that we *must* acknowledge something to be a fact or only that *if* we do, something will follow. If his answer is the former, he should be pressed to indicate his basis for stating this to be a fact; if the latter, he might be forced to concede that he cannot prove that the opposite assumption is invalid.

One of the favorites of government witnesses, to conceal the fact that they are making assumptions or merely offering personal opinions, is to use "the civil service passive". We are assured that something is "generally accepted", "is deemed to be" or "is considered to be". Each of these begs the question: by whom? Has the witness conducted a survey to discover what people generally accept, or was his phrase just another way of saying, "I accept"? The pseudo-objective phrases are used to conceal the fact that the witness is merely expressing a personal opinion.

Another way in which witnesses have attempted to objectify subjective opinions is by the personification of an unspecified theory. For example, "In economic theory, when X happens, Y will usually follow." What, or whose theory is this? Is it a novel theory of the writer, or that of some well-known economist, as distorted or applied out of context by the writer? Was the particular theory selected because it was the only one that would yield the results the witness was seeking? Another illustration is the statement that "X is consistent with the dictates (or requirements) of engineering efficiency". Dictated or required by whom?

Professional witnesses are often masters of semantic subtlety. That is how they can point the reader or listener in a desired direction without being overtly dishonest. While a semantic nod is as good as an evidentiary wink, the alert counsel will pay special attention to the witness' grammar as a clue to the detection of assumptions.

(c) Intellectual Dishonesty

It is quite common for expert witnesses knowingly to construct a chain of logic which flows impeccably from premise to conclusion, but the conclusion is invalid because some of the techniques used to arrive at the premises are inapplicable, or the theories applied are irrelevant to the circumstances of the case. In preparation for cross-examination, counsel or his expert adviser should research all theories, expert writings or authorities referred to, to ensure that they are being properly used.

Many expert witnesses see themselves as advocates for their

clients, just like lawyers, but with different training. Such witnesses would consider the legal distinction between evidence and argument as merely formal. Their evidence is essentially argument, supported on some empirical basis with evidence from the discipline in which they were trained. In his first board appearance, an advocate who expects expert witnesses to be dispassionately neutral may not be prepared for the extreme partisanship of, for example, a consultant who has made a very handsome living for the last decade testifying for a particular client.

As success in the witness box leads to large consulting retainers (or promotions for company employees), sometimes witnesses will try to defend points of view which are virtually indefensible. In his classic work, *The Art of Cross-Examination*, Francis Wellman stated:

> It has become a matter of common observation that not only can the honest opinions of different experts be obtained upon opposite sides of the same question, but also that dishonest opinions may be obtained upon different sides of the same question.[1]

Some witnesses, even with perfectly sound evidence, will try to confound and defeat the cross-examiner from a motive of personal vanity or for the sheer joy of the sport. Such witnesses see questioners as prey to be beaten at their own game.

Not all cross-examiners' questions are worded with perfect clarity, and witnesses can occasionally be expected to misunderstand the thrust of the questioning. This should produce only a rather limited amount of honest confusion. However, anyone accustomed to cross-examining before expert tribunals will recognize that some witnesses have elevated disingenuous confusion to an art form. They pretend to misunderstand, just to confuse and delay the questioner.

As the crafty witness is all too well aware, a cross-examiner is subject to two major disadvantages. First, he may not fully appreciate all the technical implications of his questions. A cunning, aggressively adversarial witness will try to exploit counsel's difficulty in manipulating the unfamiliar technical vocabulary while cross-examining. Second, there is great pres-

---

1 F. Wellman, *The Art of Cross-Examination* (London: MacMillian & Co., 1904), p. 81.

sure from the tribunal to conclude the cross-examination as quickly as possible. A clever witness will try to add to this pressure.

The basic objectives of a witness in attempting to exploit the disadvantages under which cross-examiners work are:

1. To put psychological pressure on the cross-examiner by frustrating and embarrassing him, to induce him to give up the cross-examination;
2. Confronted by a difficult and potentially damaging question, inconspicuously to gain time to think of an answer which is safe;
3. To avoid answering the question altogether, while giving the appearance that it has been answered;
4. To provide an answer that is useless to the cross-examiner, without the latter noticing it and repeating the question;
5. To discover whether the cross-examiner really understands the implications of the questions he is asking, or whether he is merely relying on a script provided by another expert; if it is the latter, then to give him a confusing and useless answer which the lawyer would not detect until after the transcript has been read by the lawyer's adviser. By then, perhaps, the witness will have departed.

These objectives are accomplished by means of a variety of games. Not all of them can be catalogued here, but a few illustrations are set out below. Unfortunately, most of these games are difficult to detect at the time they are being played, although they can be recognized after the fact. This underlines the importance of reading transcripts of previous hearings in which the same experts have testified, to see how they respond to questions from different counsel.

(d) Witness Games and Counter-strategies

(i) *Game #1 — "Repeat the question, please"*

If the witness is surprised by a particularly tough question he will often ask the cross-examiner to repeat it. The tactic is especially useful if the witness observes that the cross-examiner has not written down his questions. The witness can then exploit the probability that the question, when repeated, will be slightly differently worded. The new version may be easier to answer. At least the witness can choose between the two wordings of the question, as the questioner has treated them as equivalent.

If the cross-examiner, when repeating the question, deviates slightly from the former wording, counsel for the witness might well object that that was not what was asked the first time. Or the witness can say "That's a different question — which one do you want me to answer?" This can lead to a fruitless altercation as to whether the second question was in substance different from, or the same as the first question, which will waste time and make the board irritated — usually with the cross-examiner rather than the objecting counsel or witness. This highlights the importance of writing out fully all difficult questions, such as those which contain technical phrases the precise meaning of which are important. Then, if one is asked to repeat the question, it is simple to read it again. Once the witness sees that the questions are not being made up as the questioner goes along, the usefulness of this game as a technique for putting pressure on the cross-examiner greatly diminishes.

(ii) Game #2 — Define a common term

As an alternative to Game #1, the witness can ask the cross-examiner what is meant by a simple, commonly used word in the question: a word such as "average" or "significant". While the questioner may have a general understanding of the meaning of such terms, instantly providing a technically correct definition is often quite difficult. When suddenly put on the spot one may offer a technically incorrect, ambiguous or meaningless definition. Exploiting this definition, the witness can provide a totally useless answer; or, can turn the tables and make the questioner look foolish by demonstrating that he does not know enough about the subject to recognize that, with this definition, the question is silly. A face-saving recovery is not always possible. The result may be to increase the credibility of the witness while decreasing that of the cross-examiner.

With a witness skilled at this game, one can expect no help from the board. Board members would not themselves risk appearing ignorant by ordering the witness to answer the question when the point of the request for clarification is that the question appears unanswerable. Rare is the board member confident enough to interject that the meaning of the term must be obvious and well understood by the witness.

One effective impediment to this game is to use the witness' own words when drafting questions. For example, when asked to clarify what is meant by "average", the questioner might reply, "The same as you mean by it on page 12, line 7 of your evidence." As another approach, if asked "In what context are you using the term 'efficiency', in the economic context or the engineering context?", the response might be to quote the desired definition from a standard text. In any event, the well-prepared cross-examiner expects this game, and will have a definition of every important term used, written out on the same page as the questions. In some situations, even if the witness does not ask for the definition of a term, it is useful to define it as part of the question. It improves clarity, and denies the witness the opportunity to exploit any ambiguity and thereby to provide a useless answer.

If the questioner is caught by surprise and is uncertain as to what choice to make between, for example, engineering efficiency or economic efficiency, it is not necessary to choose: ask the witness "Give me your answer both ways." This is not as good as knowing which way one wants it, but a lot better than guessing wrong.

(iii) *Game #3 — The vague question leading to role reversal*

The witness asks the cross-examiner a vague, unstructured question in a pseudo-attempt to clarify a perfectly clear one. Of course, the cross-examiner cannot understand the question the witness is asking because it is incomprehensible. This game has two purposes: first, to test how much the cross-examiner knows or understands, and second, to distract the questioner by imposing a mental struggle to understand the meaning of a meaningless question. There is a good chance that in the confusion the cross-examiner will forget the purpose of his own question; if not, at least time can be wasted, with the result that the witness will make the questioner appear to be the time-waster who asks unclear questions.

An example of such a vague question put to a cross-examiner is: "In what context is your question asked?" Of course, the scope and limits of "context" are very difficult to define, as it is a rather vague term. If the questioner replies, "In the economic context", the quiz may continue as, "Do you mean micro-economic or macro-economic?" Indeed, whatever the reply, the questions will continue, as the purpose is not to seek clarification of the question but to reverse roles and put the cross-examiner on the spot.

There are a number of variations to this game. If the witness offers a binary choice ("Do you mean 'a' or 'b'?"), the hope is that the questioner will choose the wrong alternative. If so, a useless answer will follow; if not, the witness may continue with, "That's what I thought you meant, and by 'a' do you mean 'a' as measured at a point in time or as a trend?" The binary choices can continue until counsel makes a mistake, the probability of which increases with the number of times the game is played.

The honest response from the cross-examiner, and the way one might end the game, is to say, "I'm not sure what I mean right now, but to avoid a useless answer, why don't you answer it both ways." An alternative might be "I don't know whether I mean 'a' or 'b', but if you can tell me the significance of each to your response, I can decide." If the distinction is trivial, it makes the witness look bad; likewise if only one of the options is meaningful and the other, a useless quibble. If the questioner does this repeatedly, this is refusing to play the witness' game by refusing to choose. The witness will eventually recognize this and stop.

(iv) Game #4 — The technical "snow job"

This game is typically played by delivering a rapid-fire, technical pseudo-explanation which is literally meaningless, a torrent of words with a trickle of meaning. Incidentally, it also permits the witness to test the knowledge of the board and its staff. If they allow someone to get away with this, then it is obvious that they, too, are feigning expertise.

The best defense against this game is to train the cross-examiner to be so thoroughly expert in the subject matter as to be able to spot the fraud and to say sternly "Now you and I both know that has nothing to do with my question. Just answer the question please." If the cross-examiner cannot do this, he should at least know enough to recognize that there is something "fishy" and to ask a few more questions. For example, ask the witness to explain the relationship conceptually rather than numerically. It may be possible to have the witness dig himself a deeper hole by providing more and more explanation for something that is essentially inexplicable. Eventually, counsel may have to call his own witness to de-bunk this evidence. Obviously, success in showing that the witness attempted such a dishonest ploy can, in final argument, undermine his credibility. Unfortunately, the game usually works because the witness is not caught.

(v) Game #5 — Endless answers

The witness makes long speeches, extending over many pages of transcript, without ever answering the question. To prevent this very common game, every question which requires a choice should be worded so that it can be answered with a "yes" or "no". Even if a question is capable of being so answered, the questioner does not have the right to insist that it be answered with a *simple* "yes" or "no", as the witness has the right to qualify or explain an answer. But the qualifications should not be endless.

The witness' object in this game is to give an answer of the "on the one hand . . . on the other hand . . ." variety, without ever indicating whether the response is one of agreement or disagreement with the question put to the witness.

If the question really is simple, an effective rejoinder may be, "In other words, the answer to my question is 'yes'". Alternatively, "Subject to the qualifications you have indicated, you agree with me?" Or, try: "I can't tell from your answer whether you are agreeing or disagreeing. I'll repeat the question and ask you to indicate at the beginning of your answer, first, *whether* you are basically in agreement with the question, and then, *why* you are or are not in agreement".

With witnesses who play this game, it is very important to read the daily transcript carefully to ensure that each question has been answered. It is often easy to get the impression, under pressure to proceed quickly, that a question has been answered when it has not. A delay of a few days in discovering that might well preclude the opportunity to put the question again.

(vi) *Game #6 — Changing the question*

Often a witness will answer a question different from the one asked, but will make the reply sound close enough to the target that to the unwary cross-examiner it appears to have been answered. If counsel asks, "Is the answer X?", the response might be, "Well, it certainly isn't Y!". The questioner would tend to *infer* that the answer received was "Of course it was X", whereas the witness has said nothing at all about X. A clever witness may convey derision or indignation to distract the questioner from recognizing that the question has not really been answered. It will be necessary to repeat the question and to ask the witness simply to answer the question.

(Sometimes, without attempting to change a question, a witness will respond with a physical gesture: a nodding of the head to indicate "yes" or "no", for example. Remember that *gestures are not recorded on the transcript*, so that as far as the official record of the hearing will show, the question was not answered. Hence the questioner must ask the witness to reply verbally, for the record.)

Another species of changing a question is to slip in an assumption which is unnoticed by the cross-examiner, but which both constrains the question to a narrower scope and renders the response dependent upon the witness' assumption. For example, if the question was "Is it your recommendation that we do X?", the answer would be in the hypothetical form, "If Y occurs then it would follow that it is". Thus, the witness has made the answer dependent upon a new assumption even though the questioner was not asking for that assumption to be included. The assumption may be wrong, unprovable, or even totally absurd. The unalert questioner is lulled into believing that his question has been answered, whereas in fact it has been changed.

An artful witness, careful not to draw the cross-examiner's attention to the constraining form of the answer, may avoid using obvious words like "if," but will instead use more subtle substitutes such as "given," or "recognizing that".

To defeat this game, the cross-examiner must be both alert

enough to catch it and able to expose it. For example, ask the witness what the source of this "given" was, since it was not in the question; or, ask the witness for the answer without the constraining assumption.

Another clever way of changing the question is the redefinition trick, which uses a word in two contexts in the same series of questions and answers. To illustrate: the word "costs" is capable of several meanings, and varies in its meaning with the context. Two of these meanings are: the "cost" to a company of providing service, and the "cost" of service to a customer (*i.e.*, the price charged).

The cross-examiner, assuming that rates are based on costs, might ask whether 70 percent of costs are accounted for by transmission costs. This would be asking for the costs *to the company*. The witness' response may be that 70 percent of costs are attributable to the residential class, as evidenced by billing records. Note that the question dealt with the company's costs, but that the answer was in terms of costs *to the customer*, that is, billing. The superficial point of resemblance was "70 percent of costs". Clearly, the percentage used by the witness in reply is a percentage of an entirely different thing, totally unrelated to the percentage sought in the question.

This game (and several others like it) starts by using the word the cross-examiner provides in the same context in which it is provided. Then the witness will discuss it for a while in a rather vague, meaningless way and, after everyone has been lulled to inattention, will change the context by substituting a word that sounds the same but, in the changed context, has a different meaning (such as here "cost" versus "price").

In some cases, not only will the context change, but also the number. For example, the witness may respond that the cost is not 70 percent, but 50 percent. This may mislead the questioner and the board into believing that the cost number, in the sense the cross-examiner intended, is not 70 percent but 50 percent, which merely compounds the confusion.

The only way to beat this game is to listen very carefully to the reply, *especially* if it is long and boring. There is an understandable but dangerous tendency to tune out long speeches as containing little more than insignificant verbiage, while listening only for certain key words. Yet paying close attention to boring answers may be as important as listening to the interesting ones, because the prolixity may cover a verbal sleight-of-hand. Once the game is detected, the solution is easy: expose the shift and repeat the question.

(vii) Game #7 — The over-qualified answer

While it is dangerous for a witness to oversimplify answers, many use qualifications as a way of avoiding answering a question at all. A witness may provide a "yes" or "no" at the beginning of the answer, but will attach so many qualifications that any basic position of agreement or disagreement is hard to detect. For example, the witness might say "I agree with what you are suggesting, but in addition, an intelligent answer would have to be dependent upon the following variables [the witness then lists half a dozen variables], each of which would require detailed research and benefit-cost analysis. As a prudent witness, without having conducted all of the research or having it available to me, I could not agree that the results you are proposing would in fact occur." This answer might be given even though all the qualifications the witness has suggested, taken together, might make no more than a five percent difference in the ultimate result, whereas the factor the cross-examiner has quoted as the basis for his question might explain 95 percent of the variation.

Since it is not very difficult for a witness with extensive theoretical training to toss out variables which might, hypothetically, have some effect, witnesses who play this game with a vengeance are very difficult to cross-examine. If one tries to pin the witness down by examining each variable in turn — a slow and tedious process which sometimes works — the witness can continue to insert qualifications to each answer in turn. Of course, the witness will refuse to hazard a guess as to the relative magnitude or importance to be attached to any of these qualifications ("I would have no empirical basis for doing so"). Characteristically, a board will not order a witness to guess at something he or she has not studied. Nor is it likely that a board would substitute its own judgment for that of the witness as to what magnitude of impact to attach to each of these variables.

Ultimately, unless the witness can be forced to admit that

these qualifications are relatively minor, perhaps by getting him to agree that he could not prove that they would be significant, the best counter-strategy might be for counsel to call his own witness.

6. GENERAL DEFENCES AGAINST WITNESS GAMES

Perhaps the best defence is exposure. If one can expose the nature of the game being played, it will have to stop, and the witness may also suffer some loss in credibility if the board is at all sensitive to what is going on. The danger, however, is that most boards are remarkably unaware of the battle being waged between the witness and the questioner. They sense the tension, they recognize that the process is not very productive, but don't understand or perhaps don't even care why.

Cross-examination which appears to be very slow in extracting useful answers is all too often blamed on the ineptitude of the cross-examiner, especially if a non-lawyer. However, where a board has demonstrated an unwillingness to discipline witnesses who "beat around the bush" or play games, cross-examiners know that they can expect no support from the board. Accordingly, unless the questioner just gives up on the witness, his only weapon is his willingness to persevere until, finally, the witness answers questions. For example, one might say to the witness firmly: "Dr. . . ., I've asked you this question twice and twice you haven't answered it. It is an important question, otherwise I would not have asked it. I'm prepared to ask it as many times as it takes to get a clear answer, but perhaps you can answer it this time so that I won't have to ask it again. To refresh your memory, the question is: . . .".

With a good chair, exposure of a game should suffice to end it; with an excellent one, the board member would take the initiative and ask the witness to stop wasting time; an inept chair will suffer in silence or rebuke the cross-examiner. Unlike judges, tribunal members are not often selected from the ranks of experienced regulatory counsel. Unless and until the training of tribunal members in procedures and practices is taken seriously, much of the cross-examination of expert witnesses may be tiresome and unproductive.

If the tribunal members cannot or will not help, counsel's

best strategy may be to try a whole different approach, to go at the same issue in another way. It is rarely worth re-wording a question more than once; to continue to re-word the same question gives the impression of being unable to draft questions. If it does not work the second time, an entirely fresh approach might be warranted. How quickly a questioner can think on his feet under this kind of stress will determine how successful he will be at finding new approaches.

Many witnesses have personal mannerisms which give away their intentions, particularly when they are feeling trapped or hostile and getting ready to provide an answer which the questioner will not like. Like Pinocchio's nose in the children's tale, physical symptoms or verbal cues may give them away. Watching the witness' face and paying close attention to body movements and voice can provide important clues, as can reading transcripts of earlier hearings.

17

Cross-examination — Lawyers' Techniques

1. EXPERTISE

Although the tribunal has granted the witness recognition as an expert, the lawyer may attempt to question the depth and breadth of the witness' expertise, or its relevance to the question at hand. He may also try to suggest that the expertise has been gained all on one side of the question, implying a bias. Because these are common occurrences, actual examples can be enlightening. The following two excerpts from hearing transcripts are illustrations of attempts by opposing counsel to limit the extent of the witness' expertise.

In the first example, the lawyer tries to underline the witness' lack of practical field experience. The cross-examiner poses the question several ways, in order to drive home the point. The witness, feeling somewhat defensive perhaps, does not exploit the poor wording of the lawyer's questioning, and fails to object to the indeterminate nature of the question asked. When the lawyer tries to draw the witness into making a guess, the witness correctly avoids doing so, but sounds somewhat defensive. He could have used the opportunity to turn tables on the lawyer, exploiting the ambiguities and confusion in his questions, rather than dwelling on his own lack of field experience.

Q: Dr. . . . . , can you describe for me your field experience in the area of saltation, any investigations that you have done that have been specifically related to saltation and I am talking about large flat surface areas or with tailings?

A: In the area of saltation itself I have not worked on a specific project.

It might have been somewhat stronger for the witness to answer: "My area of expertise is in the physics of saltation. I have not spent any time running around tailings pond in the field collecting samples."

Q: Well, if you have no experience there, then your experience in respect of saltation I take it is scientific experience, is that correct?

A: I have knowledge of the physics of saltation.

Q: And you have had experience in working with saltation equations?

A: Yes.

Q: Based on your experience, does linear regression apply between aggregate measurements and observed values from tailings?

This is the key question. A better way of wording it would have been to ask what the relationship is between aggregate measurements and observed values from tailings. The question "Does linear regression apply" is weak because linear regression analysis is a technique which can be applied to almost any set of data. The fit of the line to the data may be very poor, but the technique itself can always be applied. Hence the lawyer appears confused. Perhaps what he meant to ask was: "How good is the correlation between aggregate measurements and observed values from tailings?" If this is his question, the answer obviously depends on the accuracy of the measurements and of the observed values. Hence the question cannot be answered without some clarification, if not further information. This weakness in the question permits several alternatives to the rather limp answer actually provided.

A: As I pointed out before, I have not worked on any specific project concerned with saltation, so I cannot answer the question.

Given the analysis of the question in the foregoing comment, it may not have been necessary to have any practical experience with saltation to answer the question, if the question is answerable.

Q: Do you think it might apply?

The lawyer is here pressing the witness, giving him one of two bad alternatives. If the witness speculates, he will be condemned for guessing; if he declines to answer, his inexperience will again be underlined.

A: I think all I can do is guess. If a model is good it has to be calibrated so you cannot use a model without calibration.

Is the second sentence a guess, or a general statement unrelated to the first sentence?

Q: I am sorry, I couldn't understand the first part of your answer.

A: I mean any answer to you has to be a guess which I do not want to venture.

Q: But you seem to be using those guesses here today in condemning the model developed by . . . [the witness for his client].

That is an inference from the comment about calibration, which followed immediately after an expressed reluctance to guess. Because the witness unfortunately presented a sentence about guessing with a sentence about calibration, the lawyer has cleverly linked the two and tried to etch in the minds of the board members that the witness' comment about calibration is merely a guess. The witness, somewhat defensively, in his next answer backs off condemning something he intended earlier, perhaps rightly, to condemn.

A: I am not condemning the model, I am just pointing out the fact that calibration or validation in the usual sense has not been done.

This is a frequently used evasion by a witness becoming

defensive under pressure: he professes not to condemn, but that can be the only consequence and reason for pointing out the fact that the calibration or validation has not been done. If the absence of calibration is irrelevant the witness should not be wasting the board's time with this comment; if it is relevant then, presumably, it indicates an oversight or weakness worthy of condemnation on its own. This willingness to condemn inferentially, coupled with a denial of so doing, provides beautiful rhetorical ammunition for a lawyer. A better answer would have been: "I am not condemning the model, I am condemning the result of its use because calibration or validation in the usual sense has not been done."

In the second example, the expertise of the witness has been raised as an issue by way of objection by opposing counsel during the witness' examination-in-chief. When the issue is raised again during cross-examination, the witness clearly identifies his qualifications, and does not let his area of expertise be too narrowly confined. At the same time, the witness seems totally unwilling to admit the obvious, that his evidence does in some way challenge the evidence of the lawyer's expert. He goes to such extraordinary lengths to avoid saying anything negative that his position becomes harder and harder to defend, until finally he makes a key admission of potentially great use to the lawyer.

Q: Okay. Now I would like to discuss with you your area of expertise and that is the statistics to which you referred and I would like to refer you to Table 1.

A: I would like to say something about my field of expertise. I am Professor of Environmental Studies, adjunct Professor of Environmental Studies at . . . . University and I am very conversant with the literature on radiation effects. I do not pretend to be a medical person. I do not pretend to be an expert in any way in the biological effects of ionizing radiation but it is certainly part of my qualifications that I am a scholar in this area and I am conversant with the literature.

Q: I think you have made that perfectly clear. I am suggesting to you that the area of your particular expertise and training is the area of mathematics and statistics, and if I am not mistaken, that is what you said throughout your evidence.

A: That is correct but I also said throughout the evidence that the epidemiological and experimental evidence showing non-conservatism at low doses for alpha radiation are to my knowledge . . . there is no countervailing evidence as to low doses for alpha radiation on the other side and I have asked Dr. . . . at the. . . . Commission precisely that question and he has not been able to cite any evidence and I have literature searches that I am unable to find any.

Q: That is not the area of expertise, of your particular expertise no matter how well read you may be in the area?

A: I beg your pardon, sir, it is. My field is mathematical modelling and mathematical modelling involves not only interpreting results but looking for and testing the model to see if there is evidence pointing away from that particular model.

With this answer, the witness dug a potential trap for himself because in testing a model and looking at evidence, he first has to decide what is evidence and what is not, and second, what weight to give various kinds of evidence, possibly conflicting. This must require considerable understanding of and expertise in the area of the evidence itself.

Q: Are you telling me now that it is part of your expertise to determine the legitimacy of the assumption which Dr. . . . has used, the linear dose relationship?

Of course he is! The legitimacy of any *assumption* can be questioned, with or without expertise. That is inherent in the nature of assumptions, especially where the witness said in a previous answer that he must look at evidence pointing to and away from a particular model. He has to be making value judgments about that evidence.

A: I am sorry, that is not what I said. What I said is that in testing a mathematical model you look to see whether there is any evidence which supports the use of that model and whether there is any evidence which denies the validity of that model. So what I am saying is that at low doses of alpha exposure, I as a Professor of Environmental Studies can testify before this Board that I know of numerous items which indicate the possibility of a non-linear, non-conservative model and I know of no such evidence on the other side. That is all I am saying. It is not up to me to judge whether that evidence is valid.

The witness' answer is a defensive "waffle" and, on the face of it, absurd! Of course it is up to him to judge whether the evidence is valid, or he would not know whether or not to include it as supporting the use of the model. However, by retreating to the point of denying being in a position to judge whether the evidence is valid, he has made a key concession: that he is not in a position to say anything negative about the other side's witness. Thus a feeling of defensiveness and unfamiliarity about the scope of his own qualifications and an exercise of an abundance of caution has caused the witness to neutralize his own testimony. The lawyer won an easy victory, and underlined it in the mind of the board, to emphasize it further.

Q: Okay. I think that last sentence sums it up just perfectly.

From the lawyer's view point, of course, it is just perfect.

2. FACTS

The lawyer will also question the reliability of any facts given in evidence, as well as the personal knowledge of the expert with respect to these facts — that is, the accuracy of the expert's perception, recall and expression of the data, and the sincerity of their recital. Moreover, the arithmetic and the assumptions in any quantification will be carefully scrutinized. If different assumptions or different mathematical methods yield different and perhaps opposite conclusions, the witness may be virtually assured that he will be confronted with these in as embarrassing a manner as the lawyer can muster.

3. METHOD

Expert evidence often relies on the compilation and analysis of evidence prepared by others. Thus the expert may be expected to answer questions relating to the "hardness" of the data, its accuracy and the degree of control over the observation. For example, when being questioned on research design the expert will probably be asked about sample size, methods used, why these rather than alternative methods were selected, the consequences of the use of alternative methods, the completeness of the investigation, the disclosure and suppression of data, and so on.

The expert should be prepared to explain the methods used and any generally recognized alternative methods, particularly if he has declined to employ one of these methods where it would lead to results less favourable to his position. If other studies are referred to, one should be careful not to extend them beyond the bounds of application. As well, the witness should be careful not to omit relevant information for the purpose of making the conclusion appear stronger. It is far better to present a series of alternatives, to indicate why the particular alternative which was selected for conclusions is preferable, and to understate rather than overstate the strength of the conclusion that can be based on the evidence. This will deprive the cross-examiner of the opportunity to attack the credibility of the witness for overstatement or suppression of information.

4. CREDIBILITY

The most important issue from the witness' viewpoint is credibility. Seemingly contradictory statements made in previous testimony or in published works can be used as weapons; fortunately, such occurrences are rare and the witness should be able to distinguish, on the facts, previous statements which seem to conflict with the present position. The witness should be prepared to justify current views or reconcile any apparent contradictions. Overstatements and understatements made by the cross-examiner in support of the witness' view are often effective in attacking credibility, as are half-truths in the nature of misleading innuendo or non-disclosure. Such lawyers' speeches, even if not put in the form of questions, should not be allowed to go by unchallenged. For example, if the cross-examiner makes a series of statements designed to belittle or parody the evidence of the witness, and concludes with a comment like:

Q: And that is your view of the facts. Now, my next question is . . .

The appropriate response for the witness should follow quickly:

A: I'm sorry to interrupt but I cannot let your remarks go by unchallenged, for fear of appearing to acquiesce to them. What you have expressed is your view of my view, not my view. Now, what was your next question?

5. BIAS

Another way of attacking a witness' credibility is to seek to demonstrate a bias — personal, institutional or otherwise.

In the following illustration drawn from an environmental hearing, a lawyer attempts to discredit an expert witness on the grounds of his association with a well-known anti-nuclear group. The cross-examiner is clumsy. The witness does not let himself be pinned down as an anti-nuclear zealot, and leaves the impression that he is merely a concerned scientist.

Q: You are Chairman of the group called the Canadian Coalition for Nuclear Responsibility, is that right?

A: That is correct.

Q: And you hold I think it would be fair to say strong views about what I might call, to use a cliché, the proliferation of nuclear energy?

The use of the word "proliferation" is inept because of its obvious negative connotation. Proliferation is a "loaded" word, plainly something bad. Who would be in favour of proliferation?

A: That is correct.

Q: You are against it?

A: That is correct.

The lawyer's question should have been either "What are your views on nuclear proliferation" (if he insists on using the word), or "Are you in favour of or against nuclear proliferation?"

Q: You are against the proliferation at this time, aren't you?

He has given the witness a very easy target, and the witness does not waste the opportunity.

A: I do believe the proliferation of nuclear power throughout the world is overhasty and I think that there has been inadequate consideration given to the nature of the problems and what can be done to prevent those problems from becoming extremely serious.

Note that the witness has built in some value words such as "overhasty" and "inadequate". The lawyer could then press him with questions as to what constitutes adequate consideration, what makes it adequate, how long does adequate consideration take, how much does it cost, and so on.

The lawyer then quoted a portion of the witness' testimony from a previous hearing:

Q: I am reading from the transcript there, the brief you filed, I will read you the question and answer you gave in regard to a brief you filed. Mr. . . . . , was cross-examining you at page 34:

"Presumably as you have already accepted this is a biased and selective document. You will agree that the summary of international attitudes specifically here (page 35) is itself highly biased and is in at least three incidents positively misleading.

Dr. . . . . : Certainly not misleading. I think it is definitely biased. It is showing a trend among other trends and that trend is a rising concern internationally about nuclear power and the implications of a nuclear future."

A: Yes, I think that is perfectly accurate.

Q: Well, then it is quite fair, is it not, to say that you hold strong views against the proliferation of nuclear power and that you are biased against that proliferation?

A: No, I beg your pardon. I did not say that and I would not agree to that. What I have said is that there is a growing concern and this concern is expressed at the very highest levels.

This lawyer was not able to score any points against this witness.

The same expert was then cross-examined by another lawyer, who avoided engaging the witness in an extensive and detailed discussion on the substance of his views. Rather, he made his point with one small, dramatic gesture.

Q: Is that your briefcase on the floor by the podium?

A: Yes.

Q: Would you pick that up and read the logo on the other side?

A: It says "Nuclear power? No thanks" with a picture of a smiling sun.

Q: Do you think that accords perfectly well with your views which you have expressed here today, and other places as to nuclear energy?

Clearly, the logo rejects nuclear power. If the witness accepts this as according with his views, then it means that he too rejects nuclear power. The witness tries to waffle.

A: It is a very widespread opinion in our society. If solar energy turns out to be technically viable and economically viable to meet our energy needs, the choice is clear. The real debate over nuclear power is whether we actually need nuclear power or not. That is a debate that is by no means resolved. That is a rather humorous logo here that indicates that if the sunshine turns out to be adequate to meet our energy needs, then we won't need nuclear power and I suspect that most governments would move rather quickly to disengage from the technology.

Here the witness is vacillating. He is asked either to associate with or disassociate himself from the wording of the logo. He tries to distract the questioner by including a hypothetical assumption ("*If* the sunshine technology turns out to be adequate to meet our energy needs, then we won't need nuclear power"). If the real debate over nuclear power is whether we actually need it or not, the slogan in the logo makes it plain that the answer is, we don't. The lawyer picks up the witness and sets a trap for him in the next question.

Q: Did you say *if* the sunshine technology is feasible?

Here the lawyer underlines the hypothetical nature of the witness' previous assumption.

A: Exactly.

Q: I have no further questions.

The lawyer has successfully demonstrated that the witness rejects nuclear power without knowing if solar power is feasible. This implies bias. It looks very much like the lawyer won this round because, whether he used it or not, he was in a position to say in final argument that the logo humorously but unequivocally rejects nuclear power, and so does the witness, without knowing whether "sunshine power" is feasible. If the feasibility of solar power is the pre-condition to the rational rejection of nuclear power, and if we don't know whether or not it is feasible, the rejection of nuclear power in the absence of that knowledge appears to be a bias.

A number of alternatives were available to the witness. If it were factually true, he could have said that someone merely struck the symbol on his briefcase, and he had never given it much thought. He could have likened it to someone putting a poppy or daffodil into someone's lapel for making a donation during a tag day. Alteratively, he could have said that it oversimplified rather than fully stated his views but, since it was amusing, and at least partially right, he carried it on his briefcase anyway. This, too, would have defused the appearance of bias. Finally, he could have said that he believed that solar power and other energy sources, taken together, were sufficient to render nuclear power unnecessary.

6. A HIDDEN PSYCHOLOGICAL GAME

Cross-examination involves more than a simple, direct assault on the witness. Often the cross-examiner attempts to lead the witness to one of two possible extremes: to have the witness adopt an exaggerated version of his testimony, an extreme position that may later become untenable, or to suggest a more "reasonable" interpretation which makes it appear to be in substantial agreement with that of the cross-examiner's side. The careless witness might thereby be thrust onto the horns of a non-existent dilemma. At no time should the witness feel obliged, in order to appear affable or co-operative, to agree with statements or even opinions suggested by the cross-examiner. Beware of the tactic of gross exaggeration of one side of the argument coupled with innocuous understatement of the other as a form of pressure to move one's position along the continuum to the point the lawyer's client would prefer.

7. THE EXPLOITATION OF UNCERTAINTY

In any scientific discipline a self-respecting expert witness would agree that on many points, the opinions of equally learned and honest experts may differ. Many of the predominant theories and practices of the day may well be tentative, inconclusive or wrong. Every scientist will acknowledge that there have been significant errors made in scientific discoveries and theoretical assumptions. Given these admissions, the lawyer can either attempt to show that the witness' conclusions should be taken with a grain of salt, or try to "lean on him" to be more conclusive and definitive (and perhaps excessively so). There will be rhetorical questions such as: "Do you expect this Board to reject an important project, and all the jobs that go with it, on the basis of that kind of as yet inconclusive evidence?" While this form of cross-examination may appear bombastic, the witness must avoid over-reacting, either by adopting an extreme and indefensible position in response, or by timid waffling and hedging. All that one need maintain is that in the context of present day theories and "the state of the art", this evidence is, in an uncertain world, as certain as it can be. In deciding whether to approve or reject what is often less than mathematically certain evidence both for and against the project, it is not very dangerous to concede that the evidence of environmental risk is somewhat inconclusive if the witness points out at the same time that the evidence of environmental safety as submitted by the proponent is perhaps even less conclusive.

8. EXAGGERATION

The lawyer will often attempt to persuade the witness to

exaggerate. The psychological principle at work here is that it is often easier to get a witness to state his opinions too highly than to get him to agree that he is wrong. A skillful lawyer will support his previous testimony. Surprised and pleased by this unexpected occurrence, the witness will too readily agree with opposing counsel. The cross-examiner then gradually exaggerates the expert's position until it becomes a bit outrageous. The commitment to the lawyer's line of reasoning must now be qualified by the witness, with a possible loss of credibility. One can be sure that counsel will exploit any backtracking to his own advantage, expressing marked surprise at the witness' need to keep changing his mind.

Exploiting Personal Mannerisms

The lawyer recognizes that a hearing setting is a lawyer's forum, not that of the witness. The objective is to use this to his advantage. It is also the lawyer who is asking the questions, from an undisclosed and potentially infinite list.

Lawyers may at times choose to adopt bullying tactics because nothing provokes inconsistent statements or backtracking as effectively as intimidating questions posed by a glaring counsel to a nervous witness. Thus the lawyer may attempt to exploit nervousness, belligerence, forgetfulness or, in the case of many government witnesses, an extreme unwillingness to offend, all to imply substantive uncertainty or lack of credibility. Although such tactics may backfire if the counsel takes them too far, particularly if he persists when the witness does not fall for them, unfortunately a tribunal will rarely rescue a witness who is being bullied, especially if he is retreating, because that is recognized as one of the purposes of cross-examination. Thus, the lawyer has little to risk by bullying. If it is unsuccessful these tactics can be changed quickly. If it is successful the tribunal will not rescue the witness.

Apart from tone of voice and phrasing, the questioner may attempt to direct the witness towards certain conclusions with a use of leading questions and gestures. For example: to provide subliminal feedback to the witness by nodding his head sympathetically to a favourable answer, raising eyebrows or frowning to an unfavourable one, or even walking up and down and turning his back on the witness if the witness is making a long speech which the lawyer doesn't like. All these tactics are designed to influence the nature of the witness' answers.

Friendly persuasion also takes several forms. As mentioned earlier, the cross-examiner may try to re-assure the witness that what he is saying is undisputed. This is to give the witness confidence from the friendly reception that the testimony evokes. Slowly and carefully, the cross-examiner may, through this amicable discussion, draw out mild or even major concessions from the unsuspecting witness. Alternatively, counsel may present contrary testimony or writings of other experts and politely suggest to the witness that the questions to follow provide an opportunity to modify slightly the testimony in relation to that of these other experts, out of fairness and consideration to the witness. By emphasizing subtly the expertise of those persons who hold opinions contrary to the witness, the lawyer attempts to undermine, in a backhanded way, the self-confidence of the witness. This is to apply a form of peer pressure by suggesting to the witness that his testimony is somewhat out of line with accepted scientific norms. The intimation that the witness is, out of kindness, being given an opportunity to redeem himself, coupled with the intimidating setting of the hearing itself, may result in the witness feeling that he is better off accepting the helpful reformulations of his testimony as suggested by cross-examining counsel.

9. THE FALSE ANALOGY

Opposing counsel will frequently attempt to put to the expert a complex *hypothetical* question which deals with matters similar to those of the fact situation around which the present case revolves. If this elicits an answer from the expert which the questioner feels can be helpful, in final argument there will be an attempt to draw an analogy between the hypothetical problem posed to the expert and the facts of the case. For such a technique to be effective, counsel will usually try to obtain an unequivocal answer, either a "yes" or "no", to the hypothetical question. Then, in final argument, it will be submitted that this answer also expressed the expert's opinion on the determinative issue in the actual case. Notwithstanding that the lawyer will phrase the hypothetical question so that it contains variables which significantly differ from the facts in issue (that is, it may well be a false analogy), the decision-maker may not always be sufficiently well-versed in the fine points of the technical speciality to perceive this and, thus, may be swayed by the superficial resemblance. The expert witness and, especially his own counsel must be alert to this possibility and should, during cross-examination, point out to the tribunal the features of the hypothetical situation which differ from the facts in issue.

10. "ANSWER YES OR NO"

Generally, a witness can never be required to answer a question in a form with which he does not agree. Faced with a counsel who seeks to force a "yes" or "no" choice, the witness may conduct himself as follows:

Q: On the basis of our discussion of the last few minutes, would you agree with the passage that I had quoted to you earlier?

A: Would you read the passage again, please?
[Lawyer reads the passage]

A: No, I could not agree with it entirely.

Q: Then you don't agree?

A: I cannot with certainty answer "yes" or "no".

Q: I take it you don't know.

A: I have an opinion on the subject which would necessarily be qualified which I can elaborate upon if you wish.

Opposing counsel can be quite stubborn in insisting on a "yes" or "no" answer. In the following excerpt, the cross-examiner poses a question which receives a qualified answer. He admonishes the witness twice for his verbosity, then poses the question again. At this point the witness gives a definitive response. The general impression created was that the latter answer could have been given at the outset, so that the witness was either inattentive to the question or evasive. A close reading of the transcript shows that the lawyer actually reformulated the question to change its emphasis, so that the witness found he could agree to it in its reworded and changed form. To avoid such a situation the witness should point out the precise part of the question to which he cannot respond in definite terms, and any reason why the questioner's desired response might be misleading.

Q: Dr. . . . , there are just one or two questions which I would like to ask to clarify, if I may, exactly what it is you are trying to tell the Board. Is the burden of your evidence that recent developments have suggested that the linear method of calculation which has been used by Dr. . . . . in the preparation of his appendices is not warranted?

A: It is the purpose of my evidence to say that recent publications, recent published data, if correct, may indicate that Dr. . . .'s calculations could seriously underestimate the risk of lung cancer, yes.

Q: Are you indicating in your view, whether expert or not, that these recent publications are correct?

A: As I mentioned on Friday, there are three criteria —

Q: Excuse me. I really think that question can be answered by "yes" or "no", Dr. . . .

A: I have been unable to find data which points in the opposite direction. I would not say that one can possibly conclude at this early stage with the scanty data at the present time and without proper elapse of time for the scientific community to come to a consensus on this point, I don't think it is possible to say one theory or the other theory is correct.
What I can say is my knowledge of the evidence indicates evidence on one side and I have been unable to identify evidence on the other side.

Q: Dr. . . ., I realize the difficulty in answering "yes" or "no" or "maybe" but I think it would be more helpful if you can, if you would, if you can give responses to that. If the question doesn't lend itself to that, I will try to rephrase it. I will ask the question again: Is the burden of your evidence that recent developments have suggested that the linear method of calculation used by Dr. . . . . in his appendices may not be appropriate?

A: Oh, yes, that is certainly correct. "May not be appropriate" is far less categorical than "is not warranted".

11. ASKING QUESTIONS BASED ON ASSUMPTIONS

When answering a question containing an assumption, the witness must expressly recognize this assumption and repeatedly state that his answer holds true only if the assumption is also true. The assumption might be included in a question of this type: "Given that A and B exist, would not C and D also exist?" A simple "yes" answer to an apparently simple question of logic might be interpreted as an admission by the witness that A and B *do in fact exist*, although the witness intended to answer a *purely hypothetical* question. A better answer would be: "*If* A and B *did* exist, which I will not accept without proof, C and D would also exist", leaving no doubt that the expert refuses to accept A and B as established facts.

Even assumptions which the opposing counsel clearly identifies as hypothetical may eventually be exploited to create confusion. The technique used to achieve this result is simple: once the assumptions are established, the lawyer launches into a long series of questions about the logical consequences of these assumptions. The intent, of course, is to make everyone forget that these effects are in reality merely derivations from assumptions which may or may not be true. To prevent this confusion from occurring, the witness must always — even at the risk of boring everyone with repetition — make it abundantly clear that each of his answers is based on the original hypothetical assumptions. This will reveal the lawyer's game, and thereby destroy its effectiveness.

Only close scrutiny can detect hidden assumptions, but certain words and phrases beginning a sentence are usually good indicators. Among these are: "accepting that", "since", "if", "because of", "in view of", "the fact that", "given that" and "recognizing that".

The following witness is careful to qualify his answer and emphasize the fact that he is commenting on an assumption:

Q: Tell me, what do you think your position would be if there were a friendly takeover.

A: I think there would still be very — firstly, it's difficult to foresee how it could be a friendly takeover. But let's presume for a moment that it may . . .

Often assumptions are hidden in questions seeking categorical choices, e.g.: "Do you prefer a pristine environment and massive unemployment or a bit of environmental impact and full employment in a depressed area." This is not necessarily the total range of choices available. Rather than saying that one can not answer "yes" or "no" to such a question, which may sound weak or evasive, the witness might say: "I cannot accept the hidden assumption in your question". The lawyer may stop the game, or feel obligated to ask: "What hidden assumption?"; to which the witness replies: "That those two extreme, oversimplified, hypothetical situations are the only choices available".

12. ASKING FOR OPINIONS BASED ON FALSE DATA

When asked to base an opinion or calculation on numbers already entered into evidence, the expert witness must always verify the reliability of the numbers with which he is asked to work. A very common task an expert witness is asked to perform while under cross-examination is to make computations or draw conclusions from numbers which the opposing counsel says are correct, or are already entered as evidence. The result is often contradictory to the expert's previous conclusion. This, of course, does nothing to add to the expert's credibility.

The reason for these unfortunate results is usually not incompetent witnesses but incorrect starting figures, or simply unreliable numbers drawn from crude statistical methods. By being aware of the questionable reliability of the starting figures, the witness may put the blame for unsatisfactory conclusions where it belongs, on the original figures. The answer should always be qualified by "subject to my verifying the numbers you have provided". After cross-examination, the witness should immediately go to the quoted source and check the numbers. If they are less reliable than the witness', or simply wrong, the witness' view should be put on the record.

13. PLAYING SEMANTIC GAMES

The skillful cross-examiner will sometimes try to get the expert witness to agree to a certain definition of a term. The witness, not being alert to all of the possible implications, may accept the questioner's definition. The lawyer will then confront the witness with a part of his testimony where he uses the same term in an unusual manner. The witness either has to admit that this original definition was too narrow, forcing him to change his definition (which appears to be backtracking), or to admit that that part of his evidence does not square with this definition. In argument, then, the cross-examiner will imply either that the witness was using a key term in apparent ignorance of its true meaning, or was attempting to mislead the tribunal by the deliberate misuse of a technical word.

While it is preferable for a witness in such a situation to admit that the previously offered definition was too narrow, obviously the best course of action is to avoid being locked into a restricted definition of a term.

18

How to Prepare and Submit Evidence as a Witness

1. INTRODUCTION

Preparation and submission of evidence is an extremely important part of participation in the tribunal process. In rare cases, it may be possible to anticipate that all the information necessary to support an argument will be made available by other participants, or may be elicited through cross-examination of others' witnesses. But unless this is known with certainty in advance, most prudent participants will at least prepare to submit evidence, even if it later becomes unnecessary to do so.

While a polished submission of evidence is an art which can only be mastered after some practice, anyone who is sufficiently organized and understands the distinction between evidence and argument should be able to do an acceptable job.

All evidence should be submitted with a *particular* purpose in mind, as the basis for a specific point in final argument. Therefore, the first step in preparing to submit evidence should be preparation of a detailed outline of the final argument, followed by a list of the evidence which will be before the tribunal in support of the arguments to be made. Next, for each piece of evidence in the outline, list the likely sources of that evidence. What one cannot be assured of obtaining from others one will have to be prepared to submit.

This type of outline of facts and expert opinion to be submitted can serve several purposes: to clarify before the hearing what sources of evidence should be considered; as a checklist of what has been presented during the hearing (including via cross-examination); to remind the tribunal of the evidence it has before it during argument. Using such an outline, it may become apparent during the hearing that a witness intended to be used to testify at the hearing may no longer have to be called as a witness because the gist of that evidence has already been presented by others. With a complete list of the evidence essential to final argument, it should be easier to determine which witnesses, documents or other physical evidence should be put before the tribunal; without it, there are likely to be gaps or duplication.

If some of the evidence is difficult to explain, consideration should be given to the production of charts or other aids to assist in presentation and to make the evidence more effective. Personal computers now make the preparation of charts and graphs quite easy and inexpensive.

The rules of the tribunal may impose special and unexpected requirements. For example, it may be necessary to submit written evidence some weeks in advance. Such rules may hamper interveners who are opposed to an application, since often it is impossible to make a final determination of which witnesses it is necessary to call to present what evidence until after the cross-examination of the applicant's evidence is completed. Such situations call for interveners to display an imaginative approach to the rules, usually in the form of a motion to the tribunal to permit filing evidence a set date (e.g., two weeks) after cross-examination of the applicant's witnesses.

Selection of witnesses involves careful consideration. The credibility and demeanour of prospective witnesses may be as important as their academic credentials, particularly for experts who are to give opinion evidence. It will be helpful to select experts who have given similar evidence in comparable proceedings.

The opinion evidence of an expert witness may be of little or no weight unless the evidence survives cross-examination. An important part of preparing an expert who has not testified before as a witness is a briefing on the types of cross-examination likely to be faced. Since evidence which falls apart on cross-examination is even less useful than argument which may be unsupported by evidence, use another witness if time and resources allow, or say the same things in final argument as the witness would have said. If there is serious concern that the witness may not survive the ordeal, do not file the witness' evidence. If the potential witness has serious reservations about facing cross-examination, it may be a sign of discomfort with defending the evidence. What is worse, the insecure witness may appear confident or even cocky beforehand, but may deteriorate on the stand. Careful "checking out" and interrogating the witness in advance may prevent disaster. As one experienced lawyer put it, "If he survives the cross-examination I give him in my office, he can survive anything at the hearing."

Any briefing of a prospective witness should include general suggestions as to how to respond under cross-examination. The witness should listen to questions very carefully, and ask for clarification of any question which is ambiguous. Answers should be careful and thoughtful, responding *only* to the question asked, without offering gratuitous information or opinions. If the witness is asked "Do you know what day of the week it is today?", the answer should be "yes", not "Wednesday". The latter kind of answer offers information not sought and, if incorrect, runs the risk of needlessly discrediting the witness.

Witnesses need not give simple "yes" or "no" answers to questions which cannot appropriately be answered this way. If the answer to an apparently simple question requires qualification, the reasons for qualifying the answer should be given, whether or not cross-examining counsel so desires. The witness should not be bullied or intimidated by a cross-examiner into answering "with a simple 'yes' or 'no'" questions which would give a distorted picture of the witness' views if so answered. However, a cross-examiner is entitled to know whether the witness agrees or disagrees with the point of the question, subject to whatever qualifications or reasons may be necessary. A problem often arises with witnesses (especially professors) who give lengthy, detailed answers from which it is impossible to tell whether the witness agreed or disagreed. In that situation the questioner is entitled to ask, and the witness ought to be required to say clearly, whether the answer involves agreement or disagreement — "yes, because" or "no, because", but not simply "because". Otherwise it will be difficult to tell when reading the transcript whether the question was answered at all and, if so, what the answer was.

Experts are sometimes tempted to give opinions on areas which are not truly within the realm of their expertise, and this can be dangerous. If the witness does not feel that the question put in cross-examination is properly within his or her field of expertise, it is usually best to say so explicitly, and to decline, politely, to answer.

Experts should support their opinions with logical arguments, developed step-by-step, in language which is comprehensible. The number of obscure or specialized terms should be minimized and whenever there is doubt, technical terms should be carefully defined. Conclusions should be broad enough to cover most reasonable interpretations of the facts or assumptions before the tribunal, but not so broad as to overstate or jeopardize the opinion. On the other hand, the opinion should not be so narrow that it can be ignored entirely if the tribunal finds that an assumption underlying the opinion is not entirely applicable.

Experienced witnesses will probably be quite conversant with these considerations. Experts who have no previous hearing experience should be provided with a copy of this chapter or parts of other texts for background reading.

If a witness is giving general, non-expert testimony only, his relationship to the facts should be explained to the tribunal at the beginning of his testimony. If the witness has direct knowledge of relevant facts, his evidence (but not his opinion on technical matters) is admissible.

If expert testimony is to be given then some expertise must be proved by provision to the tribunal of relevant academic, professional and other credentials, along with the evidence. Technically, the expert is not entitled to give any opinion evidence until the tribunal is satisfied with his qualifications. This can be done in several different ways. The expert can prepare a résumé for submission to the tribunal, can simply recount his qualifications orally, or can have them read aloud by counsel, followed by the question: "Does this accurately summarize your credentials?" As in a court, other participants may challenge the right of a witness with questionable qualifications to give opinion evidence, but this is quite a rare occurrence. Most often the witness will have previously been accepted for purposes of testifying on the subject before this or another tribunal; this fact will be included in the résumé, and arguments about whether the expertise is sufficient to testify will be pointless. Even a first-time witness is usually allowed to testify without fuss, given adequate academic or professional credentials. However, greater, lesser or no weight may be given to a witness' evidence by the tribunal, depending upon credentials and performance.

If the witness has not prepared a detailed written report but will be presenting evidence orally, it is generally best to confine examination-in-chief[1] to simple questions. These questions must be phrased in a manner which does not suggest the desired answer, as such questions are "leading" and unacceptable: for example, "What colour was Alexander the Great's white horse?" Tribunals may be a bit lenient on occasion, but not always. In any event, evidence which has been "led" from a witness is almost invariably less persuasive.

The questions should be simple and call for relatively clear answers. It is perfectly acceptable to ask a witness to explain an answer in more detail or in less technical language. The questions should proceed through the subject matter in logical order. For witnesses giving non-technical evidence, this will usually mean chronological order. Expert witnesses should be asked what they were retained to study, what they did study and what they found. Then they should go through the steps necessary to arrive at their expert opinions. These steps may not always be in chronological order, but the evidence will be more persuasive if the witness follows some logical process in describing the research.

Documentary evidence must usually be introduced through witnesses giving testimony. If the document was prepared by the witness (e.g., a written opinion or chart), he should be asked to confirm that he prepared such a document, and to identify a copy shown to him. Copies should be made for the members of the tribunal and other parties participating, as well as for tribunal staff, court reporters and translators. These should be distributed when the witness is testifying at the latest and,

---

1 See above, Chapter 2, under sub-heading 4(e) "Sequence of Evidence" (p. 28).

preferably, at least a few days before. It is advisable to have a few extra copies for unexpected requests.

It is important to be familiar with the tribunal's rules relating to documentary evidence. Those tribunals which require written evidence to be submitted in advance may have severe restrictions on the nature of documentary evidence which can be submitted after the deadline. When the document is admitted, it should usually be given an exhibit number by the tribunal. Well-organized participants will ensure that their own copies of all exhibits are numbered, so that when future reference is made to them by number, it will be clear what the documents are. It is a good practice to keep copies of all parties' exhibits in binders in exhibit number order.

Expert witnesses should be encouraged to prepare and make use of models, graphs and any other form of evidence which will help explain their conclusions or the methods by which they have arrived at them. Care should be taken to cite the source of all information used and to explain any processes involved. The more visually comprehensible the evidence, the more effective it is likely to be.

2. TESTIFYING AS AN ORDINARY WITNESS

There are two ways in which evidence may be presented: orally or in writing. Normally, hearings such as those before the National Energy Board or a public utilities tribunal employ fairly formal procedures because most of the witnesses are experts and virtually all parties are represented by counsel. On the other hand, less formal tribunals usually have shorter hearings, with no necessity to present one's evidence in writing. Whether evidence is usually presented orally or in writing will depend upon the rules of the tribunal. Nevertheless, it may be possible even before one of the more formal tribunals to present evidence orally by special permission of the tribunal, obtained in advance. All that would be necessary is to make a motion so requesting, indicating that because of the non-technical nature of the evidence, it would be needlessly onerous to require that it all be prepared in writing and submitted beforehand.

Let us first consider the simplest situation, in which the group has no lawyer and only one witness. In these circumstances, examination-in-chief would consist of an oral presentation by the witness. Many witnesses will feel uneasy about speaking simply "off the cuff", and will want to use handwritten notes to remind them of the various points they wish to make. That is perfectly acceptable and a good aid to memory. However, if there is another party to this hearing which is adverse in interest and represented by a lawyer, that lawyer may ask to see the notes being used, which request may be granted. If it is, the witness might be embarrassed if what was presented orally was not the same as what was in the notes. If the witness is warned of the possibility that his notes may be examined by others, he will know what not to put in them.

Going beyond notes, some people feel most secure when they have the entire presentation written out, and will try to read it. This will usually get an objection from someone present — if not the lawyer for the other side, perhaps the tribunal itself or its counsel. There is nothing more boring than listening to someone read from a written text and, since most people can read faster to themselves than witnesses can read orally, the board will invite the witness simply to leave the written notes with the board for photocopying and distribution. It will also promise to read every word faithfully. But such promises, unfortunately, are not always kept. Accordingly, the witness should not try to read the brief aloud. Either a written statement should be filed or the oral evidence presented. As an alternative, it may be preferable to leave a written memorandum with the board and to highlight or summarize its contents orally.

Any presentation to a tribunal, whether written or oral, would normally have certain standard contents. These should include, at the outset, the witness' full name and address and a statement of his interest in the issue before the board. The witness must be absolutely clear in his own mind as to what his role is. If the witness is a member of a group, is the intervener the witness personally or the group? If the group is intervening, is the witness there as a representative of the group or on his own as a separate intervener despite membership in the group? For example, a witness participating in an environmental assessment hearing of a particular project, in his capacity as an individual, should state that he lives in the area and indicate the distance between his residence and the project. After this introduction, summarize the points to be made and then make them. The presentation should reflect the three B's: be brief, be clear and be gone.

Too many people view their opportunity to be a witness as a kind of soap box or grandstand, savouring every moment of the attention they are receiving. This is particularly true of persons who might be described as "causy", that is, people with a personality which tends to be attracted towards causes, with which they become intensely and emotionally involved. Tribunals usually find such intensity tiresome. Much more effective is the witness who appears to be in just a bit of a hurry, sensitive to the fact that the tribunal's time is precious. Do not provide endless background: come to the point right away. When the point has been made, thank the tribunal for the opportunity and leave; or, if there are questions from the tribunal, or cross-examination, be ready for these as soon as the points have been made.

Whether in response to questions or as part of the affirmative presentation, exaggeration, posturing or rhetoric should be avoided. If the facts are dramatic, the drama will be evident in the facts themselves. If the facts are not dramatic, they will not appear so (at least not to board personnel, who have heard every "sob story" in the book) merely by emotional carrying on. Members of most tribunals — whether it be a Rent Review Hearing Board, Workers' Compensation Tribunal, Immigration and Refugee Hearing Board, or whatever — tend to see themselves as professional adjudicators. In this atmosphere, someone who acts as if they were on stage is likely to be more offensive than persuasive, regardless of how terribly polite and sympathetic everyone will appear. This is especially true if the witness represents a consumer, environmental or other group which people in the bureaucracy, and corporate or governmental lawyers just love to stereotype as well-meaning but emotional and naive and, therefore, not to be taken too seriously. To avoid falling into one of these rather patronizing stereotypes, community group representatives must err, if anything, on the side of being a bit too bland rather than a bit too excited.

Many years ago, near the beginning of his practice, the author requested and was granted a meeting with the chairman of a major Ottawa tribunal with a view to asking how, with very limited resources, the client group could best contribute to a forthcoming public hearing. The group suggested calling a witness in forecasting, or in one of two other disciplines. The chairman's answer was a complete surprise. "Don't call any of those, we have plenty of those experts on our own staff," was the reply, "What I would really like to see is someone who can put it all together." He then gave as an example a distinguished economist who was, at the time, the president of a major Canadian university. When it was suggested that this person lacked direct expertise in any of the particular topics conventionally addressed at such hearings, the chairman advised that this made no difference at all. What was really lacking in these proceedings was a witness with the perspective, insight, objectivity and originality of the person he had mentioned. One day's reading of the application by such an individual, plus a few hours' thought, would provide a better contribution to the policy issues to be faced by the tribunal than several weeks of number crunching by yet one more technocratic specialist.

Of course, such a "guru" is not easy to find or to persuade to testify. Nevertheless, if one can be obtained, the person would probably testify as an ordinary witness rather than as an expert witness because the evidence to be presented would be of a general policy nature, the seeming simplicity of which could only be the result of three or four decades of very sophisticated thinking.

3. TESTIFYING AS AN EXPERT WITNESS

(a) The Assignment and the Retainer Letter

Most expert witness testimony is presented in written form, as a memorandum of evidence to be submitted a week or longer before the person is to testify. The preparation of that memorandum should, if possible, be a team effort between the witness and the client. This does not mean that the client should attempt to dictate its contents, nor to distort what the witness would otherwise say. Indeed, any witness with any pride would reject any attempt by a client to compromise the witness' objectivity. Nevertheless, a witness is not called to pontificate in the abstract, but to make a useful contribution to a particular policy espoused in the intervention of the client. If the witness does not share that policy viewpoint or has no sympathy for it, another witness should be found, unless the witness can persuade the client to change its views to those of the witness.

The best witnesses are those who, when presented with a certain set of facts, would offer the same evidence regardless of who the client happened to be. For example, a witness asked to provide evidence as to what is a fair rate of return for a public utility should not attempt to manipulate the number to produce a "highball" estimate if representing a utility or a "lowball" estimate if representing a consumer group.

It should be remembered that it is open to a suspicious cross-examiner to ask questions about the nature of the assignment from the client. In one case in which a group's expert witness was being cross-examined to determine whether or not the witness was truly independent, counsel asked him to outline the initial discussions he had had with the client and its lawyer and, in particular, what the lawyer's instructions had been. Much to the chagrin of the cross-examiner, the witness responded that, although the lawyer had suggested a certain initial hypothesis, he had been able rather quickly to talk the lawyer out of it and thus, to make the assignment reflect the witness' hypothesis, which had led to his present testimony. Having thus neatly inserted the knife, the witness turned it by saying that had the group's lawyer failed to show such objectivity, he as a witness would not have testified for it.

This little anecdote highlights the importance of the initial communication between the witness and the client. Where possible, the nature of the witness' assignment should be set out in writing, with the recognition that there is a distinct possibility that the correspondence may be the subject of cross-examination. (If there is some confidentiality with respect to the per diem rate or other arrangements, these can be contained in a separate memorandum or, if not, can be blacked out, with the consent of the tribunal, before the retainer letter is introduced in evidence.) It may be worth including the retainer letter as an exhibit to the evidence of the witness when it is presented in-chief.

(b) Format of a Memorandum of Evidence

There are two formats commonly used. The first is a series of questions and answers. The questions are supposed to be those that would be asked by a lawyer during an oral examination-in-chief. The responses are those of the witness, again as if making oral replies to these questions posed by the lawyer. The second format is that of the simple essay or memorandum, with headings introducing the different parts of the evidence, much like chapter headings and sub-headings in a book.

Regardless of the format, it is desirable to have each page on which evidence is presented printed down the left or right-hand margin with line numbers. That way, during cross-examination, the lawyer can ask the witness to refer to page 27, line 16, rather than to page 27 about a third of the way down the page. Most personal computers (now used by virtually all witnesses) permit the easy printing of line numbers. Alternatively, line numbers can be typed onto a page which can then be photocopied, with these copies being used in the printer or typewriter.

One advantage of the question-and-answer format has been that it makes "old timers", who remember the days before written memoranda of evidence were used, feel more familiar. However, anybody who was appointed to a tribunal less than 20 years ago or who has not practised as a litigation lawyer in courts would not remember or know about oral examination-in-chief and could not care less which format was used. Since most members are recent appointees and are not ex-litigators, this advantage, today, is largely gone.

Questions and answers also have a certain punchiness that mere headings do not. They seem a bit more dramatic, and help to focus the mind of the reader on the question being asked. On the negative side, because everyone knows that the questions as well as the answers are drafted by the witness, it makes the whole exercise appear somewhat contrived. Also, from a cross-examiner's viewpoint, it is often easier to pick holes in badly drafted questions than in mere headings.

What expert witnesses fail or decline to say may be more important than what they do say. These holes in the evidence tend to be easier to spot with the question and answer format because that format highlights more vividly when a witness has posed the wrong question. For example, a typical question in environmental impact statements is: "What will be the impact of the project on bird-nesting habitats during the construction phase?" Note that the question does not ask what will happen after the construction phase, when there may well be continued and even more serious long term impacts. Had there merely been a heading "Impact on Bird Nesting Habitat", without specifying that this was limited to the construction period, the cross-examiner might never spot this omission.

The essay format has the advantage that it is not expected to conform to any particular set of questions, permitting the witness to use any headings considered desirable. The disadvantage may be that in the absence of specific questions to pose to oneself, the memorandum may be less focused.

(c) A Common Core of Content

To obtain the advantages of both the question-and-answer and the essay format, it is suggested that all memoranda of evidence try to answer the following three questions:

1. What were you asked to do?
2. What did you do?
3. What did you find?

The first question we have already discussed. There should simply be a heading (or question, if one wishes to use that format) identifying the witness' assignment.

The second question is necessary because in many cases the witness did not do precisely what was asked. That may be because the original assignment proved too expensive in relation to the size of the client's budget, or that there was insufficient time to carry out the work, or that interrogatory responses were inadequate to provide the full range of data necessary to do all of what was assigned. As well, frequently the assignment is, of necessity, rather open-ended, to allow the witness a considerable amount of latitude as the work proceeds. There is likely to be extensive dialogue between the witness and the client (or the client's lawyer) throughout the interrogatory process and the cross-examination of the proponent's witnesses. During this process new opportunities will be created and old ones foreclosed. Accordingly, until the memorandum of evidence is actually completed, it will be difficult for the witness to describe precisely how much of the original assignment was done or left undone.

Nevertheless, an important part of any memorandum of evidence is to specify in some detail what was done. This allows the tribunal to assess the thoroughness of the preparation of the witness, including, where this information is helpful, blind alleys or approaches which were examined or abandoned in favour of better techniques. Not only does this history show the full extent of the work done, it adds an element of objectivity to the final result because the witness has shared with the tribunal the reasons for having rejected alternative approaches. Also, it can save a great deal of time in cross-examination because the cross-examiner is always looking for weaknesses or errors in method, particularly if the witness appears to have something to hide. This is often assumed to be the case if the experts of the other party are unable to replicate the calculations of the witness because the methods or raw numbers have not been provided. Hence the answer to "What did you do?" should not be a mere sentence or two but should, perhaps in an appendix to the memorandum, set out in detail the data collected, the methods of collection and the calculations performed.

The findings should appear in two places in the memorandum. First, right near the beginning, either in the form of a brief executive summary or as a summary of conclusions. This enables the tribunal to see immediately what the witness found. At the end of the memorandum, the findings should again be set out, this time in detail, to enable the tribunal to see clearly the linkages between what was done by way of research and analysis and how this led to the expert's conclusions.

A memorandum of evidence should not contain recommendations unless for some special reason the witness is called upon to make them. Because a recommendation is essentially an *argument* as to what *ought* to be done, it should be made by counsel in final argument rather than by a witness. Otherwise, the witness appears to be an advocate and, thus, to be biased.

There is nothing wrong with a witness saying, for example, that if a particular project is constructed it will have a serious negative impact on wild fowl in the subject area. It is quite another for the witness to go beyond that and to say that therefore, the project should not be constructed. The latter is a value judgment in which the witness has no expertise. About the furthest one could go in the direction of giving a recommendation without actually doing so would be to address the issue of how the destruction of the wild fowl habitat could be avoided. If the answer is that it can only be avoided by not proceeding with the project because no mitigation measure would be adequate, that is about the strongest statement the witness can make.

(d) Major Difficulties Commonly Found in Witness' Memoranda of Evidence

Witnesses who habitually testify for large corporate clients present evidence that is very slick. It has often been finely tuned by being presented over and over again in other hearings so that virtually every sentence has been tested in cross-examination. Any aspect of the evidence which has ever given problems is likely to have been replaced. Unfortunately, witnesses for interveners do not have this same opportunity. Many interveners, particularly in environmental cases, are local groups participating for the first time. Most consumer groups, although of some longevity, can intervene only with limited frequency before a very small number of boards. All of these groups have very small budgets and cannot afford to pay their witnesses to do a large amount of work very thoroughly. There is a tendency for the witness to work for the group on a one-time basis, but not repeatedly. This means that the witness has neither the budget nor the repeat opportunity to fine-tune the memorandum of evidence to meet the specialized needs of that tribunal, that client, and that type of case. What, then, are the typical rough spots in the evidence of interveners' witnesses?

The largest single problem is the unarticulated assumption. Most interveners' expert witnesses have PhDs and work or have worked in a university setting. They tend to teach graduate students or to do their own research among their peers, where there is a high level of intelligence and great familiarity with the work they do. After some years in this environment, it becomes difficult to understand how to explain to others who lack this training the significance of their findings. In short, they have become very poor communicators with anyone but their peers.

The more intelligent the witness, usually the more difficult he finds it to understand what it is that other people do not understand about his work. He will take many ideas for granted that others do not. Something too obvious to bother saying will appear as a major leap in logic to the inexpert reader. This is where the lawyer or client can help the witness enormously. Rather than being intimidated by the witness' brilliance, the non-expert should ask the witness to explain anything he does not understand. Only in that way can the ultimate reader, who is likely to be much more like the non-expert, follow the evidence in a logical, step-by-step fashion. Undoubtedly this will make the evidence seem rather pedantic to the witness, but the reader will certainly appreciate it.

A second major problem is the failure to provide an adequate background for the evidence. A background section of basic theory is useful and, indeed, with many tribunals it is necessary to provide it regardless of how long the members of the tribunal may have held their positions. An engineer lacking a basic grounding in economics may bandy about economic concepts for years without really being able to reason very well as an economist, and vice versa. It is probably fair to say that no-one ever lost a case by underestimating the expertise of a tribunal. In many cases, the opposite has been fatal.

Given all the frustrations of working with a tribunal, staff members tend to be lured away by other government departments with more powerful policy roles, by universities, by consulting companies or major corporations. Those who do stay may find it difficult to develop or preserve their expertise in an environment in which there is no time or opportunity for original research, for study, for cross-pollination of ideas with other members of the same discipline or with those drawn from other, related disciplines. Thus, the expert witness will often find it necessary to educate the staff as well as the tribunal. It could be fatal to assume, merely because the tribunal deals with, for example, cost of capital evidence regularly, that its members really understand it and can manipulate the data. In some cases, they will either accept this evidence on faith, or reject it for lack of faith, in large measure in accordance with the impression they have of the witnesses presenting the evidence and the consequences of acceptance or rejection on the final result.

A third major problem is a lack of coordination between the witness' evidence and the final argument. There is nothing more disheartening than to see a witness prepare and present evidence which, when all is said and done, is inconclusive. The fact that the evidence is presented at all indicates a breakdown in communications between the intervener's staff or counsel and the expert witness, due to failure to plan the case strategy properly by working backwards from the ultimate order sought. It is essential that the expert witness be made party to the case strategy — which, of course, cannot be done unless there is a clearly defined strategy. Assuming that there is, the witness should understand and agree to the need to draw expert conclusions on a specified list of subjects so that these can form the basis of recommendations to be made in final argument.

If the witness is unqualified to provide such conclusions, or is uncertain about whether it will be possible at the end of the applicant's evidence to do so, a serious discussion will have to take place. The witness may have to be replaced with someone else who has different credentials. Or, the budget for the witness' evidence will have to be increased. Or, strategies for interrogatories and cross-examination will have to be changed. Or, if none of these will work, the case strategy itself will have to be changed. Ultimately, however, if the intervener is unable to find an expert witness who can in all good conscience and with sufficient data support a particular conclusion, the party may have to reconsider whether anything useful can be accomplished in the case.

(e) Timing Problems

What a witness can put in the memorandum depends considerably upon two aspects of timing; first, the amount of time permitted for preparation and, second, the stage of the hearing at which it is presented. Some tribunals, in the mistaken belief that this procedure is fairer, will require all parties to submit their evidence on the same day. The result is to prevent a dialectical process in which the interveners can respond to the evidence of the proponent. It also makes the evidence of interveners much less informed and, therefore, less useful than would be the case if the more usual practice were followed. The usual practice is to permit interveners to file their evidence a reasonable interval after the cross-examination of the proponent has been completed. In that way, the interveners' evidence can incorporate both interrogatory responses and answers to questions obtained during cross-examination. And, perhaps of greatest importance, the witness for the intervener will have had the opportunity to be present in the hearing room during the cross-examination of the witnesses for the proponent, to brief and assist the cross-examiner.

(f) The Witness as Critic

This presence during cross-examination (or reading the transcripts) should enable the witness to prepare a detailed critique of all aspects of the evidence of the opposing side's witness. This is seldom done by interveners because they fail to recognize that it can be done, or do not think of it. However, it can be a very useful thing to do because applicants' witnesses can often evade the thrust of questions during cross-examination, provide incomplete or misleading answers or otherwise render themselves effectively un-cross-examinable. A person with equivalent training in the same discipline can state in his evidence what the answer to a particular question put to the proponent's witness should have been. Similarly, he can state what the other expert's method should have been and what it would have shown had the appropriate method been used. This critique is sometimes a reasonable alternative to the witness for the intervener devising and employing his own detailed and costly study. Usually the onus is not on the intervener to provide a better study than the applicant, in which case it will suffice merely to show that what that applicant's witness has done is unsatisfactory. What follows is an interesting example of such a detailed critique from a recent telecommunications hearing before the CRTC.

A Bell Canada witness, Dr. Morin, was testifying on the issue of what would then be a fair rate of return for Bell Canada, employing a highly controversial technique called the "comparable earnings" method. As part of this technique, he attempted to look at the earnings of companies which he described as comparable, over a time period which he described as the business cycle. His conclusions[2] were:

> The group of industrials which survived those stringent quality tests has provided an average return of 14.23 percent over the last ten years as shown

---

2 Exhibit B-87-350 RR88, p. 31.

in the last column of the top panel in Exhibit B-87-357 RR88, page 2.
The reason for working with a 10-year average of realized returns is that
by averaging achieved returns over time, cyclical aberrations are dampened, and cyclical peaks and troughs are attenuated.

The National Anti-Poverty Organization (NAPO), an intervener in the hearing, retained as expert witnesses Dr. Berkowitz and Dr. Booth from the University of Toronto to examine Dr. Morin's methods and conclusions. Their study, in addition to employing several different techniques to determine the fair rate of return, provided an extensive critique of all of the evidence of the several Bell Canada rate-of-return witnesses. With respect to the particular portion of Dr. Morin's evidence we have been discussing, Dr. Berkowitz and Dr. Booth observed:[3]

> Users of the comparable earnings test generally agree that the time period over which to estimate prospective returns is an entire business cycle, yet cycles can only be accurately measured in the past, once completed. As to forecasting the business cycle, it is only the subjective judgement of the individual as to where we are presently in a business cycle.

More specifically, the time period was criticized:[4]

> Dr. Morin's comparable earnings testimony also suffers from his choice of time period, 1977-86. This ten year period covers parts of three business cycles, i.e. 1977, 1978-84, and 1985-86. While incorporating the expansionary phases of the last cycle and the present cycle within his ten year time frame, Dr. Morin does not include the corresponding troughs. Hence, his ten-year historical return figure of 14.23 percent which he applies to Bell Canada for 1988 is upward biased.
>
> . . .
>
> The importance of Schedule 5 is twofold: first, profitability and the business cycle are measured in *real* terms, in the same way that economic growth is measured; and second, it reveals quite clearly that over the past eleven years measuring from peak to peak, we have one business cycle beginning in 1978 and finishing around 1984 and the final 'up parts' of another business cycle ending in 1978 and the beginning 'up parts' of a third business cycle beginning in 1985. To treat the whole period as one cycle, as Dr. Morin has done, is to effectively include two complete peaks and only one complete trough, resulting in an upwardly biased average accounting return on equity estimate.

This observation clearly had the desired effect because the CRTC's conclusion on this aspect of the evidence stated:[5]

---

3 NAPO Exhibit 4, at p. 11.
4 *Ibid.*, at p. 12; also p. 14 and schedule 5.
5 Telecom Decision CRTC 88-4, March 17, 1988, p. 79.

The Commission also has some reservations about Dr. Morin's comparable earnings analysis. In essence, the Commission agrees with Ontario and NAPO that the 10-year period used in his analysis was chosen on a basis that is inconsistent with economic theory. It includes two peaks and only one trough. Furthermore, a substantial portion of the time period is characterized by unusually high rates of inflation. For these reasons, the Commission found Dr. Morin's comparable earnings result to be of minimal assistance in establishing an ROE range for Bell.

This illustration provides an object lesson in how an expert witness should not present evidence: by selecting a time period which will produce a biased result. Hereafter, this Commission is likely to be very careful whenever it examines this witness' evidence. It also shows the proper use of expert witnesses by the other side. NAPO could have attempted, through cross-examination, to get Dr. Morin to admit that he had selected a period which would bias the results upward, but he is far too shrewd and experienced a witness ever to be forced to concede that. The most a cross-examiner could ever have obtained from him is a comment to the effect that: "That may be your opinion, counsel, but it isn't mine". Since lawyers are not expert economists, not much weight would be given to the lawyer's opinion. Rather, the graphic depiction of these business cycles in Schedule 5 of the appendix to the evidence of Dr. Berkowitz and Dr. Booth, clearly showing two peaks and one trough rather than two peaks and two troughs, was persuasive because it was prepared by persons with comparable expertise.

It is, of course, by no means certain that Dr. Morin selected his ten-year period deliberately to bias the results. It is quite possible that it was inadvertent. Nevertheless, because he is a witness with many years' experience, unfortunately for him the more cynical view may prevail, even if unjustified. To avoid having one's evidence rejected and credibility jeopardized in this way, it is not enough for a witness arbitrarily to select a time period such as ten years and to use that, without looking at the consequences of expanding or contracting the period under examination. Thus, if, for example, 13 and seven years produced drastically different results from ten years' data, it may be desirable to provide three graphs, one for each time period, and then to select the time span the witness regards as the most appropriate, with reasons for that selection. At least that way, if the other side argues that a longer or shorter time period is better, the witness' reasons have already been provided and there is no possibility of arguing that he attempted to do something clever or misleading.

Time periods are only one way in which results can be deliberately or inadvertently biased. For example, in deciding which companies are "comparable", one must use certain criteria such as company size or volatility of stock prices. Whatever the arbitrary cut-off points for these selections, if a small but reasonable expansion or contraction of these cut-off points significantly changes the results, as it often may do, that can give the impression that the witness chose the particular cut-off with a particular result in mind. Again, the witness should include a few more companies or a few less in the sample to demonstrate that it does not make much difference. If this cannot be shown, then the technique itself is rather arbitrary and does not justify a high level of confidence.

(g) The Distortions of the Adversary Process

Despite strong reliance on technique as an aid to judgment, in virtually every field, expert witnesses must use a great deal of personal judgment both in the selection of the appropriate technique and in its employment to analyze results. Such evidence is as much art as it is science. Major corporations and government agencies are usually the applicants/proponents in tribunal hearings employing expert witnesses. These parties have virtually limitless resources in hiring a small army of the best. An expert without equivalent knowledge (if not testifying experience), of not only theory but its practical application to the issues in the hearing, would be better off declining to participate.

The public hearing forum is a very special kind of game. It is not so much an objective search for the truth as it is a modern version of the medieval trial by battle. As such, it tends to create its unique distortions in the way in which evidence is perceived. It rewards quick thinkers rather than deep thinkers. It encourages over-simplified answers rather than over-complicated questions.

Communications skills are more important than pure expertise. In many cases, a professional witness with merely a masters degree and a strong sense of "street smarts" will be much more persuasive to the typical tribunal than will a distinguished scholar with a PhD who has written a text in the field but has difficulty in communicating simply and clearly to the tribunal. To some extent, the intervener's lawyer can compensate for the lack of experience of the witness, provided that the lawyer has such experience and can communicate with the witness. However, from the witness' standpoint, the ultimate constraint is not merely "Is this conclusion right?", but "Have I communicated this right conclusion effectively?". Tribunals all too frequently have no choice but to accept theoretically incorrect answers which are comprehensible to them in preference to theoretically correct ones which they do not understand.

The role of the witness is not primarily to write a piece of evidence for peer group review (although it should withstand that too, of course), but to make a tribunal feel secure in accepting that conclusion. If the witness understands that his role is not to outsmart the other side's expert but to make the tribunal feel comfortable in adopting his conclusions, that will force concentration on communications problems. It may seem bizarre, and even unjust, that the truth does not always win. Nevertheless, the public hearing process is what it is and always will be: a very fallible human process in which human needs, like comfort with the witness and confidence in his evidence, tend to predominate over intellectual pyrotechnics. For a witness, then, it is better to be seen as trustworthy than brilliant.

4. RE-EXAMINATION

Although a considerable amount has been written on the subject of how to prepare evidence-in-chief or to prepare for cross-examination, very little has been written about re-examination. It is also used rather seldom, perhaps because it is so poorly understood.

The purpose of re-examination is to enable the witness to clarify on the record matters which have been left in a state of confusion or obscurity. This does not mean that the witness is merely to be given a "second bite at the apple"; particularly offensive would be any attempt of the witness merely to repeat or expand upon what has been stated earlier.

In a good, vigorous cross-examination there is a substantial likelihood that the witness' views will have become obscured.

It is one of the techniques of a cross-examiner to ask questions in such a fashion as to make it appear as if the witness has backed off many of the important statements made in the written memorandum, so as to be able to say in final argument that the witness was unable to withstand cross-examination. If the tribunal were to examine the evidence and the cross-examination minutely, it might recognize that this claim was a gross exaggeration. However, it would be imprudent to take the chance that the tribunal, or even its staff, was that precise. In a lengthy and exhausting hearing, more likely, all that will be left are general impressions — often wrong ones.

If the waters have been muddied during cross-examination it is important to attempt to "unmuddy" them during re-examination. But this may not always be easy to do and, indeed, if re-examination is not conducted properly the result may be to obscure completely what was merely slightly confusing.

The usual difficulty with re-examination is that it begins as soon as cross-examination is finished. Witnesses and counsel are usually unprepared. There are two suggested solutions. First, anticipate and prepare for re-examination well before cross-examination so that the techniques of communication between counsel and witness will have been worked out in advance; second, if necessary ask the tribunal for a brief adjournment to allow witness and counsel to consult as to the parts of the evidence on which re-examination will be required.

Not every tribunal will grant an adjournment, particularly if it is inexperienced with re-examination. However, an argument that only ten minutes is sought, that this will help clarify the evidence and make it easier for the tribunal to arrive at its decision, will often be sufficient.

The possibility of counsel and witness discussing evidence together at this stage of the proceedings may cause some very legalistic lawyers to react negatively. In courts of law, once a witness enters the witness box and is subject to cross-examination, conferences between counsel and witness are considered improper or unethical for fear that the lawyer will tell the witness what to say and, thus, will distort the witness' evidence. It is by no means clear that this same restriction applies to the situation of administrative tribunals. It may be argued that legal ethics are legal ethics and apply wherever the lawyer practises. True, but legal ethics are situational and different situations require different considerations. The purpose of the rule in courts of law is to prevent the lawyer, who is usually much more sophisticated in these matters than the lay witness, from influencing the latter's testimony. In most administrative tribunals, however, most witnesses know far more about the subject matter than do their counsel. Thus, it is unlikely that the lawyer can have anything useful to add to a witness' evidence. Since the expert witness is usually relatively impartial (that is, has no personal financial stake in the outcome, unlike the witness in a civil trial, and certainly is not going to go to jail, as in a criminal trial, if his evidence is rejected) the concerns of the court of law are largely irrelevant. Nevertheless, there have been cases in which lawyers have attempted to make an issue of this. While the best thing the tribunal could do would be simply to ignore these court-like strictures as vastly overestimating the knowledge and importance of lawyers, the next best thing would be to permit the witness to discuss the topics to be dealt with on re-examination, without discussing in detail the content of what the witness is expected to say.

Another problem with re-examination is that the witness cannot be asked leading questions, just as in examination-in-chief. If the tribunal applies this restriction too strictly the dialogue between the lawyer and the witness will seem contrived and the witness is likely to answer "I don't understand what you are getting at, can you put the question another way?" The lawyer may be unable, with no opportunity for prior discussion with the witness, to prepare a carefully worded list of non-leading questions which nevertheless reveal to the witness what is sought. That may be why so few lawyers even bother with re-examination, rationalizing their being intimidated by these difficulties with the excuse that by now the tribunal has heard both points of view.

Preparing for re-examination should be done by both the lawyer and the witness independently. Agree beforehand that each of you will have a pen of a certain colour at hand, and will make an asterisk or other mark in the margin of the written evidence beside a point which, after cross-examination, has been left obscure. It is a relatively easy matter during the adjournment (or even if none is permitted) for at least the lawyer to spot these marks and to re-examine on them. Where an adjournment is granted so that the lawyer and witness can confer, they should compare their lists of asterisks and decide which areas will be re-examined. In this discussion, greater weight should be given to the impression of the lawyer rather than the expert, for two reasons. First, under cross-examination the witness is more likely to be thinking about what answers to give next than to be paying attention to the overall impression left before the tribunal. Although this is not necessarily true with the best expert witnesses, who usually watch the faces of the board members rather than the opposing counsel, many witnesses are less likely than their lawyers are to notice board members frowning or scratching their heads in confusion. Unfortunately, most board members are reluctant to interrupt cross-examination, even in these circumstances, and will simply continue to be confused unless positive steps are taken by the witness or the lawyer to correct the confusion. Second, as the lawyer is usually a non-expert, he will be more sensitive to the points at which the tribunal became lost because he probably became lost at the same points.

If cross-examination has extended for several days, and if a daily transcript of the proceedings is available, the expert should be given a copy of the transcript as quickly as possible to review it for purposes of re-examination. In the absence of this, the lawyer or someone else should attempt to make careful notes of communication problems and bring these to the witness' attention.

Particular illustrations of useful types of questions which can be asked on re-examination are:

Q. On page .... of your evidence you said X and during cross-examination by lawyer Jones on this point you said XY. Is there a contradiction between these two statements? [Or, are these two statements really different?]

Q. In your examination-in-chief you estimated the amount to be 12.52 but during cross-examination you conceded that you had overestimated one of the variables by 50 percent. Can you clarify what the impact of this error in estimation would be on the final result and, therefore, on your conclusion?

Since this answer may require new information not already on the record, it may make the witness liable to further cross-examination on the new information. Nevertheless, the evidence that the error was immaterial to the conclusion is usually important enough to justify the further risk.

Q. During cross-examination lawyer Smith asked you a question and wanted you to answer "yes or no", and then did not give you an opportunity to explain your answer. [Or interrupted you before you were finished.] Had you been allowed to complete what you were going to say on that point, what would you have said?

The latter technique is effective revenge against those cross-examiners who try to bully witnesses to say only what they permit them to say.

Q. During cross-examination you were asked the question "Given the facts X and Y, would your conclusion not be disproved?" and you stated that it would. However, you were not asked to state your views on those factual assumptions which you were asked to make. Would you care to comment on these now?

The latter is a very good defence against the clever cross-examiner's technique of forcing witnesses to accept assumptions in which they do not believe, or to make choices between two equally unattractive alternatives when there are better options available.

The effect of a good re-examination can frequently be devastating to what appeared until then to be a very successful cross-examination. A competent witness will usually not be forced by a cross-examiner to repudiate his evidence, although a clever cross-examiner can make it *appear* as if that is what the witness had done. A good re-examination can correct that appearance. Moreover, a witness who is confident that his lawyer is skilled in the inevitable scramble that is re-examination will feel more confident during cross-examination that he will be given a fair opportunity later to correct inaccurate impressions left by the cross-examiner. This confidence will permit the witness to be less defensive and argumentative during cross-examination, which will leave a better impression with the tribunal.

19

The Management of
a Major Regulatory Case

The overwhelming majority of cases before administrative tribunals are short. Some tribunals can hear and decide several cases a day. This chapter deals with the opposite extreme, hearings which may occupy several weeks or even months. Such cases are particularly important before tribunals which determine major environmental assessment or public utilities rates; also royal commissions. Very few lawyers and even fewer citizens' groups have had any significant experience in dealing with such tribunals. Hence, there will be a tendency to underestimate the nature and kinds of resources involved. Accordingly, this chapter, which attempts a functional analysis of the management process, begins with the first and most important function, planning.

1. PLANNING

(a) Timing and Schedules

It is necessary to plan all aspects of the case, taking into account timing deadlines and the human and financial resources needed to meet them. And the plans will keep changing throughout the case.

On the assumption that every intervener will wish to take advantage of the opportunity to file interrogatories, submit expert evidence and final argument, certain lead times will have to be built into the overall schedule. It will also be assumed that the intervener has not participated in a case such as this before and, therefore, does not have counsel and expert witnesses who are familiar with this work already on retainer.

As a general principle, the intervener should try to do as much of the administrative or clerical work as possible within the organization, since employing a law firm to do this is extremely expensive. For example, law firms typically charge 25 cents or more per page for photocopying. If the client can do its own photocopying it can probably enjoy considerable savings. As well, the more keyboarding done on a volunteer basis (particularly by volunteers who have access to and are knowledgeable about computers) the better, likewise delivery of documents. Keep in mind, however, that tribunals do not like to accept sloppy work; and documents which must be delivered on a certain date cannot be late. Therefore, once someone undertakes to carry out these functions they must be done competently.

Few people recognize how long it takes to recruit counsel and expert witnesses. It is safe to assume that this process could take as long as two weeks or even a month, particularly in summer, when many people are on holiday. The Canadian market for expert witnesses is very thin, with relatively few experts available in any particular specialty. Many of these will already have been retained for several years by another party. It may be possible, in rare cases, to share such a witness with others. In most situations, however, recruiting an appropriately qualified expert witness may be the largest single challenge of the case. Of course, the rather limited resources likely to be available to the group will not make the task any easier.

It may not be possible to find an appropriate expert in the same city as the hearing or, indeed, anywhere in Canada. It may be necessary to recruit someone from the United States, where the talent pool is much larger. United States experts, however, tend to charge higher *per diem* rates and are accustomed to working with much larger budgets. To find one of them interested in the budget available to a Canadian intervener group may take a lot of very persuasive arguments. Moreover, U.S. experts have to be paid in U.S. dollars, which increases their cost in Canadian dollars very substantially. An intervener seeking an award of costs may also raise a lot of eyebrows on the part of the tribunal as to why the group was unable to obtain a suitably qualified

Canadian expert who could be paid in Canadian dollars. Nevertheless, because the U.S. experts seem to spend more of their time testifying than their counterparts in Canada, and will have more of the relevant comparative information at their fingertips, a higher *per diem* rate will still be worth while if they can accomplish proportionately more in fewer days.

Recruitment of counsel is also a difficult task, particularly in the less populous provinces or smaller cities. Even in the larger cities it may be difficult to find an experienced regulatory counsel who is not already retained by one of the other participants. If the group can afford it, it may be necessary to retain someone from outside the province with direct experience before that type of tribunal. Obviously, one's chances of recruiting the best lawyer at the least cost are likely to be increased by starting the search sooner rather than later. As well, lawyers will often know who are the best experts. Accordingly, it is advisable to retain the lawyer first, and to use him to help recruit the expert witnesses. However, if one happens to know and to have a good relationship with an experienced expert witness, one could proceed the other way around and have the witness suggest the names of lawyers.

It is fair to assume that it will take at least two weeks, and probably twice that long to examine initially a major submission of a proponent or applicant. It will, of course, have to be re-examined several times with the assistance of lawyers and various experts as the case progresses. The initial examination referred to here is only enough to allow someone to understand what the basic issues are and are not, so as to enable him to prepare to retain the appropriate lawyer or experts for more detailed advice and assistance.

Ideally, if time permits, the intervention statement should not be filed until the experts have been retained and have gone over the application (or environmental impact statement, or whatever) carefully, so as to ensure that the intervener is not precluded from raising any essential arguments or lines of cross-examination by an intervention statement which has failed to focus its attention on any issue of concern to the group. If the search for the lawyer and for the experts proceeds in tandem, the total process, from receiving the information to the completion of the intervention statement, should be approximately four to six weeks.

Then, the process of preparing interrogatories in a complex case would normally take approximately two weeks. The responses to these are rarely required to be provided in less than two weeks and, often, the other side will be allowed a month to respond. During that time, there is not much that the intervener can be doing if the interrogatories filed are numerous and if the evidence does not make much sense without them. However, assuming a reasonably good initial submission by the other side, the absence of interrogatory responses should be no impediment to the preparation of such portions of the evidence as can work around the gaps.

The preparation of a witness' memorandum of evidence normally takes at least a month, and often two. Therefore, the preliminary research and writing must begin virtually immediately, at least for the portion critiquing the application. It should also be written on the assumption that the interrogatories will provide few responses of any value because, sad to say, that is all too often the case.

The length of the hearing itself is almost impossible to forecast. Experience suggests, however, that most tribunals grossly underestimate the length of time their own hearings will take. This is in part because they add the estimates of the parties' lawyers and most lawyers grossly underestimate how long their cross-examinations take. A fair rule of thumb is to take the estimated cross-examination time for a particular witness and to double it. If a lawyer advises that it will take two days to cross-examine a particular witness, assume three or four days because the answers will never be quite what the lawyer expected or wanted.

Part of the difficulty of forecasting is created by a large number of parties. Sometimes, each party will have planned a unique and different cross-examination, so that each will cross-examine as if the others do not exist. In many other cases, however, there is a sufficient overlap in the positions of the parties that after the first one or two cross-examiners have finished, there will be a lot less for the others to do. The subsequent cross-examiners will have overestimated how long they will take and, therefore, the total time to be taken by the cross-examination of that witness may be less rather than more than the total of the time estimated by the various lawyers.

Nor does experience help in forecasting. One lawyer may be quite inaccurate in estimating cross-examination for the first three witnesses and be very accurate thereafter, and vice versa. Since cross-examination is an interactive process, as much depends on the witness as on the lawyer. For that reason, asking a lawyer to estimate the length of his cross-examination is a bit like asking a boxer how many rounds a boxing match is likely to last. So much depends on the other person that there is no real way to forecast accurately.

During the course of the hearing, the tribunal will set various deadlines. One of the more important ones is the relationship between the close of interrogatories and the opening of the hearing. Logically, an applicant should not be permitted to proceed to a hearing until all interrogatory responses have been properly completed. But some tribunals seem more interested in speed than quality of cross-examination and assume that somehow it can all be made up, even if some interrogatory responses arrive right in the middle of the cross-examination! That is because it is not often understood by tribunal members (few of whom have had any practice experience before tribunals) that it may take as long as a week of research and analysis to prepare an hour of good cross-examination, whereas slow and tiresome cross-examination can be prepared much more quickly. Ideally, there should be an interval of at least a week or two from the time satisfactory interrogatory responses are received to the time cross-examination begins so that one may prepare cross-examination using the interrogatory responses.

Another critical interval is the time between the conclusion of the cross-examination of the witnesses for the applicant and the calling of the evidence by the interveners. Ideally, this should be at least two weeks and preferably as long as a month. In that way, the experts working for the interveners can analyze all of the cross-examinations, interrogatories and memoranda of evidence and perform such mathematical calculations and text writing and editing as may be necessary to prepare a coherent memorandum of their own. Unfortunately, many tribunals are unaware of what it takes to prepare a coherent memorandum of evidence and, although the proponent's experts may have had several months to prepare, insist that interveners' evidence should be presented almost immediately after the conclusion of the applicant's witness' cross-examination. This is often unfair to interveners because their witnesses may be asked by the applicant's lawyer whether they were aware of a certain answer having been given in cross-examination by the applicant's witness, and may have to state that they were not because the cut-off date they had to use for the preparation of their evidence was several weeks earlier. This then unfairly damages the credibility of the intervener's evidence. It also means the tribunal does not get the best evidence.

The final important interval is the time between the conclusion of cross-examination of the expert witnesses called by interveners and the commencement of final argument. Ideally, this should be no less than two weeks but is often not more than a few days. Two weeks is necessary to permit the interveners' experts (as well as those of the applicant) to analyze the cross-examination of their own evidence in the context of the rest of the evidence and to assist counsel in the preparation of final argument. Even with the world's best indexing system, final argument requires a kind of serenity of thought, a detachment not possible when one is working around the clock merely to organize the data necessary to buttress the final arguments.

What should happen rarely happens in practice. Timetables are rushed and the quality of evidence and argument suffers accordingly. Nevertheless, the key to presenting an intervention which is at least coherent and credible (as opposed to one which gets further and further behind and ultimately falls apart) is a combination of planning and flexibility. The original timetable will have to be revised periodically as new events take place. Sometimes a tribunal will announce a deadline (such as Christmas) in the hope that everyone will want to finish by then. Things may be right on track until fairly shortly before then and, to ensure that the deadline is met, the tribunal may be encouraged to telescope several steps into one, chopping out time for preparation by reducing some of the critical intervals discussed above. A panicky tribunal may extend the hearing to evening sittings, rendering effective preparation for the next day well-nigh impossible. The ability to cope with these accelerated timetables requires contingency plans. As the possibility looms that the tribunal may cut down on these crucial preparation intervals, plan for that, rather than assuming that all will continue to be well.

(b) Personnel

We have so far been discussing only timing and must now consider staff resources as well. A key problem with interventions in major cases is that there are never enough people to do all the work. It will often be necessary to have more than one competent secretary available on a full-time basis. If the forecast was that the hearing will end in three months and Mrs. Jones can act as secretary on a volunteer basis until September, when her baby is due, it is not impossible that the hearing will still be in progress when her baby reaches its first birthday. This is especially true if the tribunal has been given a firm, fixed deadline by the government. Such deadlines are notoriously unrealistic and are almost always exceeded, sometimes by a factor of two or more.

If Ms. Brown is going to be the lawyer for this hearing until September, when she has to go to Yellowknife to handle a major environmental hearing which will last six months, it should not be assumed that she will be able to complete the first hearing. If the hearing continues two or three times longer than was forecast it will be very difficult for a new lawyer to arrive just at the time the first one leaves, and to take over immediately. Too much evidence will have gone by for an easy change in counsel. Accordingly, a client should seek a commitment from the lawyer that she can finish the hearing however long it takes, or can provide adequate alternative counsel who can be briefed early enough, and can overlap for a while, to take over when necessary.

In major regulatory cases the quantity of paper is usually such that anyone who is working at the hearing all day will find it difficult to keep track of it all. The author has found it useful to hire persons such as librarians with cataloguing skills or persons who are competent in preparing computerized indexes of the materials. (Some tribunals themselves prepare an index of the evidence for their own use but this may be of limited use because the issues they may be interested in are not the ones the intervener is interested in. This in itself is a problem which a party should attempt to redress by asking the tribunal to include this party's issues in the index but, in any event, some indexing and cataloguing based on the party's own priorities will be essential.) Similarly, while one person is busy at the hearing, paperwork such as writing notices of motion, opening piles of mail in the form of interrogatory responses from other parties, or service of various documents will require considerable clerical time. It is extremely expensive to have lawyers or expert witnesses doing this. Some sort of paralegal, junior economist, junior lawyer or experienced volunteer would be very useful. Just as a good general must always have a few troops in reserve, a wise intervener will recognize that its resources are likely to be stretched and to keep a few people on standby.

2. ORGANIZING THE PAPER

Participants at regulatory hearings often are unaware that they will need several copies of the information and evidence collected during the hearing. One copy will usually have to be kept at the hearing room itself, either on the table assigned to the participant or in a filing cabinet or storage boxes kept on site. That is because the volume of paper will be too large to carry back and forth between the hearing room and the office or hotel room the hearing team will be occupying. Typically, in a hearing in which there are five or more parties, each filing interrogatories, the interrogatory questions and responses will fill from three to ten three-ring binders of the 2-inch size. (A better alternative may be to use special catalogue binders which are much stronger and can be expanded by several inches.) If these interrogatories are not all available at the hearing, Murphy's Law will surely apply and the witness being cross-examined will refer to the interrogatory which was left in the office. The author's practice in major hearings is to make an arrangement beforehand with the clerk or secretary of the tribunal to permit the storage of a three or four-drawer filing cabinet (at the back of the hearing room or in some adjacent storage room or cupboard) so that the papers used at the hearing can be put away, locked, every night.

Since the time of lawyers and expert witnesses is expensive, it will not be cost effective to have only one set of materials to be shared. Each expert should be given a complete set of the materials relevant to his specialty, and a complete set of everything should be stored in the office as well as at the hearing.

This may mean four or five sets of some materials and at least two sets of everything. This amount of photocopying is not inexpensive. Resources can be saved, however, if an arrangement is made with the applicant early on to provide as many copies as will be required. Since the applicant usually prints or photocopies these in bulk, it will be more economical for the applicant to provide two copies of everything and three or four copies of some things than for the intervener to photocopy the entire mass of materials to make one copy. Not all applicants, of course, are willing to cooperate in this way. If the tribunal awards costs, the applicant can usually be persuaded that it will have less to pay at *its* photocopying cost than if the intervener charges the going rate (about 25¢ per page).

If the applicant is uncooperative, a letter to the tribunal setting out the reasons for requesting not one but two copies of all of the materials may assist in obtaining that cooperation as the applicant may not wish to appear to impose higher costs upon an intervener than it itself would incur by providing an additional copy. Moreover, as most applicants are large government institutions or major corporations, the cost of an additional photocopy is normally trivial in comparison to the amounts they will be spending on the hearing itself.

With respect to the transcript, there is a greater problem. It is convenient to maintain one copy at the hearing room and one in the office. However, under the copyright arrangements usually made between court reporters and their customers one is not permitted to photocopy a transcript. A second copy of the transcript is not as expensive as the first (usually $1.50 per page for the first, .50¢ for the second), but still far more expensive than the photocopying cost itself. There are a number of options.

First, one may request the court reporter to provide a computer diskette instead of or in addition to a hard copy of the transcript. With a computer diskette, one can print as many copies as are necessary, either using the computer's printer or a combination of the printer and the photocopier. But at the present time, relatively few court reporters offer diskettes on a timely basis and, in some cases, they are prepared using equipment which is not compatible with ordinary personal computers. This is a matter it is to be hoped that the tribunals will rectify as the new contracts with their court reporters are negotiated.

Another option would be to transport back and forth the transcripts of the last few days only, keeping the earlier transcripts in the office. This runs the risk that an unavailable volume will be referred to at the hearing and one will have to scramble to borrow an extra copy of it from another participant, the court reporter or the tribunal itself. Then, one will have to find the page referred to by the witness and read the prior page to ensure that the reference is in context and accurate. This can cause an embarrassing few minutes' delay, and can make the questioner appear disorganized.

There is no doubt that it is to the cross-examiner's advantage to have every volume of the transcript, every interrogatory and every piece of evidence available at the counsel table throughout the hearing. That is also why it is very helpful to have a junior counsel, articling student or other qualified assistant sitting with the cross-examiner throughout the hearing. If a question is asked and the witness, in reply, refers to some material not currently being used, the assistant will obtain a copy from the court reporter or tribunal and check the validity of the reference while the cross-examiner can go on to ask the next question.

Another option is to purchase one copy of the transcript, take it back to the office and photocopy it. While this may be a breach of the court reporter's right to sell a photocopy, many will agree to waive this right, especially for a public interest group, because they know that there is no money to purchase a second copy in any event. Therefore, by precluding photocopying, all they are doing is making it less convenient than it otherwise would be for advocates of such a group to use their product. They are not really depriving themselves of any source of revenue that they could realistically expect to obtain. That is why if one asks nicely, many of them will say only that they do not officially want to know about it. As a practical matter, the court reporter is unlikely to find out what anyone does with the transcript back in their office and, even if he did, is unlikely to sue for breach of copyright. Nevertheless, it is always better to ask and to obtain the consent.

During the course of the hearing, almost daily, new information will be filed. There will be at least one daily volume of the transcript. As well, interrogatory responses, updates to evidence and new pieces of evidence will be filed routinely.

Again, an arrangement should be made with the applicant to provide more than one copy, if needed, to keep down photocopying costs. These materials should be inserted in appropriate three-ring or catalogue binders daily, in the proper numerical sequence. Different colours of covers could be used for interrogatories and evidence, or for submissions by different parties. As well, a running index or table of contents should be made and kept up to date, listing by number and title each exhibit that is filed. Ideally this should be done by the applicant and circulated to all the parties, revised frequently to include each additional piece of information filed. If this is not ordered by the tribunal, each party will have to undertake this exercise on its own. If the indexing is not done, a need to refer to a particular interrogatory or exhibit will require a lot of fumbling and turning of pages. It is also helpful to put in coloured or numbered tabs between every 10th exhibit (or whatever) or at the beginning of key items which will be frequently referred to.

Thus far we have been considering only collecting and filing *paper*; it is now possible to do much of this electronically. Although it is not yet a regular feature of tribunal hearing rooms in Canada, the technology is already available to permit computerization, even using personal computers, to put all of the interrogatories, exhibits and transcripts into a computer with something as small as a 20-megabyte hard disk. A very large hearing could be handled in 40 megabytes. There are laptops which can be purchased or leased with hard disks of that size. It is also possible, with the use of the modems, to keep a computer in the office loaded with a large amount of information and another at the hearing which can obtain access to it by telephone line. As well, in the same way as one can keep a set of papers at the hearing and a set in the office, a group which can afford it can use two computers, one at each location. (There is always an active market in used computers, particularly as offices upgrade, so that a good quality PC with 40 megabyte hard disk and software should be available for between $500 and $1,000. Stores have recently opened which sell last year's models and demonstrators at certain times of the year at a substantial discount.) The only difficulty may be to persuade the tribunal to provide appropriate facilities. Both courtrooms and tribunals in the United States regularly make use of computer facilities in this way, so Canada cannot be too far behind.

3. PREPARING THE EVIDENCE

(a) The Intervener's Own Evidence

As has been mentioned throughout this work, good case preparation depends on a fully articulated case strategy based upon the end result or order one wishes to obtain. Working back from there, one comes to the evidence that is necessary to produce the conclusions which will lead to that order. Assuming that the intervener will call expert evidence, a detailed outline or table of contents of that evidence should be prepared in several alternative versions, depending upon what evidence is or is not obtained through the interrogatory and the cross-examination stages. The witness should start by writing those portions of the evidence which are not dependent on this information, in particular the general explanatory portions and the description of the methods of research employed. Then, once the interrogatories are in, further portions can be prepared employing them. Finally, the whole memorandum can be assembled when the cross-examination of the other side's witnesses has been completed.

While one's expert is working on drafting one's evidence, it is necessary to be preparing for cross-examination of the applicant's witnesses.

(b) Preparing the Material for Cross-examination

For each witness to be cross-examined, prepare a three-ring binder containing the materials that are relevant to that witness. Include all of the interrogatories relating to that witness' evidence, and place tabs before those to which it is intended to refer the witness to introduce specific questions. As well, of course, include the witness' own written memorandum of evidence and perhaps examples of other testimony the witness has given in previous cases, if there has been time to examine these, or transcripts of cross-examination of this witness where he may have given contradictory or damaging answers. Finally, include the necessary question-and-answer sheets described above in Chapter 15.

Of course, when one's own witness is being cross-examined the same procedure should be duplicated. Provide the witness with a three-ring binder containing the same sorts of materials as one's own, including, for example: answers to any interrogatories the witness may have had to provide, as well as relevant interrogatory responses by other parties or by the applicant. The binder should begin with a table of contents for easy reference. All the pages should be numbered sequentially and there should be tabs at convenient locations.

(c) Organizing Final Argument

However reasonable the tribunal's time interval between the close of evidence and the presentation of argument, argument cannot be prepared adequately if left entirely to the end of the case. The interveners' hearing staff must be thinking throughout the case as to what the content of final argument will be. Some of the discrete topics within the final argument should be written as the hearing proceeds, while the memory of the key admissions and their location in the transcript is still fresh in counsel's mind. Ultimately, these preliminary portions of argument may have to be revised at the end as new issues or pieces of evidence may become even more important. However, this occurs infrequently enough that final editing is often all that is necessary to polish the argument.

Just about the worst thing to do is to wait until after the argument of the applicant. At that point, one may have at most a day or two in which to prepare a response and that clearly cannot be done adequately if references to the evidence are to be included.

In some cases, the tribunals do not stagger the final argument (that is, with the applicant preceding the respondents) but insist that the final arguments all be submitted in writing on the same day. This is not a very effective procedure because it prevents a dialogue: applicant's argument, interveners' response and final reply. Nevertheless, in those tribunals which insist upon this procedure, particularly royal commissions, before whom there may not be any formal "applicant" or "proponent", the early and continuous preparation of final argument is especially important.

(d) Management of Finances

The most difficult part of the management of a regulatory hearing is managing the money. It is not easy to offer useful advice on this since the amount of money interveners have, or will spend, can vary so enormously. Nevertheless, some general techniques which may be helpful can be summarized.

First, it is usually important to establish a budget for the entire case. This should be broken down to include individual line items such as transcripts, photocopying, transportation, long distance, courier and delivery, travel and accommodation, lawyers' fees and experts witness fees. As well, one should keep track of the intervener's own staff time and calculate an hourly rate or cost for those staff members. This is particularly important if the tribunal awards costs. Careful time logs detailing activities to the nearest 0.1 of an hour will have to be kept by all those for whose time one intends to seek costs. A reasonable overhead component can also be added to that time to cover rent, computers, stationery, etc. A rough rule of thumb might be to take the hourly cost of that employee (salary plus benefits) and to double it to cover the overhead. Specific items such as photocopying are disbursements and do not form part of this overhead calculation. Local telephone costs would be included within the overhead, whereas long distance calls would be billed separately.

When a budget of specific items has been calculated, it should then be broken down on a monthly basis in accordance with two categories: spent and committed to spend. Typically, it will be found that during the first month, virtually nothing has been spent but a substantial portion of the budget is already committed to be spent. Usually, by the time the hearing opens, as much as a third or a half of the budget may already have been spent or committed, even if all the bills are not yet in and paid. The amount of money spent and committed each month should be tracked against the budget.

If the intervener finds itself going far over budget, tough questions must be asked about why. Was the original budget completely unrealistic? Has the intervener lost control of its counsel? Has counsel lost control of the witnesses? Has the hearing suddenly taken on a life of its own with new issues not previously anticipated? Or, more typically, is the hearing simply taking much longer than everyone expected and, therefore, because time is money, becoming much more expensive? If so, there are certain — but limited — economy measures which can be introduced.

It is not always necessary to order the transcript every day. There may be some days in which what occurs may be of very little or no interest. If that is the case, instruct a court reporter very clearly not to deliver a transcript or otherwise they will do so and bill for it. Not ordering a transcript can save $200 - $300 in disbursements that day. This runs the risk, however, that something of importance will occur that day and one will not have a transcript of that day when the other side refers to it in final argument.

Also, if it is not too late, it may be possible to ask one's expert witness to decline to develop a certain portion of the evidence intended to be submitted. The risk of course, will be that one cannot deal as effectively with that issue in final argument. (If that is not the case, that portion of the witness' evidence is probably redundant.) As well, because counsel and expert witnesses are paid by the day, attendance at the hearing can be reduced, although this should only be done as a last resort. It may be possible to instruct counsel not to attend the hearing on days when evidence that is not clearly relevant to the intervener's interests is going to be submitted or cross-examined. This technique, however, has its dangers and is often false economy. If Murphy's Law is in operation, that will be the day that an important motion is made and decided and the absentee's interests will not be represented; or an important new piece of information or evidence will pop out and, if the transcript for that day is not ordered, one may not even find out about it until it may be too late.

There is also a subtle, but important, image problem created if an intervener is absent for a substantial portion of the hearing. Since the applicant and the principal interveners will be there every day throughout the case, one creates the impression of being a peripheral party if counsel for the party is consistently absent for substantial portions of the hearing. Not much money is actually saved because most competent counsel who sit at hearings while evidence of marginal relevance is being heard will not merely sit there in a state of boredom. Rather, they will listen with one ear only, while preparing final argument or drafting cross-examination questions for their next turn at cross-examination. The saving by asking counsel to stay in the office is likely to be very limited or non-existent in any hearing which is intensive and in which the intervener seeks to play a significant as opposed to a peripheral role. Since most lawyers bill the same whether they are preparing in their offices or attending at the hearing, a party may as well leave it to the discretion of its counsel to determine whether the preparation can be more effectively done at the hearing or in the office. If the team is large enough to contain a junior counsel, on certain days it may be more economical to leave junior counsel at the hearing to keep an eye on things while senior counsel is back in the office preparing for the next day's cross-examination.

The budget planning aspect of a public hearing is very much like a roller-coaster ride: once you get on it, it is very difficult to get off; but if you do jump off, you certainly cannot get back on again. Hence the budget savings and adjustments one can make are likely to be relatively minor and the intervener is, basically, along for the ride. That is why it is so important to try to budget accurately at the beginning and to keep track of the budget — both spent and committed — throughout. Insist that expert witnesses and lawyers — the largest single items of expense — provide a monthly billing or, at least, a monthly tally of hours worked. (One can then multiply by the hourly rate which has been agreed upon in the retainer to obtain a fairly good idea of the amount committed to date.) Comparing the budget one had estimated would be spent and committed at the end of each month with the actual of these expenditures and commitments will enable a party to prepare an over/under report for each item and for the total.

(e) The Planned Approach

Given the limitations of space and the wide variability in tribunal procedures and intervention situations, it would not be practical to try to anticipate every possible item for which it would be desirable to plan. Accordingly, the foregoing should be seen as illustrations only. What is important to learn from this chapter is the need for planning itself: the planned approach. Even the best plans will sometimes go awry because of unanticipated contingencies. The tribunal may reject a motion which was expected to be a sure winner, or an interrogatory response which was expected to be helpful turns out to be useless. These events may cause re-juggling of priorities. However, the need to plan for all three important elements — money, time and people — is undisputed among competent and experienced participants. If the hearing is treated like a spontaneous happening which can be made up as one goes along, that is courting disaster. On the other hand, planning with alternative strategies and fall-back positions will give greater confidence and peace of mind. To the extent that it is possible, the party will then have its participation in the hearing under its control instead of out of control or under the control of others. As a participant gains more experience at these hearings and learns to anticipate almost every possibility which might arise, his effectiveness will increase.

20

Appeals — to the Courts and to the Political Process

1. TO THE TRIBUNAL ITSELF

Some tribunals have review committees or review processes which, on request from a party at the hearing, will review the decision if certain criteria are met (e.g., new evidence which could not have been available at the time, some significant error of law or fact, or a substantial likelihood that the decision was wrong). If the decision is made to review the tribunal's decision, the review committee is usually composed of persons other than those who heard the case the first time. If the original decision is modified or reversed, that may end the matter. If not, there may still be other avenues of appeal.

2. OUTSIDE REVIEWS

There are two important distinctions between an appeal and an application for judicial review. First, an appeal may be either to a court, to a minister or to the Cabinet. Judicial review is only to a court. Second, if an appeal is successful, the court, minister or Cabinet may not only set aside the decision of the tribunal, but may also substitute a different decision of their own or may remit the matter to the tribunal for reconsideration in accordance with certain instructions. With judicial review, normally the court has no power to substitute its judgment for that of the board, but merely has the power to determine that it was improperly made and therefore should be set aside. (However, section 28 of the *Federal Court Act*[1] permits the Federal Court not only to set aside a decision of a federal tribunal, but also, to refer it back with specific instructions, which gives this specialized court, in judicial review, one of the powers of an appeal. But it does not go the further step of allowing the Federal Court to substitute a decision of its own for that of the federal board or tribunal whose decision is being quashed.) The criteria for determining when there should be an appeal or an application for judicial review, and the proper forum for each, are numerous and varied.

(a) Appeals to Minister or Cabinet

Most tribunals' decisions are final, absent serious errors of law of jurisdiction. Contrary to popular belief, there is no general right to a political appeal to a minister or to the Cabinet from decisions of most tribunals, whether federal or provincial. Such political review power is required to be expressly granted by statute. If such power exists, the grounds can be virtually anything, other than a pure question of law. Politicians will not normally entertain appeals on legal grounds because that is the function of the courts. Arguments made on appeal to the Cabinet or to a minister are usually policy and political arguments, and are discussed in greater detail below.

Since legal issues should properly be brought before the courts, it is understandable that neither the minister nor the Cabinet will want to play judge. On the other hand, since courts will only review decisions of tribunals on questions of law or jurisdiction, errors of policy or principle can only be appealed to the minister or Cabinet. The statute will determine in every case what avenues of appeal are open.

The political dependency of many tribunals makes them particularly sensitive and vulnerable to appeal to their political superiors. The federal Cabinet, in its reasons for decision in numerous cases, has stated that it will not interfere with the decision of a tribunal unless the error is a grave and weighty one and the decision is contrary to public policy. More realis-

1 R.C.S. 1985, c. F-7.

tically, perhaps, if the decision of the tribunal appears unjust or is a political liability for the government of the day, there is a chance that the appeal will succeed. The real or perceived power of the appellant together with the quality and quantity of publicity it is able to bring to the appeal may also be important factors in determining the outcome. *Nevertheless, the percentage of appeals to the minister or to the Cabinet in which the appellant is successful is extremely low.*

Carrying out an appeal to the minister or to the Cabinet can be either very simple or very complicated. At the federal level there is *no set procedure* for Cabinet appeals, so one must be worked out by the parties in consultation with the relevent minister's office. Usually the appeal will consist of a simple letter addressed to the Clerk of the Privy Council, with a copy to the appropriate minister. A copy should be sent to the tribunal and the other parties in the case. Also, a meeting with the relevant minister or his or her advisers is often permitted. Sometimes the appeal may involve the preparation of long and complicated memoranda which highlight the evidence.

Procedures vary in individual provinces. For example, in British Columbia, several statutes provide for appeals to the Cabinet or to one of its committees and in some cases this involves an oral hearing. In Ontario, the process is entirely in writing, but is well organized to ensure that all affected parties have the opportunity to make submissions.

Appeals, particularly to the political level, can be a two-edged sword. If one is successful in the appeal, there is a good chance that the tribunal will be more respectful the next time. The treatment received from *some* tribunals is in direct proportion to their perception of a party's power and influence. Others resent political interference with their independence and are likely to create the same result, but with more politically appealing reasons. However, if an intervener appeals everything and wins nothing, it can expect to be treated with very little respect.

(b) Appeals to the Courts

Most laws establishing tribunals provide expressly for some avenue of appeal to the courts for errors of law or jurisdiction.

Appeals[2] from federal regulatory tribunals go to the Federal Court of Canada and from provincial tribunals to the Court of Appeal of the province, where the statute so provides.

If the statute is silent as to an appeal, that does not mean that there is no avenue of judicial review. Although judicial review is not, strictly speaking, an "appeal," the opportunity for judicial review and setting aside of the decision is still there, through the inherent powers of the court. Indeed, this may be so even if the statute says that there is to be no judicial review, as courts will sometimes ignore such clauses.

Preparation of appeals or applications for judicial review to the courts are *highly complex, even for lawyers experienced in the field.* Such work could not be done by a non-lawyer unless he or she spends so much time training as virtually to become one. Often, too, if the case before the tribunal was not conducted by a lawyer (or was, but poorly), errors of law may not have been clarified or "set up for appeal" in the transcript. The result will be that it will be very difficult — if not impossible — to prove the error of law to the court.

If a party used a particular lawyer during the hearing it may wish to use a different lawyer for the judicial review or appeal. It is not suggested that one jump to the conclusion that because one was unsuccessful at the hearing, the lawyer did a poor job. However, not all lawyers who are good at trial advocacy are good at appellate advocacy. Moreover, if the lawyer has become emotionally involved with the result of the hearing, objectivity in the appeal may be impaired. It must, however, be recognized that bringing a new lawyer into the case involves the expense of familiarization with the evidence and the issues and, if it was a long, complex hearing this may be quite costly. A compromise may be to use the lawyer from the hearing as junior counsel to a more senior appellate counsel who has an established reputation before the court. If this court is the Federal Court of

---

2 Technically, judicial review applications are not the same as appeals, causing some difficulty as to the correct way to begin review or appeal proceedings in the Federal Court. In Ontario, certain proceedings may start in the Divisional Court; in other provinces, in the Supreme Court or Court of Queen's Bench. These technical niceties are primarily of concern to lawyers at the point of initiating proceedings, and hence of little relevance here as the standard works on judicial review, some of which are cited at the end of Supplement I below, cover this subject adequately.

Canada, the lawyer selected should have had experience before that court since its jurisdiction is extremely complex and its rules are somewhat unusual.

On the basis of statistical probabilities alone, chances of a successful judicial review application or appeal from an administrative tribunal to the courts are not very good. Nevertheless, it may be important to undertake an appeal simply to clarify what the law is. If the appeal court makes it clear that one's interpretation of the law is wrong, one is in a better position to do something constructive about it. One possibility is an appeal to a higher court (such as the Supreme Court of Canada, from the Federal Court of Appeal). Alternatively, and perhaps preferably, if there is a valid argument that the law, as now authoritatively defined by the appeal court, is unfair, the party should proceed to make a vigorous and widely-publicized presentation to the minister to change the law.

(c) When There is a Choice: Court or Politicians?

In certain circumstances an appeal may be possible either to the political level (minister or Cabinet) or to the courts, or to both. How should one decide which course to take?

When the statute permits a political appeal on a question of policy or to the courts on a question of law or jurisdiction, if the objectionable aspect of the tribunal's decision is that it ignored the evidence before it and made its decision failing to take into account some important pieces of evidence or aspects of the argument, there may be two avenues of appeal:

1. It can be alleged in an appeal to the minister that the tribunal's decision was wrong in policy;
2. It can be alleged in an appeal to the courts that the tribunal made its decision in an arbitrary, capricious or perverse manner and contrary to the evidence; in law this constitutes either an excess of jurisdiction or declining to exercise jurisdiction by deciding a matter other than the matter properly before it.

While it may appear that success can be achieved in either of two ways and, therefore, success is more likely, in fact, the opposite may be the case:

1. The minister may not wish to intervene because the argument about the evidence may sound like an argument which should be decided by the court; but by the time the minister informs the parties of this, the time to commence an appeal to the courts may have passed.
2. The court will often be sympathetic to the argument of the other side that what it is being asked to do is to substitute its judgment on a technical matter for that of the tribunal, which judges are neither qualified nor willing to do. The more complicated the evidence looks, the less likely the court is to deal with it. Since the brief time permitted to argue an application for leave to appeal is grossly insufficient to provide a cram course in chemical engineering, economic forecasting or petroleum geology to a judge who has spent a full professional life in legal matters, it will probably be difficult to show that there is even an arguable case that the tribunal decided contrary to the evidence.

If the evidence were no more complex than that something is black and the tribunal held that it was white, the court would readily find that this was a perverse decision, and would set it aside. But the evidence is rarely that simple. An equally perverse finding may be hidden in the complexities of equations or technical jargon. When the evidence is complicated, a decision based on a perverse finding of fact may be virtually unappealable.

Tribunals are often aware of this. Tribunal lawyers who help the members of the tribunals write decisions are quite clever in writing judgments that will be very difficult to appeal. If the tribunal wishes to make its decision effectively appeal-proof, all it may have to do is to summarize some of the technical evidence presented by each of the parties, indicate that it has considered and weighed all of the evidence most carefully and then put forward its conclusion — however perverse it may be. The very sight of this evidence in the tribunal's reasons for decision will be intimidating to a court. It is for this reason that appeals to the political level are important.

Unlike a judge, who usually has no expert technical staff (at most a judge will have a law clerk), the minister has access to the full resources of the department and the rest of the government. This includes both staff experts who are able to analyze the evidence and the funds to retain outside experts if necessary. When faced with what appears to be an appeal-proof judgment in the courts, consider trying a political appeal if the legislation allows it.

From the foregoing discussion one can conclude that administrative tribunals are difficult to overturn through the courts except on fairly narrow questions of law or jurisdiction. If the minister, for various political considerations which may be unknown, supports the tribunal's decision or simply does not want to become involved, a party will not go far with the political route either. All of this points to the grave importance of preparing and conducting the case effectively the first time: do not count on the appeal.

(d) Meetings with Politicians and the Tribunal

After the public hearing has concluded and after the decision has been released, there is nothing wrong with meeting with the politicians or their staff or officials or with the tribunal to discuss any matter, at least until another application has been filed with the tribunal. Because of the absence of any set procedure at the federal level, even while there is an appeal before the Cabinet itself, there is nothing wrong with meeting Cabinet ministers (or their advisers) and attempting to lobby them. Everyone does this. In provinces which have a set procedure, such as British Columbia, where a committee of Cabinet provides an oral hearing to the parties similar to that before a tribunal, making private submissions outside of this process is legally questionable.

If a tribunal no longer has before it any undecided cases involving a person, for him to discuss with the tribunal the subject-matter of anything other than the next hearing is acceptable.

Supplement 1

The Law of Administrative Procedure

1. INTRODUCTION

Administrative tribunals exercise substantial powers of decision-making. But courts have for centuries insisted on a right to review almost any decision of a tribunal when it affects the rights of individuals. We now have a large and complex body of case law which indicates when the courts will review the actions of tribunals and, upon review, what standards will be imposed. This supplement is intended to convey a very general sense of this area of law; for any detailed consideration of the law, a selected bibliography is provided at the end.

Tribunals usually derive their powers through the statute which creates the tribunal and directs it to make certain decisions. The tribunal only has such powers as are granted to it. Therefore, the most obvious basis for reviewing a decision of a tribunal is that it exceeded its statutory powers.

A second and similar basis for a court setting aside a decision of an administrative tribunal is that the tribunal failed to observe explicit statutory rules or requirements which have been imposed upon it. Such failure is another form of jurisdictional error.

Even if tribunals observe all the explicit statutory rules or requirements, and do not exceed statutory powers, that is not enough. The courts themselves impose a further set of requirements, which have traditionally been considered to be an "implied" part of the grant of powers to the tribunal. These are referred to in some cases as the "rules of natural justice", in other cases, as "fairness" and now, in the *Canadian Charter of Rights and Freedoms*, as "fundamental justice".

There are two broad rules: the rule against bias and the rule protecting the right of a party to a full and fair hearing. While neither of these rules can be defined with precision, a large body of administrative law cases provides relatively clear guidelines for acceptable conduct.

It is important for anyone who participates in administrative proceedings to have a general understanding of the rules and restrictions which both protect them and govern their conduct. Individuals who know when a tribunal's breach of statutory or common law duties may result in a successful court challenge will be more fully aware of their duties, rights and options.

2. JURISDICTION AND "ULTRA VIRES"

Historically, there has been a tendency for governments to be protective of the administrative tribunals they have created, and to give them virtually unlimited powers. Therefore, when English and Canadian courts started to review and, sometimes, to set aside the decisions of tribunals, legislatures tried to exclude the courts by legislating that the decisions of certain tribunals were to be final and unreviewable. But this intended barrier has not proved a major impediment to the courts. It is now universally accepted that with limited exceptions (particularly in the labour law field), a tribunal cannot hide behind such a statutory provision to make its decision unreviewable if it does not stay within the boundaries of its statutory powers. Furthermore, it is a question of law (for the courts to determine) whether the tribunal did in fact stay within its powers. Although the courts will defer to an expert tribunal's interpretation of its own Act unless this interpretation is "patently unreasonable", the tribunal can never be the final arbiter of this question of law, for that would be to usurp the role of the courts. The difference between what is patently unreasonable or merely wrong is often a rather fine line.

As no tribunal's statute can anticipate every situation which may arise, the statute may have to be examined as to implied powers. This can work both ways: powers not expressly stated will be implied if it appears reasonably necessary to do so to achieve the aims of the statute; and limitations not expressly stated will be implied if their absence does violence to the objects and powers in the Act and, also, to other laws (the *Charter of Rights*, other statutes and principles of common law such as natural justice). For example, a tribunal may exceed its jurisdiction if it considers and relies upon evidence which is irrelevant or totally ignores or refuses to consider evidence which is relevant. Similarly, fair treatment of all parties has been held to be almost universally implicit,[1] so that serious unfairness to any party can lead to a finding that statutory powers were exceeded.

There are other examples of conduct which can constitute excess of a tribunal's jurisdiction. A tribunal cannot hear and decide a question or issue not properly before it. Similarly, a tribunal may not "decline jurisdiction" by refusing to consider and determine a question which it has an obligation to decide.

Some of the legal mistakes which a tribunal can make may violate more than one principle or rule. For example, a decision may both exceed the jurisdiction of the tribunal and also be in breach of the principles of fairness. This is why it is difficult to specify what conduct by a tribunal may be found to constitute an excess of jurisdiction rather than a violation of some other principle.

3. SPECIFIC PROCEDURAL RULES

Many administrative tribunals are governed by rules which apply uniquely to them. These rules may be found in the statute which creates the tribunal, in regulations made pursuant to the statute, in rules written by the tribunal itself (the latter are usually required to be approved by the Cabinet) or in a combination of these sources. Furthermore, a government may pass general

---

1 A rare exception is the peculiar situation of the federal Cabinet acting under s. 64 of the *National Transportation Act*, R.S.C. 1970, c. N-17 [now R.S.C. 1985, c. N-20, ss. 67-68]. Because of the unfettered political nature of the discretion conveyed by that section, the Supreme Court of Canada held that there was no duty of fairness (*Inuit Tapirisat of Can. v. A.G. Canada*, [1980] 2 S.C.R. 735, 115 D.L.R. (3d) 1, 33 N.R. 304). However, the recent case of *National Anti-Poverty Organization v. A.G. Canada* (1988), 32 Admin. L.R. 1, 21 C.P.R. (3d) 305, 21 F.T.R. 33 (F.C.T.D.) recently reversed by the Federal Court of Appeal (Doc. No. A-798-88, May 15, 1989), raises questions about the correct interpretation of *Inuit Tapirisat*.

legislation intended to govern the procedures of a number of administrative tribunals (e.g., the *Statutory Powers Procedure Act*[2] in Ontario). Although a tribunal is generally free to vary or waive any rules which it has set to govern its own procedures, it is bound to follow all the rules in the form of legislation or regulations.

However, rules of procedure, whether statutory or informal, are not intended to be applied in a rigid, technical manner; they should be applied flexibly, to achieve a result which is fair to all parties in the circumstances of each case. Legislative rules of procedure take priority over implied rules of fairness which courts impose. But many tribunals do not have any formal rules, and any rules they may draft for themselves will be subject to the principles of procedural fairness. Since many tribunals have no written rules of procedure at all, the only principles which restrict the conduct of the tribunal may be those of fairness.

4. NATURAL JUSTICE

The term "natural justice" is used to describe the collection of duties which courts will impose on a tribunal even though they may not appear in any statute. "Natural justice" is in the process of being replaced by "fairness", but the process is not yet complete, and natural justice is, for technical reasons, still of great importance in the Federal Court. The rules of natural justice have evolved during a period of over 100 years of consideration and re-consideration by English and Canadian courts. It has often been suggested that the "rules of natural justice" are not really rules, that they are not particularly natural, and that in practice they are not always just. In fact, the rules of natural justice are a group of somewhat vague general principles which may actually be little more than a sophisticated judicial attempt to balance the competing considerations of fair procedure against the necessity for relatively quick and inexpensive regulatory proceedings.

Some tribunals have a variety of functions which may include investigating certain questions or advising the government. These functions may or may not give rise to a duty of

---

2 R.S.O. 1980, c. 484.

fairness, depending upon the likely impact of these functions on the rights or interests of individuals. When a tribunal exercises powers which clearly affect a person's interests, privileges or rights — even if it is only making a recommendation which is likely to be relied on by the government — the courts will usually impose upon the tribunal a duty to act in accordance with the rules of natural justice or fairness. When the rules of natural justice apply, the tribunal is said, in the jargon of the court, to have been acting "quasi-judicially". While this does not necessarily require the tribunal to adopt the full range of formalities and complex procedures used in a court of law, the tribunal must conduct its affairs in a "just" manner, without bias to one side or another, and must give each side a fair opportunity to present its case.

The courts have long recognized that tribunals were established by governments precisely because they were less formal and, therefore, presumably more efficient at certain tasks than the courts. It was recognized, particularly in criminal cases where proof had to be "beyond a reasonable doubt", that the courts had to apply procedural safeguards and rules of evidence which were designed to protect the individual against a miscarriage of justice resulting in an innocent person being convicted; they were not designed to be particularly efficient. Different priorities apply in administrative tribunals. Although the rules of natural justice are used by courts in assessing the legality of tribunals' procedures and decisions, courts apply them with an enlightened understanding of the special role of administrative tribunals. The common law acts as a guide to the tribunal and the parties, to keep proceedings within certain absolute limits; it should not be considered as a source of hard and fast rules.

There are two main branches of natural justice (or fairness): the bias rule and the fair hearing rule.

(a) The Bias Rule

This rule is somewhat difficult to define simply because of the variety of ways it has been applied. Obviously, a person sitting as the judge of important matters must not have a direct financial or other material interest in the outcome of the hearing (this is known as "actual" bias). For example, the decision-maker must not own any shares in a company appearing before him to seek permission to proceed with a project. He would have to disqualify himself from hearing the case or in any way participating in making the decision. The other members of the tribunal would have to make the decision without any discussions with the member who had the bias; indeed, he cannot even be physically present in the room in which such discussions take place, to avoid creating an appearance of bias.

There is also a second kind of bias. The conduct or background of a decision-maker must not be such as to raise in the mind of an ordinary, objective person a reasonable apprehension of bias. Obviously, it is hard to decide what such a hypothetical person is like. However, the rationale behind this test is that it is not possible for the judge to get into the mind of the decision-maker in the manner of a psychoanalyst, to determine whether or not bias existed as a mental phenomenon. Rather, the law holds that the public has the right to have confidence in judicial and quasi-judicial proceedings; the appearance of impartiality cannot be compromised to the point that a reasonable person would lose confidence in the tribunal's impartiality.

If one member hearing a case is found to have had a bias, the entire panel who participated in the hearing with him becomes "tainted". In such a case the decision will be set aside, and the case must commence anew with a different panel of members.

An apprehension of bias can arise in a variety of ways. In the leading case, Marshall Crowe, then chairman of the National Energy Board, was held by the Supreme Court of Canada to be disqualified from sitting as part of a panel to hear the applications for the Mackenzie Valley pipeline because his former position as a senior public servant included responsibilities for working toward the construction of the very pipeline which was before the National Energy Board. The fact that as a civil servant he had had no monetary interest in the pipeline proposal was held to be irrelevant, as was the two-year interval between his civil service job and the hearing on the pipeline application.

Another way in which the appearance of bias may be created is if one or more of the board members have participated in private meetings with any of the parties before or after a public hearing, at which anything of substance related to the subject-matter of the hearing was discussed. A fortunately rather rare form of bias which occasionally manifests itself is the situation of a tribunal member who prevents one party from adequately participating in the proceedings. This may involve persistently rude and harassing conduct, preventing the party or its counsel from effective presentation of the case, and other grossly abusive behaviour.

Since the only totally open mind is a totally empty mind, obviously there are practical limitations to the application of the bias rule. Tribunal members are not expected to be totally ignorant of the matters which are discussed before them; quite the contrary, they are often selected precisely because of their expertise in the industry. Hence a general connection with the regulated industry itself, or even the making of a speech suggesting a certain policy viewpoint of a broad, general nature, would not, in the absence of something specific to the case before it, be sufficient to raise a reasonable apprehension of bias. The courts will tend to presume that, notwithstanding earlier industry connections or speeches, the decision-maker would deal objectively with the evidence.

(b) The Fair Hearing Rule

The second principle is the obligation to hear both sides fairly and completely. "Hear" in this context means more than merely sitting and listening passively. It involves the positive duty to ensure that each side is given a fair opportunity to present its case at the hearing, and to respond to arguments against its interests. This duty has been well developed by the courts, and is elaborated under the subheadings set out below.

(i) Notice

Even if a statute stipulates that a tribunal shall give notice to all who might be interested in a forthcoming public hearing by means of newspaper advertising or the placing of notices in the *Canada Gazette* or a provincial Gazette, the common law would add a duty to notify personally particular parties whom the tribunal knows are especially interested or will be particularly affected by a decision. For example, a group of ratepayers had a zoning decision set aside on the basis that they were not specifically notified of the public hearing. This was based on their special interest in the application and their history of previous interventions before the same body on similar matters.[3] Once a person has been given standing to be a party, or has interests affected by a public hearing, and the tribunal becomes aware of this, it has the duty to give him or her notice of any steps which may be taken which may affect his or her interests.

Where a statute specifies certain notice provisions, the notice must be given or the ensuing hearing may be a nullity. Notice must be clearly descriptive of the area affected by the proposal, sufficient to enable residents in the area to know whether or not they will be affected.

(ii) Evidence

Although a tribunal is allowed to apply its own expert judgment to the evidence it receives, it is not permitted to make a decision based on no evidence whatsoever, or on "secret" evidence obtained on its own or withheld from any of the parties. It need not apply the rules of evidence strictly the same way as in courts of law, but it should neither refuse to admit evidence which is relevant to the case of any party, nor rely on worthless evidence which can have no probative value. Of course, a tribunal may exercise its discretion as to which evidence to admit and how much weight to attach to it, as long as it does not exercise this discretion in a grossly unreasonable manner.

As part of the notion of hearing the other side, every party must, within reasonable limits, be given an opportunity to prepare and present its own case. Sometimes the evidence with which to do so is not within its possession, but is uniquely within the possession of the other side. In these cases, the lawyer for such a party will usually make some form of motion for disclosure, such as the submission of a list of questions sought to be answered, usually called interrogatories, or a request for the production and inspection of documents. In the absence of

---

3 *Re Harvie and Calgary Regional Planning Comm.* (1978), 94 D.L.R. (3d) 49, 8 Alta. L.R. (2d) 166, 12 A.R. 505 (C.A.).

established interrogatory or production and inspection procedures, there may simply be an application to be given access to certain documents or to have the party with the information conduct certain further studies and present their outcome. Additionally, the advocate may request an opportunity to cross-examine opposing witnesses in order to extract this evidence, if it has not been made available in any other form.

Depending on the circumstances, a court may take a very serious view of a tribunal's failure to order disclosure. For example, the Canadian Radio-Television and Telecommunications Commission, when hearing a rate-increase application by a cable television company, refused to order disclosure of the financial statements of that company to a consumers' group because the company, although it filed them as evidence, requested that they be treated as confidential. When the consumers' group appealed this decision to the Federal Court of Appeal, the court held that the Commission had failed to conduct a meaningful public hearing as required by the Act and, therefore, that the hearing was a nullity. The decision was rendered void, the rate increase was deemed to have been held in trust for the subscribers and, thus, was repayable to them.[4]

Normally, evidence must be subject to cross-examination to see how it withstands scrutiny. Evidence sought to be presented in confidence (i.e., without the opportunity for the other side to attack it) should not be received by a tribunal. If there are genuinely important reasons why the evidence should not be heard in public, an *in camera* hearing may be held. At such a hearing the general public is excluded, but all the parties are permitted to perform as usual. Thus their interests are protected. However, they must undertake not to disclose the information they have learned at the *in camera* hearing. Motions for confidentiality without *in camera* hearings will rarely succeed, but may be granted when information, if made public, would be so damaging to the party giving it that it would considerably outweigh the need of the other party to be able to criticize it.

---

4 Re C.R.T.C. and London Cable TV Ltd., [1976] 2 F.C. 621, 13 N.R. 292, 67 D.L.R. (3d) 267, 29 C.P.R. (2d) 268 (F.C.A.), leave to appeal refused (sub nom. Cdn. Cablesystems (Ont.) Ltd. v. Consumers Assn. Can.) [1977] 2 S.C.R. 720, 30 C.P.R. (2d) 76, 77 D.L.R. (3d) 641, 15 N.R. 111.

Yet some tribunals, rather than relying on untested evidence, will send it back to the party which submitted it, and will disregard it. This often results in rapid voluntary disclosure.

5. THE FAIRNESS DOCTRINE

In theory the principle of "fairness" (first articulated in Canada in the *Nicholson* decision[5]) requires only that the procedure followed be fair to all parties, but it does not necessarily require that the decision itself be fair. Yet there are a few cases which seem to suggest that the principle could even be extended to require that the result or decision be fair.[6] For this reason, a distinction needs to be made between "procedural fairness" and "substantive fairness". The notion of "procedural fairness" is now solidly entrenched in Canadian law.[7] The status of "substantive fairness" is less clear. It has been the subject of vigorous criticism by legal academics, notably Professor David Mullan, on the ground that it is inappropriate for courts to second-guess regulators in this way on matters of substance rather than procedure or law. Cases are few, at lower court levels, and the Supreme Court of Canada has yet to express its opinion.

In theory, fairness is supposed to be a less demanding procedural standard than natural justice because fairness may be required even in some administrative decision-making where the rules of natural justice do not apply. In practice, however, since the courts are accustomed to applying the standards of natural justice, fairness will, in most cases, very closely resemble natural justice. Indeed, the two terms are, in Canada, virtually synonymous, except for the special jurisdictional problems created by the *Federal Court Act*.

---

5 *Nicholson v. Haldimand-Norfolk Police Commrs. Bd.*, [1979] S.C.R. 311, 23 N.R. 410, 78 C.L.L.C. 14,181, 88 D.L.R. (3d) 671.
6 See, e.g., *Re Trans-West Developments Ltd. and Nanaimo*, 107 D.L.R. (3d) 68, [1980] 3 W.W.R. 385, 17 B.C.L.R. 307, 11 M.P.L.R. 254 (S.C.), and (1980), 116 D.L.R. (3d) 420, 24 B.C.L.R. 340 (S.C.).
7 *Innisfil v. Vespra*, [1981] 2 S.C.R. 145, 37 N.R. 43, 15 M.P.L.R. 250, 12 O.M.B.R. 129, 123 D.L.R. (3d) 530.

6. SUGGESTED FURTHER READING

The law of administrative procedure may be based on long-standing legal principles, but it is evolving relatively quickly. The state of both statutory and common law varies between Canada and England, and it may even be applied differently in various provinces. Care should be used in relying on legal texts; Canadian texts may rapidly become obsolete, while United States or English texts may be inapplicable because of different statutory or common law development.

Given the limitations of such materials, the following are still reasonable references for questions on administrative law or procedure:

— D.J. Mullan, *Administrative Law*, (2nd ed.) (Toronto: Carswell, 1979). A Canadian book, relatively straightforward reference, now a bit dated but the third edition is in preparation and should be published shortly.

— *de Smith's Judicial Review of Administrative Action*, 4th ed. by J.M. Evans (London: Stevens & Sons, 1980). Focus is on English law. Once "the Bible" of administrative law, frequently cited by courts, but may rely on old and isolated case law. Law organized under obsolete headings and analysis often gives too much weight to a single 19th century lower court English decision.

— R. Dussault & L. Borgeat, *Administrative Law: A Treatise*, 2nd ed. (Toronto: Carswell, 1986). An encyclopedic work in three volumes, available in French or English. An up-to-date Canadian work covering every aspect of administrative law (e.g., access to information legislation, the organization of government). Volume 3 concentrates on judicial review issues.

— D.P. Jones & A.S. de Villars, *Principles of Administrative Law* (Toronto: Carswell, 1985). A modern analysis of Canadian administrative law, with emphasis on judicial review.

— R.W. Macaulay, *Practice and Procedure Before Administrative Tribunals* (Toronto: Carswell, 1988). A new loose-leaf service examining issues of procedure, practice and jurisdiction in a down-to-earth, practical way.

— J. M. Evans, H.N. Janisch, D.J. Mullan & R.C.B. Risk, *Administrative Law: Cases, Text and Materials*, 3rd ed. (Toronto: Emond Montgomery, 1989). A useful casebook with good analysis of the major issues in administrative law.

— Law Society of Upper Canada, Bar Admission Course Materials, *Public Law: 1988 - 1989* (Toronto: Carswell, 1988). A good overview of the important issues in administrative law. Designed for students, but useful to most newcomers to administrative law.

Supplement 2

The Law of Evidence

1. INTRODUCTION

Evidence is the testimony of witnesses and the production of physical things (including documents, charts and photographs as well as actual objects) which are presented to a court or tribunal for the purpose of proving a fact or supporting an argument.

The rules of evidence stipulate the types of evidence that may be admitted and the manner in which they are to be presented. Once the evidence has been properly introduced, it is up to the tribunal to consider what value or weight to give it.

Courts generally apply very formal and strict rules of evidence. Although tribunals are not confined strictly to the same rules of evidence (which evolved with a jury in mind), some tribunals are also quite formal in their treatment of evidence. Other relatively informal tribunals may be inclined to treat most things sought to be introduced as "admissible", but may use analogies to the rules of evidence to determine what *weight* they will assign to evidence that would not ordinarily be admissible in court. This does not mean that a tribunal has the attitude that everything and anything is evidence. The tribunal can only rely on evidence which has *some* cogency; a decision based on no evidence, or evidence that no reasonable person would possibly have found helpful, might be subject to being set aside by a court.

Participants in hearings should be familiar with the rules of evidence, both to know what evidence may be introduced and to judge the weight that may be assigned to it by the tribunal.

2. TYPES OF EVIDENCE

(a) Direct Evidence

Direct evidence is defined as testimony relating to things or events which the witness has perceived by the use of one of the five senses. This is the most common form of evidence given in civil and criminal trials, but far less use of it is made in the hearings before some administrative tribunals, where expert opinion evidence is used more extensively. Nevertheless, there are still instances when a witness will be required to give an account of a specific occurrence. The indispensible requirement for admissibility is that the witness did, in fact, personally observe the event; otherwise it will be unacceptable hearsay. All other considerations, such as the quality of the witness' memory and perceptual abilities, and any other factors affecting observation, go to the weight to be given to the evidence. Other things being equal, the greater the "direct" component of a witness' evidence, the more weight is likely to be assigned to it.

(b) Real Evidence

Real evidence is the presentation of physical objects. These must be identified, substantiated and explained by a witness. The witness must not only describe the evidence and outline what it purports to represent, but must also indicate its origin and, in the case of a physical model, diagram, photograph or other such representation, the method and theory behind its production. The manner in which real evidence is verified by a witness can best be illustrated by examples relating to the sort of real evidence that is usually sought to be introduced.

(i) Documents

Usually when a document is introduced in court it is necessary to present the original. This is because of the "best evidence rule". Exceptions to this rule include judicial documents bearing official seals and copies of original documents certified to be "true" (i.e., exact or accurate) by their original custodians. In the case of administrative tribunals, copies of documents are admissible whenever the board is satisfied as to their authenticity, but it is always tidier to file the original of a document, if it is available. If there is some doubt as to the potential admissibility of a document, it is best to consult with counsel for the tribunal.

(ii) *Photographs*

A photograph should be introduced by a person who can verify its accuracy and fairness. The witness presenting the photograph should usually be prepared to provide information relating to the time, date and place of the photograph, and perhaps the lens and camera type, camera height, angle and setting, the type of film, the physical conditions under which the picture was taken, the method of film processing, and so on. Motion pictures and video-tapes are similarly admissible, provided that they can be shown to be actual reproductions of the events as they occurred. The courts have held that tapes which have been edited are not admissible; tribunals may be less stringent in their rulings, but if anything important could hinge on it, they will have to be satisfied with the reason for the editing, and the accuracy and fairness of the edited version.

(iii) *Diagrams and tabulated charts*

Any diagrams or tabulated charts should be introduced by explaining any theories or methods that underlie their production. Also, any numbers that are used must be identified either as hypothetical figures or, if they represent actual evidence, must be substantiated at some time in the course of the hearing. If the chart is a large one, placed on an easel and discussed by a witness during oral testimony, a copy of this chart on ordinary paper should be filed with the tribunal and provided to each of the parties, to the court reporter and, in a federal tribunal, to the simultaneous translator. Otherwise, any transcript reporting the witness' description or explanation of the chart may be incomprehensible.

(c) Hearsay

Hearsay evidence is testimony of a witness containing a statement (oral or written) by another person, where the intention

312   EFFECTIVE ADVOCACY BEFORE ADMINISTRATIVE TRIBUNALS

of the witness is to suggest that the statement being quoted is true. Such evidence is usually inadmissible in court. A witness may, if it is otherwise relevant, be permitted to testify to having *heard* another person say "I shot the sheriff"; but the witness cannot say that the statement itself is true. To establish the truth of the statement, the original speaker must give that testimony. There is always a danger that a jury might mistakenly infer that if the witness heard it there must be some truth to it. That is why normally a judge would treat the statement as inadmissible. The danger is not that the wrong evidence will be admitted, but that a potentially inaccurate or self-serving second-hand account may be believed, especially if there is no opportunity to hear from or to question the original speaker.

Administrative tribunals do not usually apply this rule; hearsay evidence is often admitted. However, they will often exclude evidence where the nature of the evidence demands direct personal knowledge of the event. Or, when deciding the case, they may apply the concern behind the hearsay rule to reduce the weight given to hearsay testimony that is admitted. Generally, the less reliance on hearsay evidence the better, unless the cost or inconvenience of bringing the person who made the statement or wrote the letter is excessive having regard to the probability of its correctness. For example, the stock market report in yesterday's newspaper may quote the price of Moosepastures Mining shares at $1.25 each. To quote the newspaper would be hearsay, yet to call the editor as a witness, as well as the editor of the stock price service, would be more trouble than it is worth unless there was some serious question as to the price of the shares on that date. Most tribunals would allow the newspaper quotation to be admitted as evidence without concern about its hearsay character.

(d) Opinion Evidence

Normally, even in tribunals, only experts are permitted to testify as to opinions (as distinguished from facts). Non-expert opinion is usually inadmissible unless it can be shown that the opinion is in relation to a matter an ordinary person with average knowledge and experience could ordinarily comment upon. An expert is defined as a person qualified as an expert in the area being considered on the basis of some special skill, training, education, experience or achievement. The opinion is admissible only after such qualifications have been established. Considerations relating to credibility and the depth and breadth of the expert's qualifications contribute to the weight given to the testimony.

3. ADMISSIBILITY

Once the nature of the evidence has been established and the qualifications of the witness to render that testimony determined, there may still be certain questions as to its admissibility. Broadly, the categories that should be considered are: (a) relevance; (b) privileged communications and information; (c) Crown privilege; and (d) public policy exclusions.

(a) Relevance

The relevance of a given piece of evidence, if challenged, may have to be established by showing that it is of demonstrable value to proving some issue before the tribunal. Evidence that is not relevant is of no value and is not admissible; similarly, evidence that tends unduly to prejudice or embarrass a witness or a party before the tribunal, but which is otherwise of highly dubious value, may be held to be inadmissible.

Tribunals are likely to be more lenient than courts in admitting evidence of questionable relevance. This is due in part to their relative informality and, in part, to their greater difficulty in determining what ought to be considered inadmissible in hearings which often involve broad issues of public policy.

(b) Privileged Communications

The law in some instances recognizes the existence of certain special relationships, the confidential bonds of which the law declines to disturb. The only important "privileged" relationship that has an unchallenged legal recognition is that of the solicitor-client relationship. The law holds that a person is not required to answer questions relating to the substance of a communication between himself and his lawyer.

The privilege rests with the client, and without the client's waiver of that privilege the client cannot be required, nor will the lawyer be allowed, to divulge the contents of any communication made in the course of their professional relationship, be it oral or written, in anticipation of litigation or not. But if the lawyer or the client repeats or discloses the communication outside the context of their relationship, the privilege may be considered to have been "broken" and the client may lose his right to refuse to disclose the communication. Tribunals are unlikely to question privileged communications which would be recognized by a court.

(c) Crown Privilege

Information in the possession of the Crown which arguably should be withheld in the name of some public interest may also be considered as privileged. The law in this area is not entirely clear, with the outcome of particular cases being hard to predict. Recent federal and, in some provinces, provincial legislation covering access to information has caused some change.

The categories of information covered by Crown privilege are, generally, the following:

1. affairs of state, including matters relating to national security, international and federal/provincial relations;
2. information relating to the detection of crime;
3. information held by judges or jurors relating to proceedings before them;
4. certain Cabinet proceedings, including policy advice received from the public service.

In addition, certain cases stand for the proposition that some routine documents of the public service may be covered by this privilege *if* it can be shown that withholding these documents is necessary for the proper functioning of the public service.

The fact that *some* Crown information may be privileged cannot be used as a reason to rule out *all* evidence from such sources.[1]

As this area is both rapidly evolving and of great legal

---

1 *Innisfil v. Vespra*, [1981] 2 S.C.R. 145, 15 M.P.L.R. 250, 12 O.M.B.R. 129, 123 D.L.R. (3d) 530, 37 N.R. 43 at 62.

complexity, it would be wise to consult with legal counsel if a question arises or can be anticipated.

(d) Public Policy

Even if evidence is relevant and is neither privileged nor Crown information, courts have retained and occasionally used a power to exclude the evidence for reasons of "public policy" or in the "public interest". This usually occurs where a specific relationship or operation, at least in the particular instance, works for the good of society at large and the court ordered disclosure of such information or communications would be detrimental to the public.

The courts, in such situations, usually consider the impact on the parties and society generally of admitting or excluding such evidence, and the decision is made by weighing the benefits and detriments of the alternatives.

Administrative tribunals are generally free to make such decisions as well. They may, for example, decide that if a party is forced to disclose certain evidence (which may be of questionable weight or relevance), then every individual or corporation in a similar situation may have to consider altering its practices, ultimately to the detriment of the public.

4. CONFIDENTIALITY

"Confidentiality" is a species of privilege not normally recognized in a court of law, but of considerable importance before some regulatory tribunals. The usual subject-matters for which it is claimed that confidentiality precludes the disclosure of evidence include salaries of individual employees, labour relations (e.g., corporate forecasts of wage costs before wage negotiations are concluded) and trade or proprietary secrets (e.g., patents, recipes, or special computer programmes which it would be difficult or expensive for competitors or customers to develop).

A few tribunals have statutory provisions permitting them to keep confidential certain information which enables them to see evidence while precluding the parties from doing so. This unusual departure from the fair hearing rules is to be used sparingly, and the power itself will be narrowly interpreted by the courts. Some tribunals have drafted procedural rules supposedly permitting them to do the same, but whether such rules can do this is questionable if the power to do so is not spelled out in the Act itself (rules are always subordinate to the statute, and cannot be used to enlarge statutory powers). To date we are not aware of any cases directly deciding this issue but, for a tribunal lacking the statutory power to treat certain evidence as confidential, the alternatives would be either to send the evidence back to the party submitting it (or otherwise to refuse to receive it), or to make it available to all parties. This need not be the same as making the evidence totally public, as an *in camera* hearing can be held from which the public is excluded.

5. "JUDICIAL" AND "OFFICIAL" NOTICE

Judicial notice may be taken of facts which are so well known and indisputable among reasonable persons, or which are capable of such immediate and easy verification that the decision-maker can waive the submission of evidence to prove such facts. Judicial notice, in the ordinary sense of the phrase, may not be taken of matters which merely happen to be within the personal knowledge of the decision-maker; rather, these must be matters that are well known to the population as a whole.

Judicial notice is a term which applies to courts; in administrative tribunals it is sometimes called "official notice". Because tribunals are expected to have some expertise of their own, they can frequently take notice of facts within their field of general knowledge with greater freedom than a court of law. How far this may be taken is not easy to determine. It is inadvisable for a tribunal after a hearing to attempt to take notice of anything which is both factual and potentially controversial. Nor should the tribunal simply "look it up" in the files of prior hearings or in technical literature without giving the parties an opportunity to comment. That is because it is inappropriate for anyone sitting in judgment of the evidence to be introducing evidence to fill gaps in the record. Only the parties can do that.

6. JUDICIAL REVIEW OF TRIBUNALS' TREATMENT OF EVIDENCE

Generally, courts will not overrule a tribunal's procedural or final decision simply because of the tribunal's handling of evidence, and this has reinforced the freedom of tribunals from strict observance of the rules of evidence as applied in courts. But there are several important exceptions.

A tribunal is not free to make a decision based on a finding or an assumption of fact where there is absolutely no evidence to support the finding (unless it is a fact of such notoriety that it may take official notice). Furthermore, a tribunal cannot base its decision on irrelevant evidence, nor exclude evidence which is relevant.

A court may set aside a tribunal's decision if it refused to consider evidence in other instances: where the exclusion was, in effect, a refusal to hear a party; where it is found to be an "error of law" on the face of the tribunal's record; and where the rejection of the evidence is equivalent to declining to exercise its jurisdiction to make decisions.

These are all quite narrow, technical considerations, but they are the only major limitations on tribunals' treatment of evidence.

7. SUGGESTED FURTHER READING

A full description of the law of evidence in courts and tribunals is beyond the scope of this manual.

There are many sources one can consult on the law of evidence as it applied in courts. Unfortunately, there are no readily available books on the use of evidence before administrative tribunals, in large part because the practice varies so greatly among tribunals. Therefore, court-oriented materials on the law of evidence should be used very cautiously, with full understanding that tribunals are rarely, if ever, bound by the common law rules of evidence. The only useful reading material may be the previous decisions or procedural rulings of the particular tribunal.

Supplement 3

Costs

1. INTRODUCTION

The term "costs" has several different but related meanings, depending on both the context and the speaker. Individuals who become involved in legal proceedings may consider their costs to be all the expenses or losses sustained as a result of that involvement. Others may use the term more narrowly to mean "legal costs", which may be the account rendered by a lawyer, including professional fees and disbursements (which are expenses incurred on behalf of the client). But there are more precise meanings of the word within various parts of the legal system.

In most Canadian courts costs are amounts which one party in litigation may be ordered to pay to another party, as partial reimbursement for some of the expenses of becoming involved in litigation. A judge decides which party, if any, is entitled to an award of costs. If the amount is disputed, it is initially settled by an officer of the court (a "taxing officer" or "registrar"). The amount allowed ("taxed") usually does not equal the actual expenses incurred, but is based on certain formal rules and schedules. The amount to be determined consists of legal fees, together with disbursements (which may include filing and service fees, photocopying costs, expert witnesses' bills and other such expenses for which the party may be billed). The legal fees to be paid as court-awarded costs are usually based on fixed schedules of fees for various services of lawyers. The schedules of fees are usually obsolete and may bear little or no resemblance to amounts actually charged to a party by the lawyer. A lawyer's account may well be several times higher than the costs which are allowed by the court for such services. The party who is "awarded costs" is still responsible for paying the lawyer's account directly, so the costs award will provide only partial reimbursement.

Under Quebec's civil law system, costs which are awarded go to the lawyer for a party, and not to the party. In all other provinces, the award is to the party who is entitled to costs, and it is up to the party, with or without the assistance of a lawyer, to collect the costs from the other party.

While the basic purpose of costs is to compensate the justified litigant, there is a policy reason for the failure to provide full compensation. It is considered to be in the public interest to induce parties in disputes to settle their differences without resorting to litigation. For this reason, United States courts usually award no costs at all; each side pays its own, regardless of who won. Canadian courts, for the same reason, award costs well below most lawyers' fee levels, and there are other rules of court which further use costs to induce settlements. For example, if a defendant pays money into court as an offer to settle and the plaintiff ignores the money, presses on to trial and is awarded less than the payment, the plaintiff will usually be deprived of the costs of trial.

For administrative tribunals the term "costs" may have any of several meanings. Most tribunals do not have the power to award costs or expenses of any kind, hence the term has absolutely no meaning to them. A few tribunals treat costs much as the courts do, even if they apply their own rules in awarding costs. Others use the term to mean the actual expenses incurred, with no use of preset schedules of fees. A very few can and do award costs to interveners who make a useful contribution to their hearings. It is important to clarify exactly what a tribunal means by "costs" when determining how and when a tribunal will award them.

The policy which underlies the absence of costs in U.S. courts and the lack of full reimbursement in Canadian courts (i.e., the inducement to settle disputes) may apply to some of the tribunals which most resemble courts (e.g., labour relations boards), where the issues only involve two or a few parties to the disputes. For tribunals concerned with broad questions of public policy and public interests, there is no reason to discourage responsible participation or encourage private resolution of the issues. One cannot "settle" a telephone rate case or environmental assessment. This strongly suggests, first, that the rationale for awarding costs in administrative tribunals justifies full compensation for expenses incurred, not just partial reimbursement; and second, that the court's usual winner/loser analysis may, in most cases, be inapplicable.[1]

2. COURTS: THE LAW OF COSTS

There is a substantial amount of case law indicating how courts should handle awards of costs. The following brief outline is given in large part as a background against which the evolving question of costs before administrative tribunals is unfolding. Few if any tribunals are likely to apply the common law rules as to costs.

(a) Costs Are Discretionary

The most important aspect of costs awards is that such awards are always entirely left to the discretion of the court. Of course, the court must exercise its discretion properly. Irrelevant matters should not be taken into consideration.

The most important reason for awarding costs is the partial reimbursement of an individual who was forced to become involved in litigation in order to assert a legal position.

(b) Costs Follow the Event

The general rule is that the successful party should be awarded costs. Accordingly, the party who is only partially successful may be awarded only a corresponding proportion of the costs and, if success is approximately equal, no costs may be awarded.

---

1 *Bell Canada v. Consumers' Assn. of Can.*, [1986] 1 S.C.R. 190, 17 Admin. L.R. 205, 9 C.P.R. (3d) 145, 65 N.R. 1, 26 D.L.R. (4th) 573.

(c) Exceptions

There are several recognized exceptions to the rules that costs should be awarded to the successful party:

1. *Conduct of the successful party:* Where the successful party was unreasonable or dishonest at any relevant time (*i.e.*, from the original dispute through to the end of the trial), courts will frequently decline to award costs. Such behaviour might include giving misleading or false evidence, refusal to expedite proceedings, harsh treatment of the other party, or partial responsibility (though not necessarily legal responsibility) for his or her involvement in litigation.
2. *Causing unnecessary costs:* If the successful party has, through his conduct of the litigation, caused unreasonable delay or incurred unnecessary expenses, a court may deny a part or all of the costs otherwise receivable.
3. *Unreasonable allegations:* If the successful party has made totally unfounded allegations of fraud or other conduct which remain completely unsubstantiated and could injure the other party, costs may be denied. This is also true where a successful party made absurdly high monetary claims or other allegations which are found to be "frivolous", "vexatious", or "oppressive".
4. *Important question of law:* If the unsuccessful party has raised an important question of law (*e.g.* a constitutional issue), and it is not unfair to the successful party, a court may make no award of costs.
5. *No request for costs:* Sometimes the successful party will not request the award of costs.

(d) Level of Costs

Many Canadian courts have two distinct schedules of costs. The basic and most often used level of costs is usually referred to as "party and party" costs. This is the level at which the unsuccessful party must normally reimburse the successful party. The "solicitor and client" level of costs is generally higher, and it may be awarded if the unsuccessful party's conduct should entitle the successful party to greater costs than would normally be allowed.

(e) Party Must Be Liable for Costs

Generally the successful party is only entitled to a cost award if legally liable for the legal expenses necessary to participate in that litigation. This means that if the party received free legal services or was unrepresented, it cannot receive an award for costs which would include an allowance toward legal fees. (Most legal aid clients are a statutory exception to this rule, since legal aid legislation usually makes the costs awarded to a successful legal aid client payable to the legal aid plan.) It has been held by the Supreme Court of Canada that this privilege of indemnity applies to administrative tribunals too, but costs can be awarded and taxed even if the intervener uses a staff lawyer or counsel provided by a public advocacy group, even on the understanding that such counsel will be paid only if costs are awarded.[2]

It is important to note that some courts (e.g., most small claims courts) substantially limit the costs that can be awarded. This is largely an effort to put parties on an equal footing by discouraging the use of lawyers.

Quebec's civil law system differs somewhat from the common law rules. Costs, which generally go to the successful lawyer, may be denied or reduced due to deficiencies in that lawyer's participation in or contribution to the proceedings. This approach is substantially closer to that likely to be used by most administrative tribunals. If the presentation of the lawyer (or expert witnesses) did not assist the tribunal or was unnecessary in parts, costs may not be awarded.

(f) Costs Against Advocates

In certain very rare circumstances, courts have awarded costs personally against a lawyer involved in a case. Generally this only occurs if the lawyer has acted without being given proper authority by a client, or has caused the other party loss through serious abuse of the process or wasting of time and it would be unjust to penalize the client for the incompetence of the lawyer. There is no known instance in Canada of a tribunal making such an award, but the possibility might pose a risk to an incautious advocate.

---

2 *Bell Canada v. Consumers' Assn of Can.*, *ibid.*

There may be other instances in which a court might be tempted or asked to assess costs against an advocate. In 1975, an Ontario County Court was asked to award costs personally against a staff solicitor (of record) of a government-funded legal clinic, in part because the clinic's unsuccessful clients (who were low income tenants) obviously would be unable to pay full costs. The decision ultimately awarded nominal costs against the impoverished clients, but not without noting that there are "dangers inherent in an organization undertaking and sponsoring litigation without the need of having any regard to the legal costs incurred".[3] The judge also observed[4] that if legal aid plans do not meet the legal needs of "lower income groups", then "more radically oriented groups will fill the gap". He suggested that the clinic in question appeared to be "one such group", but conceded that it was "trying to fulfil a social need". These considerations suggest that advocates for such clients should be careful of the images and impressions they project.

3. TRIBUNALS: THE POSSIBILITIES

The majority of Canadian tribunals currently have no power to award costs or expenses. Those few tribunals which have such power have explicit statutory provisions dictating how costs decisions should be made. This is in the form of a general power to award costs to parties without dictating the criteria to be used or the levels at which costs should be paid. The few tribunals which look like and conduct themselves like courts, resolving differences between two individuals, may adopt criteria similar to those of courts. All the more usual administrative tribunals have rejected the common law court approach.

There seems to be a healthy trend towards allowing costs or other financial assistance to improve the quality and impact of public participation in the administrative process. A 1979 Study Paper of the Law Reform Commission of Canada,[5] a 1980 Report by the Special Committee on Regulatory Reform of the House of Commons, and a 1981 Report of the Economic Council

---

3 *Re Pajelle Investments Ltd. and Booth (No. 2)* (1975), 7 O.R. (2d) 229 at 241.
4 *Ibid.*, at 240.
5 D. Fox, *Public Participation in the Administrative Process.*

of Canada[6] have all strongly supported greater funding of public participation, whether through costs or through diverse grants to advocacy groups. The wisdom of these recommendations has been recognized by a long list of federal and provincial independent royal commissions and other public inquiries each of which saw fit to assist financially the participation of members of the public. For these reasons, it is possible that more administrative tribunals will be awarding costs in the near future. Ontario enacted Bill 174 (proclaimed into force April 1, 1989) to permit three tribunals (the Municipal Board, the Environmental Assessment Board and the Energy Board) to award costs before the end of a hearing. This is intended to be in effect for a three-year trial period, after which the law must be re-enacted if it is to remain in force.

Tribunals which already have established patterns of allowing costs include the Canadian Radio-Television and Telecommunications Commission (CRTC) (in telecommunications matters only), the Alberta Public Utilities Board, the Manitoba Public Utilities Board and the Ontario Energy Board. Other tribunals which have power to award costs include the Newfoundland Motor Carrier Board, the Quebec Transport Commission, Nova Scotia's Board of Commissioners of Public Utilities, Saskatchewan's Local Government Board, the Yukon Electrical Utilities Board, and several other provincial tribunals.

To a more limited extent, certain costs may be available from provincial human rights and other tribunals. But not all of the tribunals which have the power to award costs have shown a willingness to do so. Yet the weight of opinion clearly indicates that more tribunals should be awarding costs to more participants.

In tribunals which have the greatest need to consider the public interest, and which should, therefore, encourage public participation, the use of costs is necessarily different from that in courts. Courts use costs in a manner which is intended to encourage settlements without proceeding too far into litigation. In disputes involving only the private interests of several parties, the public saves money when no trials are necessary. But there is no corresponding reason to discourage responsible partici-

---

6 *Reforming Regulation.*

pants in public interest issues from contributing to the process, and it makes no sense to try to induce private settlements on issues which are heard by administrative tribunals largely because they should be aired publicly. As noted earlier, one cannot settle a public utility's application for higher rates "out of court".

While common law courts, in making an award of costs, place primary emphasis on the "success" of the parties, administrative tribunals have found consideration of the nature and quality of participation to be a more appropriate basis for awarding costs. Thus, tribunals will frequently award costs to an intervener whose case was well handled and helpful, even though the decision was "against" it. This is logical because the participation may have contributed to the decision-making process, even though the intervener did not get the result it sought.

Many administrative tribunals, most notably the "regulatory" ones (e.g., utilities, environment, communications, etc.), recognize that representation of consumer interests is a public benefit even when the tribunal's decisions do not directly reflect such input. The assumption is that tribunals need competent, reasonable and helpful participation to ensure that their decisions take into account all important and relevant considerations. Since regulated industries and large user interests before tribunals have immense resources, many tribunals now recognize that smaller parties need substantial assistance to enable them to make effective contributions to tribunal hearings. Therefore, such tribunals have reason to award costs to interveners whose participation has been constructive and helpful.

Courts have upheld the right of tribunals to apply their own costs criteria. The tribunals which have the most experience in awarding costs, most notably the Alberta Public Utilities Commission and the CRTC (and including the utilities or energy boards of Nova Scotia, Newfoundland, Ontario and Manitoba), have developed their own guidelines. Such guidelines may vary from tribunal to tribunal, so it is important to read them and the past decisions of the tribunal. Nevertheless, since tribunals which award costs have substantial discretion to vary their practices, it is worth learning about and referring to the practices of other tribunals.

There are three ways in which the expenses of a party or

intervener in administrative proceedings can be paid. Some parties may receive direct grants, either from government or private foundations, to cover those proceedings. Such support obviously does not require the tribunal to consider an award of costs or expenses. A second approach is for the tribunal to make a grant to the party, using its own funds. This can be done before, during or after hearings, and some tribunals make grants at several different times. Such grants will rarely if ever depend on the "success" of a party, although they may depend in part on the value of the party's contribution. The third approach, most commonly used by regulatory tribunals which award costs, is to make an order that the regulated industry pay the costs of certain other parties. Frequently, such awards are based on the actual expenses of the party, and not on any pre-determined scale or schedule of fees.

It has been argued that if an organization received any financial support from government it is not really liable for its own costs and, applying the common law rule, it should not be entitled to an award of costs. This position has already been rejected by the courts and publicly funded organizations generally receive the same costs as any other participant would receive.

To summarize, any party considering an appearance before an administrative tribunal, especially in a public interest capacity, should determine:

1. whether the tribunal is, by statute, given the power to award costs (or expenses) or give grants; or, if a one-time tribunal, empowered expressly by its Order-in-Council or otherwise so authorized;
2. what the tribunal's rules, guidelines and past decisions, if any, say about grants and costs;
3. whether grants or costs are available before or during hearings, to help meet the party's expenses as they are incurred;
4. whether the circumstances of the party or the issue in the present case may prompt the tribunal to consider altering its past practices or criteria;
5. whether the tribunal should be asked to consider the decisions and criteria of other tribunals.

Finally, there is one major concern which participants seeking costs must bear in mind: discretionary decisions are likely to favour those who are compliant and not too aggressive. If a participant is depending on receiving costs, it may be necessary to accept without question the procedural rulings of the tribunal at times when effective advocacy might mandate taking a stronger position — perhaps even a judicial review application — in the face of reluctance or opposition by the tribunal. In such situations, costs awards become a reward for the meek, their denial, a punishment for insisting upon fair treatment. This quandary may require some participants, in some cases, to question the wisdom of seeking costs at all.

4. JUDICIAL/POLITICAL REVIEW

Where the awarding of costs or expenses is left to the discretion of the administrative tribunal, courts will be reluctant to reconsider and reverse any decision of the tribunal as to costs. But courts will review some such conduct by tribunals, including:

1. a tribunal's refusal to exercise its discretion either for or against a request for costs;
2. a tribunal's reliance on irrelevant or unlawful considerations in awarding or denying costs;
3. a tribunal's failure to consider factors expressly or impliedly required to be considered by its statute when requested to award costs;
4. a tribunal's "fettering its discretion", where the tribunal refuses to consider the specific circumstances of each request and insists on automatic application of practices it has chosen to adopt in earlier decisions; and
5. a tribunal's capricious or arbitrary use of a discretionary power to award costs.

If the statute permits a political avenue of review, it should be considered. The Ontario Cabinet, for example, reversed a decision of the Ontario Municipal Board (OMB) awarding costs against a local intervener group, and ordered the OMB to develop and publish criteria for future costs awards. The Ontario Cabinet also sent back to the Ontario Energy Board for reconsideration a costs award of only 40 percent of the costs incurred by a consumer group because the reason given was that all parties were to be given only 40 percent except a large users' group, which was awarded 60 percent because that was all that it sought. The Board was expressly ordered to consider the need of the intervener as well as the need for balanced intervention.

5. SUGGESTED FURTHER READING

There are numerous references for the law of costs generally, but few of them consider the awarding of costs by administrative tribunals. Furthermore, there are no materials which attempt to cover costs for all administrative tribunals.

The single most useful source of further information is a publication of the Regulated Industries Program of the Consumer's Association of Canada entitled *Costs Awards in Regulatory Proceedings/A Manual for Public Participants*. This unique work was published in October 1979 and is somewhat dated. It nevertheless covers most of the matters dealt with in this supplement in somewhat more detail, and it provides general procedural assistance for parties who are actually applying for costs.

As well, Robert W. Macaulay's new looseleaf service, *Practice and Procedure Before Administrative Tribunals* (Toronto: Carswell, 1988), deals with costs in Chapter 27 and with intervener funding in Chapter 26. R.J. Anthony and A.R. Lucas, in their excellent, comprehensive work, *A Handbook on the Conduct of Public Inquiries in Canada* (Toronto: Butterworths, 1985), deal with participant funding in Chapter IV and Appendix B-8. The only current report on the subject by an administrative tribunal is that of the Ontario Energy Board: E.B.O. 116, June 12, 1985. This was the result of a generic hearing on the subject, heard by all the then-sitting members of the Board. It provides a useful review and analysis of several policy issues in the area of costs awards.

Appendix

Sample Forms

The author gratefully acknowledges the kind assistance of Cheryl Cottle, counsel to the Ontario Automobile Insurance Board, Stan Thomas, Secretary of the Ontario Energy Board, Jack Klenavic, Secretary of the National Energy Board, Greg Van Koughnett, counsel to the Canadian Radio-Television and Telecommunications Commission and Nicole Pelletier, Chief Administration and Assistant Secretary of the Canadian Import Tribunal for providing copies of the forms used by their boards. These forms are "typical" examples of forms used across Canada, although each tribunal has its own unique form and perhaps even specialized variants of the forms set out below.

The purpose of including these forms is to illustrate that:

1. they are neither difficult nor intimidating;
2. the information sought is rather basic and general because anything more complex is provided in evidence at the hearing;
3. there is a broad variety of forms, for virtually every imaginable use;
4. if a tribunal does not have one or another of these sample forms, the reader can design one to suit the particular purpose, using the samples.

FORM 1

Notice of Interested Party

[Date]

Secretary General,
Canadian Radio-television
    and Telecommunications Commission,
[Address]

TAKE NOTICE that [name of person or association] desires to be registered as an interested party in respect of any application(s) of the kind described below, which may be made to the Canadian Radio-television and Telecommunications Commission by [name of regulated company]. This notice is filed in accordance with section 7 of the CRTC *Telecommunications Rules of Procedure*.

The type of application(s) for which notice is sought is as follows: [describe nature of application(s)].

[Name of person or association] is interested in such application(s) by reason of the fact that [describe nature of interest].

The name, mailing address, address for personal service, [and telephone and Fax numbers, if applicable] of the individual or agent authorized to receive notices on [my or our] behalf are as follows:

[Name and Particulars]

Signed

_____
[Name, title]
[Name of person
or association]

FORM 2

Response to Interrogatory

[*Full name of party furnishing response*] Response to Interrogatory [Code no., e.g.: Bell (NAPO) 23Jan88-100] Page 1 of 10

[*Date of response*]

Q. [*Reproduce original interrogatory*]
A. [*Set out response*]

FORM 3

Tariff Notice

[*Name of company*]
[*Address*]
[*Date*]

Director General, Telecommunications,
Canadian Radio-television and
    Telecommunications Commission,
[*Address*]

Dear [*name*]:

TARIFF NOTICE NO.

In compliance with the requirements of the *Railway Act* and section 29 of the *CRTC Telecommunications Rule of Procedure*, [*name of company*] applies herewith for approval of the following tariff amendments:

Tariff CRTC [*number*] [*Proposed effective date*] [*Description*]

Enclosed herewith are copies of the proposed new or revised tariff pages and a letter of explanation for the changes requested.

Signed

_____

[*Name, title*]

FORM 4

Notice to Interested Party under Part II

[Name of company]
[Address]
[Date]

[Name, address
of agent for
interested party]

Dear (name):

[Name of company], Tariff Amendment
under Notice No......

In accordance with section 32 of the CRTC Telecommunications Rules of Procedure, we have enclosed herewith a copy of an application filed on [date] with the Canadian Radio-television and Telecommunications Commission for the approval of new or amended tariff pages.

On [date] the Commission issued public notice [reference] with respect to the above noted tariff filing. A copy of the public notice is also enclosed.

Yours truly,

_____
[Name, title]

FORM 5

Directions on Procedure

[Date]

[Style of cause]

Directions on Procedure

[Name of company] proposes to apply to the Canadian Radio-television and Telecommunications Commission for a general increase in rates, to be effective on [date]. Having considered the submissions of the company with respect thereto, the Commission directs as follows:

1. The filing date of the application shall be [date].

2. Letters of intervention and notices of intention to participate at the central hearing are required to be filed by [date].

3. Interrogatories addressed to the applicant are required to be filed and served by [date], provided that supplementary interrogatories may be permitted after that date with the consent of the Commission. The applicant is required to respond to interrogatories received within the specified time limit by [date].

4. A pre-hearing conference is scheduled to take place in [location] on [date].

5. Provided the application file is completed to the satisfaction of the Commission, the central hearing shall commence in [location] on [date].

6. Regional hearings will be held in the period from [date] to [date].

   [Note: Where a regional and a central hearing are expected to be consolidated pursuant to subsection 43(5) of the CRTC Telecommunications Rules of Procedure, paragraph 5 above should omit the word "central", paragraph 6 should be deleted, and paragraphs 7 to 10 should be renumbered 6 to 9 respectively.]

7. The application shall be provided in [names of official language(s)].

8. In addition to those persons entitled to a copy of the application under the CRTC Telecommunications Rules of Procedure, the company shall mail or deliver a copy of the application forthwith on filing to the following:

[Insert names]

9. The newspapers in which the applicant is required to publish a notice to subscribers are as follows:

[Insert names]

10. These Directions supplement the *CRTC Telecommunications Rules of Procedure.*

[Name]

Secretary General

FORM 6

Notice to Subscribers

[Author's Note: This notice is required to be mailed to each telephone subscriber as a billing insert.]

Notice to *[name of company, type of service]* Subscribers

[Name of company] has filed an application with the Canadian Radio-television and Telecommunications Commission for an increase in its rates. The company has proposed that the increases come into effect on *[date]*.

Q. BRIEFLY, WHAT IS THE APPLICATION ALL ABOUT?

A. *[State highlights of application, including estimated revenue increase on an annual basis]*

Q. HOW WOULD MY RATES BE AFFECTED BY THE APPLICATION?

A. Some examples of how rates would be affected by the changes being applied for are set out below. A detailed schedule of the proposed changes, which indicates specifically how rates would be affected in your community, is provided in the application itself.

[Provide particulars of increases for each service category, including representative changes by rate group, if applicable]

Q. WHY IS THE COMPANY ASKING FOR A RATE INCREASE NOW?

A. The full details of the company's justification for the increase are set out in its application. By way of summary, the company has made the following statement:

"[Provide brief statement]"

All of the assertions above, and the application itself, will be subject to questioning and examination at CRTC public hearings in which any [name of company] subscriber may participate.

Q. WHERE CAN I SEE A COPY OF THE APPLICATION?

A. Part A of the application, consisting of the Request for Increase in Rates, is available for public inspection during normal business hours at every [name of company] business office and at the offices of the CRTC, [addresses]. Part B of the application, consisting of Memoranda of Support, is also available for inspection at the CRTC and at the following [name and company] business offices: [addresses] and will be sent to anyone filing a notice of intention to participate.

Q. HOW CAN I COMMENT ON THE APPLICATION?

A. You may express your comments in one of three ways:

(1) BY SENDING A LETTER TO THE COMMISSION

If you have a comment or matter that you feel the Commission should take into account in viewing the application, including such matters as quality of service, availability of service, billing practices, or any other matter relating to the company's operations, you can write directly to the Commission. Your letter should clearly state your views and should include any relevant information that may be useful in explaining or supporting those views. Send your letter so it will be received by [date] to: [name], Secretary General, Canadian Radio-television and Telecommunications Commission, [address]. A copy of your letter should also be sent to: [name, title, address]. In the case of delivery by hand, you may use any of the locations listed above for public inspection of Part B of the application.

(2) BY APPEARING AT A REGIONAL HEARING

The Commission will be holding regional hearings, which will take the form of public meetings normally held in the evening in a number of different communities within [name of company]'s service area during [specify time period]. The locations will be selected depending on the response to this notice; these locations and the precise times of the meetings will be announced later. If you would like an opportunity to appear at one of these hearings, at which you may expand on your letter or make further submissions, you should follow the procedure described above for sending comments to the Commission, making sure to include a statement of your desire to participate at a regional hearing.

(3) BY APPEARING AT THE CENTRAL HEARING

In addition to the regional hearings the Commission will be conducting a more formal central hearing that is tentatively scheduled to take place in [location], commencing [day, date, time] provided the application file has been completed to the satisfaction of the Commission. Participation in this part of the hearing, which generally requires being present on a daily basis, involves presentation of evidence by both the applicant and interveners, often through expert witnesses, and includes cross-examination. If you wish to participate at the central hearing, you must file a notice of intention to participate with the Commission on or before [date], with a copy to the company. This will entitle you to receive a complete copy of the application. The deadline for the submission of inter-rogatories to the Company, with a copy to the Commission, is also [date].

[Note: Where a regional hearing and a central hearing are expected to be consolidated pursuant to subsection 43(5) of the CRTC Telecommunications Rules of Procedure, the first sentence of the response above would read "A. You may express your comments in one of two ways:" and the following would be substituted for entries (2) and (3) above:

(2) BY APPEARING AT THE PUBLIC HEARING

The Commission will be holding a public hearing into the application that is tentatively scheduled to take place in [*location*], commencing [*day, date, time*] provided the application file has been completed to the satisfaction of the Commission. The first part of the hearing will be devoted to hearing representations from subscribers. If you would like an opportunity to appear and expand on your letter, or make further submissions, you should follow the procedure described above for sending comments to the Commission, making sure to include a statement of your desire to appear. Following these representations, the second part of the hearing will be devoted to a detailed review of the company's evidence. Participation in this part of the hearing, which generally requires being present on a daily basis, involves presentation of evidence by both the applicant and interveners, often through expert witnesses, and includes cross-examination. If you wish to participate at this stage, you must file a notice of intention to participate with the Commission with a copy to the company on or before [*date*]. This will entitle you to receive a complete copy of the application. The deadline for the submission of interrogatories to the company, with a copy to the Commission, is also [*date*].

Q. WHOM MAY I CONTACT FOR FURTHER INFORMATION?

A. Read the *CRTC Telecommunications Rules of Procedure* to find out the rights and obligations of parties to a hearing. Copies are available at a cost of [*charge* from [*name and address*]. For additional information on the application or the hearing procedure, please contact [*name of company*] or the CRTC.

FORM 7

Directions on Procedure

[Date]

[*Style of cause*]

Directions on Procedure

[*Name of company*] proposes to apply to the Canadian Radio-television and Telecommunications Commission for approval of [*describe type of application*], to be effective on [*date*]. Having considered the submissions of the company with respect thereto, the Commission directs as follows:

1. The filing of the application shall be [*date*].

2. Letters of intervention are required to be filed by [*date*].

3. Replies to letters of intervention are required to be filed by [*date*].

4. If after having reviewed all relevant documentation submitted in connection with the application the Commission determines that it is necessary to hold a public hearing, such hearing is scheduled to take place on [*date*].

5. The application shall be provided in [*name of official language(s)*].

6. In addition to those persons entitled to a copy of the application under the *CRTC Telecommunications Rules of Procedure*, the company shall mail or deliver a copy of the application forthwith on filing to the following:

[*Insert names*]

7. On filing the application, the company shall deposit and keep on file, for public inspection during normal business hours, a copy of the application in its offices at [*insert location(s)*].

8. On receiving a copy of an intervention the company shall, if it has not already done so, serve on the intervener forthwith a copy of the application.

9. The newspapers in which the company is required to publish a notice are as follows:

[*Insert names*]

10. These Directions supplement the CRTC *Telecommunications Rules of Procedure.*

[*Name*]
Secretary General

FORM 8

Public Notice under Part V

Ottawa, [*date*]

[*Name of company, style of cause*]

The Canadian Radio-television and Telecommunications Commission has received an application from [*name of company*] for approval of [*describe type of application*].

[*Provide a summary of the proposed issue, etc. including an explanation of the reasons for it*].

The application and accompanying documents are available for public inspection during normal business hours at the offices of [*name of company and appropriate address(es)*]; and at the offices of the CRTC, [*addresses of appropriate offices*].

INTERVENTIONS

Any interested person or association who wishes to comment on this application may do so by mailing or delivering by hand a letter of intervention to the Commission with a copy thereof to [*name of company*]. The mailing addresses to be used are: [*name of Secretary General*], Secretary General, CRTC, [*address*]; and [*name and address of appropriate officer of the company*]. In the case of delivery by hand, the locations listed above for public inspection of documents should be used.

A letter of intervention should clearly state the intervener's views regarding the application together with any relevant information that may be useful in explaining or supporting those views. It may also include a statement of intention to appear at a public hearing should one be held. In order to be considered, all interventions must actually be received by [name of company] and the Commission on or before [date].

Similarly, copies of replies from [name of company] to any interventions must actually be received by the interveners concerned and by the Commission on or before [date].

PROCEDURES TO BE FOLLOWED

[Note: Two alternative texts are provided for this section of the notice. If the application is of the type where an approval in principle will be required before final details as to price, etc. are to be submitted, use text A. If the application is of the type where approval in principle is not necessary, use text B.]

[TEXT A]

Depending on the nature of the interventions and replies received within the time periods set out above, the Commission will determine whether or not a public hearing will be held to deal with the application. If, in the Commission's view, a public hearing is not necessary, the Commission will render a decision "in principle" on or before [date].

If the Commission determines that a public hearing is necessary, it will take place on [date] at an exact time and location to be specified by the Commission. All persons or associations who have expressed an interest in the application will be notified by the Commission should a public hearing be convened.

Such a hearing would be held to examine the details of the proposed [type of application], with the exception of [describe information to be filed later], which will be determined by the applicant's Board of Directors [describe when]. The CRTC will render a decision in principle forthwith on completion of the hearing.

If the Commission approves the application in principle, the applicant will provide the Commission on or before [date] with [describe final details]. Provided this information does not depart materially from that set out in the application, final approval will be granted on [date].

[TEXT B]

Depending on the nature of the interventions and replies received within the time periods set out above, the Commission will determine whether or not a public hearing will be held to deal with the application. If the Commission determines that a public hearing is necessary, it will take place on [date] at an exact time and location to be specified by the Commission. All persons or associations who have expressed an interest in the application will be notified by the Commission should a public hearing be convened.

The Commission will render a decision on or before [date].

FORM 9

Form of Endorsement on Application under Part VII

[Not Shown]

FORM 10

Form of Endorsement on Answer under Part VII

[Not Shown]

FORM 11

[file number]   [Telephone number]

November 29, 1988

Ontario Energy Board
2600, 2300 Yonge Street
Toronto, Ontario
M4P 1E4

Attention: [name]
           Board Secretary

Dear Sir:

RE: E.B.R.O. 452-3

We enclose the Supplementary Intervention of the Canadian Petroleum Association ("CPA").

As the document indicates in paragraph 2, its purpose is to advise all parties of the CPA's intention to participate actively in the Cost of Gas phase of this proceeding.

Yours very truly,

[Signature]
[Name]

encl.
cc. Consumers' Gas
cc. All Interested Parties

FORM 12

E.B.R.O. 452-3

ONTARIO ENERGY BOARD

IN THE MATTER OF THE *Ontario Energy Board Act*, R.S.O. 1980, Chapter 332;

AND IN THE MATTER OF an Application by The Consumers' Gas Company Ltd. and selected consolidated subsidiary companies, for Orders approving rates to be charged for the sale of gas.

SUPPLEMENTARY INTERVENTION OF THE CANADIAN PETROLEUM ASSOCIATION

1. The Canadian Petroleum Association ("CPA") is a body corporate, incorporated under the laws of Canada, the active membership of which comprises companies engaged in Canada's oil and gas industry. The producer-members of the CPA account for the majority of natural gas produced in Canada. The producer-members of the CPA are major marketers of natural gas in the domestic natural gas market. In addition, members of the CPA are major users of natural gas within the Province of Ontario. Therefore the CPA has an interest in the within proceeding.

2. The CPA is a registered Intervener in this proceeding. The purpose of this Supplementary Invervention is to put the Board,

the Applicant and all Interested Parties on notice that the CPA intends to participate actively in the Cost of Gas phase of the proceeding.

3. In response to Procedural Order No. 7 the CPA advises that it is the intention of the CPA to appear and participate at the hearing, for the purposes of cross-examination, presentation of direct evidence, and presentation of argument, all as the interests of the Association may require. The nature and extent of the participation by the CPA will be influenced by the additional evidence yet to be filed by the Applicant and the issues which the Ontario Energy Board includes in the List of Issues to be provided in a future Procedural Order.

Once all the Applicant's evidence has been filed, the CPA will complete and file its direct evidence, if any.

4. The CPA wishes to receive copies of the Prefiled Evidence of all other participants as well as any other materials filed in connection with this proceeding.

5. Communications with respect to this Intervention should be addressed to:

Attention: Mr. [Name]
Canadian Petroleum Association
3800, 150 Sixth Avenue S.W.
Calgary, Alberta T2P 3Y7

Telephone:
Telecopier:

— and —

Attention: Mr. [Name]
Fenerty, Robertson, Fraser & Hatch
Barristers and Solicitors
2900 Western Canadian Place
700 Ninth Avenue S.W.
Calgary, Alberta T2P 4A7

Telephone:
Telecopier:

DATED at the City of Calgary, in the Province of Alberta, this 29th day of November, 1988.

> CANADIAN PETROLEUM
> ASSOCIATION
> by its agent in this proceeding
> FENERTY, ROBERTSON,
> FRASER & HATCH
>
> PER: [Signature]
> [Name]

FORM 13

1988-05-19

National Energy Board
Trebla Building
473 Albert Street
Ottawa, Ontario
K1A 0E5

Attention: [Name]
            Secretary

Gentlemen:

Chevron Canada Resources hereby applies for a short-term, small volume permit for the export of natural gas from Canada. Approval for removal from the Province of Alberta was received under Permit GR88-119 dated 1988-05-11. In support of this application to the NEB the following is provided:

1. Exporter   Chevron Canada Resources
                     500 — 5th Avenue S.W.
                     Calgary, Alberta
                     T2P 0L7

2. Importer   Chevron Natural Gas Services, Inc.
                     P.O. Box 2100
                     Houston, Texas
                     77252

3. Term   Two years
                     July 1, 1988 through June 30, 1990

4. Type of Service   Interruptible

5. Estimated Volume   Total volume of 2 059 10^6 m³ (73 BCF)
Maximum daily volume 2 830 10^3 m³/d
(100 MMcf/d)

6. Points of Removal   International Border at either
(a) Huntingdon, British Columbia, or
(b) Kingsgate, British Columbia

7. Sales Contract   The sale and purchase will occur under contract dated 1987-06-26 between Exporter and Importer, a copy of which is included.

FORM 14

25 May 1988

VIA COURIER

Mr. [Name]
Secretary
National Energy Board
Trebla Building
473 Albert Street
Ottawa, Ontario
K1A 0E5

Dear [Name]:

Re: The Consumers' Gas Company Ltd.;
Application for an Order under
§ 8(1)(b) of the National Energy Board
Part VI Regulations

I am writing on behalf of The Consumers' Gas Company Ltd., to apply for an order under § 8(1)(b) of the *National Energy Board Part VI Regulations* authorizing Consumers Gas to import gas from the United States. In accordance with the Board's instructions in this regard, I am filing 20 copies of this application.

In support of this application, I am providing the following information:

1. <u>Name of importer:</u> The Consumers' Gas Company Ltd.

2. <u>Name of exporter:</u> Access Energy Corporation.

3. <u>Point of import:</u> Ojibway, Ontario (near Windsor), at the point of interconnection of the pipeline facilities of Panhandle Eastern Pipe Line Company and Union Gas Limited.

4. <u>Commencement date:</u> 1 June 1988.

5. <u>Termination date:</u> 30 September 1988, subject to a 1-month extension to correct any imbalances existing on the termination date.

6. <u>Type of service:</u> interruptible and reasonable efforts.

7. <u>Estimated term volume:</u> From 56 million cubic metres (approx. 1.98 billion cubic feet) to 68 million cubic metres (approx. 2.4 billion cubic feet), depending upon availability of supply, access to pipeline capacity, and market conditions.

8. <u>U.S. export authorization:</u> DOE/ERA Opinion and Order No. 147 issued 26 September 1988 to Yankee International Company, which was transferred to Access Energy Corporation by DOE/ERA Order issued 24 February 1988. A copy of these documents was filed with you in connection with a prior application for an import order (see my letter to you dated 29 March 1988).

9. <u>Import sales contract:</u> The parties are in the process of finalizing the contract, with a view to mutually executing and delivering the contract before the commencement date (1 June 1988). As soon as it is available, I will file a copy of the executed contract with you.

If you require additional information in connection with this application, please advise me and I will make it available as promptly as I can.

Yours very truly,

[Signature]
[Name]

cc. [Name]
Manager, Gas Supply
Western Canada
The Consumers' Gas Company Ltd.
[via telefax]

[Name]
Vice President
Access Energy Corporation
[via telefax]

FORM 15

12 September 1988

VIA MESSENGER

[name]
Secretary
National Energy Board
Trebla Building
473 Albert Street
Ottawa, Ontario
K1A 0E5

Dear [name]:

Re: Hearing Order No. GH-7-88;
ProGas Limited and Western Gas Marketing Limited:
Applications to Extend Gas Export Licences GL-81 and GL-90;
NEB File No.: ER1537-P38-2 and ER1537-T1-12

In accordance with § 32(1) of the *NEB Rules of Practice and Procedure* (revised draft) and ¶¶ 2 and 15 of Hearing Order No. GH-7-88, I am filing with you 30 copies of the written intervention of The Consumers' Gas Company Ltd. ("Consumers Gas") in this proceeding. I request that your list of interveners for this proceeding include the two persons identified in ¶ 5 of the written intervention, indicating both mailing addresses and addresses for personal service.

For the purposes of the order of appearances in this

proceeding, Consumers' Gas prefers to be listed as "Consumers' Gas Company Ltd., The" (that is, to appear under the "C's"). This would comport with recent practice in this regard.

As required by § 32(1) of the *NEB Rules of Practice and Procedure* (revised draft) and ¶¶ 2 and 15 of Hearing Order No. GH-7-88, I am serving three copies of the written intervention on the Applicant by serving the four persons designated for service in Appendix I to Order No. GH-7-88.

As I am filing and serving this written intervention after the date prescribed by the Board in ¶2 of Hearing Order No. GH-7-88, I hereby request the Board's leave to do so. If the Board requires a formal application to extend the prescribed date in accordance with § 7 of the *NEB RULES OF PRACTICE AND PROCEDURE* (revised draft), please advise me and I will file and serve a notice of motion in this regard.

Yours very truly,

[*Signature*]
[*Name*]

Encl.

cc. [*Name*]
ProGas Limited
(via courier)

[*Name*]
Western Gas Marketing Limited
(via courier)

[*Name*]
Western Gas Marketing Limited
(via messenger)

[*Name*]
Bennett Jones
(via messenger)

FORM 16

NEB File No.: ER1537-P38-2
ER1537-T1-12

NATIONAL ENERGY BOARD
Hearing Order No. GH-7-88

ProGas Limited and Western Gas Marketing Limited
as agent for TransCanada PipeLines Limited
Applications to Extend Gas Export Licences GL-81 and GL-90

WRITTEN INTERVENTION
of
THE CONSUMERS' GAS COMPANY LTD.

1. Appearance: The Consumers' Gas Company Ltd. ("Consumers Gas") intends to appear at the public hearing of the Applications of ProGas Limited and Western Gas Marketing Limited as agent for TransCanada PipeLines Limited ("Applicants") under § 17 of the *National Energy Board Act* for orders varying Licences No. GL-81 and No. GL-90, respectively (or in the alternative, under § 82 of the *National Energy Board Act* for new gas export licences). In this regard, Consumers Gas asserts a right to be heard, to appear by or with counsel of its choice, to adduce evidence on any relevant matter, to conduct a complete cross-examination on all relevant matters, and to submit argument.

2. Interest: Consumers Gas is a large natural gas distribution utility that purchases most of its gas supply from domestic sources. The proposed variance of Licences No. GL-81 and No. GL-90 (or in the alternative, the proposed new licences) may affect the gas supply that would otherwise be available to Consumers Gas and thus its sales customers during the proposed term of the licences and thereafter.

3. Issues: At the public hearing, Consumers Gas intends to address any issue that is germane to the Board's "Market-Based Procedure" for determining surplus under § 83(a) of the *National Energy Board Act*. Consumers Gas reserves the right to address any other issue that may arise from any document

filed with the Board by the Applicants or another intervener in this proceeding.

4. <u>Language</u>: Consumers Gas intends to use the English language at the public hearing.

5. <u>Communications</u>: Communications in regard to this proceeding should be directed to Consumers Gas and its counsel as follows:

(a) Consumers Gas:

[Name]	Telephone:
Vice-President,	Telecopier:
Regulatory Affairs	Telex:
The Consumers' Gas	
Company Ltd	

Mailing Address:	Address for personal service:
P.O. Box 650	500 Consumers Road
Scarborough, Ontario	Willowdale, Ontario
M1K 5E3	

(b) Counsel for Consumers Gas:

[Name]	Telephone:
Smith, Lyons, Torrance,	Telecopier:
Stevenson & Mayer	Telex:

Mailing address:	Address for personal service:
P.O. Box 420	Suite 3400
2 First Canadian Place	The Exchange Tower
Toronto, Ontario	First Canadian Place
M5X 1J3	Toronto, Ontario

Dated at Toronto, Ontario this 12 September 1988.

THE CONSUMERS' GAS
COMPANY LTD.
by counsel in this proceeding,
[Name]
[Signature]

TO: [Name]
      Secretary
      National Energy Board
      [30 copies]

AND TO: [Name]
      ProGas Limited
      [3 copies]

AND TO: [Name]
      Western Gas Marketing Limited
      [3 copies]

AND TO: The persons included in the list
      of interveners to be issued by the
      Secretary in accordance with ¶ 4
      of Hearing Order No. GH-7-88
      [1 copy]

FORM 17

CANADIAN IMPORT TRIBUNAL

Inquiry No.: CIT-10-87

APPEARANCE, DECLARATION AND UNDERTAKING

IN THE MATTER OF: Drywall screws originating in or exported from France

APPEARANCE

I appear as counsel for: H. Paulin & Co. Limited
a party before the Tribunal in the present matter.

My address for service is:
      Grey, Clark, Shih and Associates Ltd.
      804-141 Laurier Avenue West
      Ottawa, Ontario K1P 5J3

[Author's note: The part which follows is used for in camera hearings.]

DECLARATION AND UNDERTAKING

I have taken communication of the provisions of section 75(3) of the *Special Import Measures Act* relating to the treatment of confidential information.

I hereby declare that I am a Canadian resident and am not an employee, officer, director or major shareholder of the party for which I act or of any other known participant in this inquiry.

I hereby undertake that:

1. I will maintain the confidentiality of any information or evidence that I receive during the course of the Tribunal's inquiry and which is in its nature confidential;

2. I will not copy or reproduce such confidential documentation without prior approval from the Secretary; and

3. I will return all confidential information including any notes taken during the in camera proceedings to the Secretary of the Tribunal at the end of the hearing.

Signature: [Signature]

(Print) Name:

Firm:

Dated at Ottawa, Ontario
this 17th day of November, 1987

FORM 18

CANADIAN IMPORT TRIBUNAL

IMPORTER'S QUESTIONNAIRE

DRYWALL SCREWS

The information requested in this questionnaire is for use by the Canadian Import Tribunal in connection with its inquiry into drywall screws originating in or exported from France. The information is needed to supplement data available from other sources and is requested pursuant to section 72(2) of the *Special Import Measures Act.*

If you have imported the product in question at any time since 1983 you are requested to complete this questionnaire and return it to the Secretary, Canadian Import Tribunal, 19th Floor, Journal Tower South, 365 Laurier Avenue West, Ottawa, Ontario, K1A 0G5, Telex No. 053-3336, Telecopier No. (613) 998-4783. The questionnaire should be received by the Secretary not later than October 16, 1987.

Information which is in its nature confidential will be treated in accordance with section 75(3) of the *Special Import Measures Act* which requires that it shall not be made public in such a manner as to be available for the use of any business competitor or rival of the reporting person, firm or corporation.

Name (in both offficial languages, if applicable) and address of reporting company:

BAILEY METAL PRODUCTS LIMITED
151 BENTWORTH AVENUE
TORONTO, ONTARIO
M6A 1P6

If your firm is a wholly or partly owned subsidiary, please list the name and address of the parent company and the extent of ownership.

CERTIFICATION

The undersigned certifies that the information herein supplied is complete and correct to the best of his/her knowledge and belief.

Date: OCTOBER 1st, 1987   [Signature]
                            Signature of Authorized Official

Telephone: 416-781-9371   [Name]
                            Comptroller
                            Name and Title of Authorized
                            Official

PART I

PUBLIC INFORMATION

Note: Information requested in this section usually is

> public in nature and will be treated as such
> unless otherwise requested

(1) GENERAL

Please give a brief history of your company with particular emphasis on the importation, marketing and distribution in Canada of drywall screws.

Bailey Metal Products Limited was incorporated on 29 July 1953. In the first few years the principal product was metal lath. With the advent of gypsum board replacing plaster, there was a product shift to metal drywall studs. Screws are frequently sold as an accessory along with drywall studs.

In April 1973, importation of drywall screws increased. Sources were Canadian imports of Japanese screws. The "notched or slotted" screw was more popular than the "plain or twinfast" drywall screw.

In May 1975, Yuko Industry, which was developing a special Point screw with the second thread beginning where the point tapers, started shipping "s" point screws which were distributed by Bailey Metal Products under the label "speed tec". In 1976 the "speed tec" screw was satisfying the requests for "notched or slotted" screws. In 1977 and 1978 the plain screw had been virtually phased out by the "S" point screw even though there was a premium for this screw.

In March 1981, Bailey Metal Products rather cautiously swung over to Yuko's "ss" point which was being distributed world-wide as it was faster and favoured by the end users.

On October 11, 1979 Mantane Construction Products Limited was incorporated and has the same management as Bailey Metal. The inventory of Mantane Building Products (Western) was acquired and the operation throughout British Columbia continued intact. In May 1980 Mantane started importing and distributing screws from Yuko.

(2) PRICES

Please submit complete price lists covering drywall screws for the years 1983 to date.

See Attached (Confidential).

FORM 19

CANADIAN IMPORT TRIBUNAL

MANUFACTURER'S QUESTIONNAIRE

DRYWALL SCREWS

The information requested in this questionnaire is for use by the Canadian Import Tribunal in connection with its inquiry into drywall screws originating in or exported from France. The information is needed to supplement data available from other sources and is requested pursuant to section 72(2) of the *Special Import Measures Act*.

As a manufacturer of the product in question, you are requested to complete this questionnaire and return it to the Secretary, Canadian Import Tribunal, 19th Floor, Journal Tower South, 365 Laurier Avenue West, Ottawa, Ontario, K1A 0G5, Telex No. 053-3336, Telecopier No. (613) 998-4783. The questionnaire should be received by the Secretary not later than October 16, 1987.

Information which is in its nature confidential will be treated in accordance with section 75(3) of the *Special Import Measures Act* which requires that it shall not be made public in such a manner as to be available for the use of any business competitor or rival of the reporting person, firm or corporation.

Name (in both official languages, if applicable) and address of reporting company:

H. PAULIN & CO. LIMITED,
55 Milne Avenue,
Scarborough, Ontario
M1L 4N3

If your firm is a wholly or partly owned subsidiary, please list the name and address of the parent company and the extent of ownership.

CERTIFICATION

The undersigned certifies that the information herein sup-

plied is complete and correct to the best of his/her knowledge
and belief.

Date: October 8, 1987   [Signature]
                               Signature of Authorized Official

Telephone: [Name]
                               Vice President

                               Name and Title of
                               Authorized Official

GENERAL INSTRUCTIONS

1. This questionnaire is divided into two parts.

PART I   — deals with information
                               which is public in nature and
                               will be treated as such unless
                               otherwise requested.

PART II   — deals with information
                               which is in its nature confiden-
                               tial.

2. If the answer to any question is "none", so indicate rather than
   leave the space blank.

3. Where information is requested on a calendar year basis and
   your fiscal year ends at a different date, please make the
   appropriate adjustments and identify significant seasonal
   fluctuations, if any.

4. If the information requested is not readily available from your
   records in exactly the form requested, furnish prepared estimates, properly identified as such.

5. Necessary comments or explanations with respect to any
   question should be made in space provided or on separate
   sheets and attached to the questionnaire.

NOTE: You will note that some information and documents
      requested have already been provided to this Tribunal
      with respect to previous inquiries held into the same
      goods but from different countries; however, in order to
      provide a complete record for purposes of this inquiry,

it is necessary that you provide the necessary responses and documents, as requested, for the period 1983 to date.

Should you require copies of your prior submissions to the Tribunal in order to reply to the present questionnaire or have any questions relating to the questionnaire, please contact [name] at [phone number] or [name] at [phone number].

PART I

PUBLIC INFORMATION

Note: Information requested in this section usually is public in nature and will be treated as such unless otherwise requested.

(1) GENERAL

Please give a brief history of your company in terms of corporate set-ups, ownership, production, product range, product distribution and marketing with particular emphasis on drywall screws.

H. PAULIN & CO. LIMITED, established in 1920 as a privately-owned Canadian Company, and since 1972, a Canadian Public Company, has its headquarters at 55 Milne Avenue, Scarborough, Ontario. The company has four Manufacturing Divisions located in Scarborough (2), Milton and Mississauga, and 6 Distribution Warehouses in Vancouver, Edmonton, Winnipeg, Scarborough, Montreal and Moncton. At each of these locations, the company employs both inside and outside Sales personnel to handle the inquiries of industry.

For the year ended 31st December, 1986, Sales for both the Domestic and Export Markets totalled over $39,000,000.

The company manufactures and distributes Fasteners and related products for the Automotive, Industrial, Plumbing, Hardware and Construction Industries. Our 2 Divisions involved in the manufacturing of Drywall Screws are:

(a) Capital Metal Industries, located at 61 Milne Avenue, Scarborough, Ontario

(b) Precision Fasteners, located at 470 Harrop Road, Milton, Ontario

Both Divisions manufacture a complete line of Screw products. In addition to Screws, Capital Metal Industries also manufactures Bolts, Nuts, Washers and other special Construction Fasteners. The company has the capacity to manufacture, and is currently manufacturing, Drywall Screws in the 3 common diameters, and in all required lengths. To our knowledge, we are the largest Canadian producer, and the only one currently manufacturing the full range of sizes. Further, we wish to state that our Drywall Screws are equal to, or better than, any Drywall Screws imported from France, and are recognized by the Trade as being of the highest quality available.

As a result of the findings of the Anti-Dumping Tribunal on 14th June, 1982, H. PAULIN & CO. LIMITED re-entered the production of Drywall Screws on a large-scale basis. Since that time, Drywall Screws have become a significant part of our business. Not only do many of our employees' jobs rely on the manufacture and distribution of Drywall Screws, but we have become a major customer to our suppliers of raw material, heat-treating, plating, packaging material and transportation.

We currently market our Drywall Screws across Canada through our Warehouses in Vancouver, Edmonton, Winnipeg, Scarborough, Montreal and Moncton. The Screws are sold to Hardware Wholesalers, Industrial Distributors, Special Mass Merchandisers, Building Supply Dealers and Drywall Contractors. Our customers sell to small Dealers, Retail outlets and small Contractors.

2. PRICES

Please submit complete price lists covering drywall screws for the years 1983 to date.

See Exhibit "A" (Confidential).

Index